Mike Milotte is a multi award-winning journalist, former senior reporter and presenter on RTÉ's *Prime Time*, and before that Investigations Editor at the *Sunday Tribune*. He lives in London and has a PhD in modern Irish History.

This book is dedicated to the memory of my friend and colleague, Mary Raftery who did so much to expose clerical crimes against defenceless children, and to Rachel, Saoirse, Caoimhe and Mallaidh.

Banished Babies

Banished Babies

The secret history of Ireland's baby export business

Second Edition

Mike Milotte

NEW ISLAND

BANISHED BABIES
This edition published 2012 and reprinted 2021 by
New Island
Glenshesk House
10 Richview Office Park
Clonskeagh, Dublin 14
D14 V8C4, Ireland
www.newisland.ie

First published in 1997 by New Island

Print ISBN 978-1-84840-133-4
Ebook ISBN 978-1-84840-372-7

British Library Cataloguing Data. A CIP catalogue record for
this book is available from the British Library.

Typeset by Mariel Deegan
Cover design by Mariel Deegan
Cover image (c) Shutterstock / Natalia van Doninck
Printed by SprintPrint, Dublin

7 6 5 4 3 2

Contents

Acknowledgements

Most of the personal stories featured in the first edition of *Banished Babies* were drawn from interviews originally conducted by the author for an RTÉ *Prime Time* documentary, *The Secret Baby Trail*. Thanks to RTÉ, I was able to reuse that material in full for this book, although RTÉ bears no responsibility for its contents. New stories based on further interviews and correspondence have been added to this second edition. An enormous debt of gratitude is due to all who were willing to share with me those aspects of their private lives that have made this book possible.

As the bulk of the historical material in this book comes from State papers, with the addition of further information from the archives of the late Archbishop John Charles McQuaid, it has remained unchanged from the first edition. I am grateful to Caitriona Crowe of the National Archive for making the official papers so accessible, and to David Sheehy for providing copies of the McQuaid papers.

For the first edition I utilised information about the racial and commercial nature of adoption in America that was kindly provided by Professor Patricia Williams of Columbia University. For the second edition I have had the benefit of further documentary material provided by Marie

Hechter in New York. In addition, I have drawn freely on articles by Conall Ó Fátharta in the *Irish Examiner* in the summer of 2011 which deal authoritatively with the most recent developments in the wider area of adoption.Others who deserve thanks for their invaluable practical help in the production of this new edition include: Ita Collins, Jim Jackman, Susan Lohan, Claire McGetterick, Grainne Mason, and Mari Steed. And I remain grateful to Anne, Enda, Kevin, Fran, Maggie, Mary, Nora and Therese who taught me much about the complexities of adoption.

Finally, thanks to Edwin Higel and Conor Graham at New Island Books for the enthusiasm they have shown for this expanded and updated second edition.

Note on the Updated and Expanded Edition

When this book was first published in 1997, it revealed – for the first time – the extent to which Church and State had stood side by side in organising the banishment of thousands of babies and toddlers – the country's most vulnerable citizens – from the land of their birth. But it also proved that, far from imagining themselves to be sending these hapless children to a land of milk and honey in the United States, those responsible – clerical and lay – had abundant evidence that many of the children they dispatched across the Atlantic were sent to people whose suitability as adoptive parents had not been sufficiently investigated, if investigated at all, or who had even been rejected previously as adoptive parents by America's own child welfare authorities. The book also revealed that successive Irish governments were fully aware of a substantial and lucrative – but entirely illegal – black market in Irish babies, running in parallel with the 'official' American export programme. Yet, throughout the 1950s, when the great bulk of Ireland's baby exports took place, the official response was not to seek out and rescue the children who had been put at risk, but was rather to do nothing – other than conceal the truth and hope it never entered the public domain. Child welfare mattered less than ensuring there was no bad publicity.

Although the first edition of *Banished Babies* enjoyed a wide readership, this aspect of the story failed to win general acknowledgement or arouse widespread concern. Outrage over the Church's abuse of children in other areas of Irish life did not stretch to adoption practices. Adoption was seen as something separate, not part of the continuum of abuse and domination. I suspect that the reason for that has much to do with public perceptions of adoption in general. The prevailing attitude among the public at large was – and probably still is – that adoption is primarily an act of kindness by selfless individuals towards unfortunate children. While there can be no doubt that this is often the case, for the greater part adoption is simply the means by which people who are unable to produce their own children legally acquire those produced by others. That of course does not preclude the provision of a loving and caring home for the children involved *per se*, but it is, nevertheless, a very different starting point. When the needs of those who want children outweigh the needs of the children themselves, that is when the whole process is much more likely to turn out badly. Adoption must always raise concerns about the circumstances in which the natural parents gave their children up for adoption, especially when – which is usually the case – the adopters command greater resources and wield more authority than those whose children they are acquiring. Issues such as informed consent and financial duress are constantly present. And whatever the outcome of individual adoptions, adopted children and their natural mothers – each victims of a traumatic loss – are expected by the rest of society to display gratitude to their supposed benefactors for the rest of their lives.

Given the somewhat naïve view of adoption as intrinsically child-centred, and therefore, by definition, 'good', the attitude towards the sending of thousands of children to America for adoption remained one of broad acceptance based on the notion that it must have all been done in the best interests of the children involved. Who, after all, could dispute that life with well-heeled American adopters was preferable to life in an Irish religious-run institution?

Superficially this might appear to be a convincing argument. But when its surface is scratched, when its sentimentality is pared away and when its 'taken for granted' view of the world is challenged – as it is by this book – a different reality emerges. Yet despite the revelations in this book, there were no calls for an investigation into the fate of the children concerned, no demands that those responsible in the great institutions of Church and State be held to account for their blatant negligence. The State has never acknowledged that, in its desire to accommodate the Catholic Church, it put the welfare of countless children in jeopardy, and while it may have acknowledged to some extent the suffering of their young and often frightened mothers, it has never admitted its own share of responsibility for the damage done. Nor has the Catholic Church ever recognised that its involvement in the whole affair was the cause of widespread pain and suffering.

By comparison, the Catholic Church in Australia issued an apology in July 2011 for its role in affecting what has been termed 'forced adoptions' in that country involving thousands of children from church-run homes. Reports quoting the Australian mothers of these children will be immediately recognisable to many of the Irish mothers whose experiences are recounted in this book: 'The women said they were alone and frightened and were not told about their rights to revoke adoption consent. They said they were pressured to sign adoption papers before consent could legally be obtained. In some cases documents are said to have been forged.'

If that is what amounts to forced adoption, then Ireland has had more than its fair share of this shameful practice. But Ireland isn't Australia, and no apologies are even hinted at here. Indeed, the very existence of forced adoption in Ireland – let alone its prevalence – isn't yet acknowledged in official discourse.

Yet in the years since this book first appeared, the public's attitude to the Catholic Church and its domination of Irish life has shifted inexorably. We now know, from countless inquiries and investigations, that the abuse of children by Catholic nuns, priests, and Christian Brothers was endemic, even systematic in Ireland, and that the dominant ethos within the Church was to place the avoidance of scandal above the welfare of children. The Irish State has sought to deny any share of responsibility for the direct physical and sexual abuse of children in the care of the religious. But, as the pages that follow make abundantly clear, it cannot escape responsibility for the fate of the children it helped send out of the country for adoption. And in the case of these adoptions too, the avoidance of scandal, at whatever cost, was uppermost in the minds of State authorities.

Perhaps by retelling this story in these changed times its impact will be greater and the taboo on naming adoption as part of the spectrum of Church-State abuse will be broken. In the interest of all those who suffered – the children and their natural mothers – it is certainly to be hoped so.

PART I
Church and State

Prologue
A Surprise for the Wife

It was the 12th of July 1949 when wealthy American businessman Rollie William McDowell flew into Ireland with his personal attorney Michael Ebeling. Their arrival attracted no particular attention, but the same could not be said of their departure some two weeks later.

Forty-year-old McDowell, whose ancestors were Irish, had made his money as a property dealer in St Louis, Missouri, but he wasn't in Ireland in pursuit of real estate. He had come in pursuit of a child. More specifically, he and his attorney had come to investigate the possibility of obtaining a child from an Irish orphanage. If the signs were hopeful McDowell intended sending for his wife, Thelma, who was waiting to hear from him back in St Louis, so they could search together for a suitable infant. The McDowells were realistic. They expected to be in Ireland for quite a while, knowing that adoption, especially inter-country adoption, was likely to be a long, slow process. Yet just two weeks after his arrival in the country, Rollie McDowell returned home, disembarking at New York's La Guardia airport from the Trans World Airlines flight from Ireland. 'Never far from his sight,' according to the *New York Times*, 'were Patricia Frances, four months old, and Michael James, four years old, recently of the Braemar House Orphanage in Cork.'

'I found the children at the first orphanage we went to and they were the first children I saw,' a proud and beaming McDowell told a reporter at the airport. 'I liked the girl right away. Then Michael James came over and put his arms around me and said, "I like you," and he kissed me. He was so very affectionate,' McDowell went on, 'I liked him right away. I suppose you can say he adopted me.' Within days of his first encounter with the children McDowell had taken custody of them. Now, back at La Guardia airport, Rollie McDowell had just enough time to phone Thelma and ask her to meet him when his connecting flight arrived at St Louis at 4pm. He didn't mention the fact that he had two children in tow. 'How nice it is to surprise your wife occasionally,' remarked the *New York Times*, without a hint of irony.[1]

The remarkable story of Rollie McDowell's effortless acquisition and removal of two Irish children was syndicated to newspapers across America, complete with beguiling photographs of the two infants. Fortunately, perhaps, Michael's bright green trousers and cap weren't revealed by the black and white newsprint. But for the American media this was an unashamedly happy story, almost a fairytale come true: two little Irish waifs rescued from a life of poverty and misery by a wealthy benefactor who would give them a chance in life for which anyone in their position would be eternally grateful.

In acquiring two children for immediate shipment to the United States, Mr McDowell had broken no laws. Yet the fact that the whole business had been conducted without his wife's involvement – let alone knowledge – indicated that no one with responsibility for the children's welfare had bothered to investigate the would-be adoptive parents and their motives, nor the circumstances in which the children would live and be reared in the States. The Braemar Orphanage may have had day-to-day responsibility for the two children, but as citizens of the new Irish Republic, declared just a few months earlier, ultimate liability for their well-being rested squarely with the State as represented by the Government of the day. But the Government, as we shall see, was reluctant to curtail a babies-for-export affair that was primarily the preserve of the Catholic Church.

Rollie McDowell, of course, was just one of many. Close on his heels came US naval airman Eugene Perry. In November 1949 Perry returned from a European posting to his home in California accompanied by two Irish infants, three-year-old James Kearney and two-year-old Mary Dillon, whom he had obtained from the mother-and-baby home run by the Sacred Heart nuns at Castlepollard in County Westmeath. Like many American armed forces personnel who were acquiring babies from Ireland at this time, Perry had made contact with the nuns through a Catholic military chaplain with Irish connections. Like Rollie McDowell, Perry had made the journey to and from Ireland unaccompanied by his wife. Perry's story, too, received much publicity. One newspaper described the children as 'Irish war orphans'.[2] Another spoke of them as 'tousled redheads with eyes big as dollars'.[3] A third waxed lyrical about the 'beautiful but homeless orphans' who departed from 'the little convent of Sacred Heart... through the streets in a donkey cart'.[4] The Castlepollard home was, in fact, an ugly purpose-built institution of 1930s vintage, but that wasn't going to interfere with a colourful story. And the language got even more saccharine. It was, said one paper, as if '... a faery crept through the darkened streets of Castlepollard and through the convent gates and into the convent itself and waved a magic wand and whispered: you shall fly through the air and over an ocean and across a great new land'. From then on it was a story of 'great winged planes' and 'endless Irish laughter'.[5]

Rollie McDowell and Eugene Perry made the headlines – but only in America. Their exploits were barely mentioned in Ireland where the steadily growing practice of sending children abroad for adoption was not a matter of any significant public debate or comment. Yet it was a practice that had been going on for a number of years before McDowell's well-publicised coup of 1949, and it was set to continue, without interruption, until the 1970s, by which time thousands of babies, virtually every one of them born to an unmarried mother, had been exported. When this baby trafficking finally faded out its passing was as unremarked as its beginning, and another twenty-five years were to elapse before the story of Ireland's banished babies finally hit the headlines of the Irish newspapers.

When it did – in 1996 – the facts were initially unclear and tangled, while those who knew the truth kept silent. It was a long time before the realisation dawned that the practice of sending 'illegitimate' children to America for adoption had been a highly organised affair rather than a series of random acts by unconnected individuals.

1. A Happy Hunting Ground

'Almost 500 babies were flown from Shannon for adoption last year.'
The Irish Times, 8 October 1951

'It would be interesting to know how The Irish Times *obtained the figure.'*
Department of External Affairs, internal memo

The children involved in Ireland's transatlantic adoptions were frequently referred to as 'orphans', and the institutions they came from as 'orphanages', yet almost without exception they were the children of unmarried mothers – 'illegitimate' children in the stigmatising language of the day. A review of 330 foreign adoption cases in 1952, for instance, revealed that 327 of the children were 'illegitimate' and only three were orphans.[1] What was more, 99 out of every 100 were the children of Catholic mothers; children with few rights in Irish law, and little hope of acceptance in Catholic Irish society. The practice of dispatching such children abroad began at a time when there was no legal adoption in Ireland, but it continued for 20 years after adoption was introduced in 1953.

The export of 'illegitimate' children to America was organised by nuns, with full official sanction. It was regulated by the Catholic Archbishop of Dublin, John Charles

McQuaid, and facilitated by the State, with the Department of External Affairs issuing passports so the children could be taken out of the country. As far as possible the whole business was conducted in conditions of secrecy – on orders from McQuaid himself – and although individual government ministers were well aware of what was going on, the matter was only discussed once, and briefly, by the full cabinet. It was rarely mentioned in the Irish press, although foreign papers reported and commented on it from time to time. The civil servants who were involved lived in constant fear of awkward parliamentary questions or an angry public outcry. When Archbishop McQuaid asked the Department of External Affairs in November 1951 about the number of 'adoption passports' being issued, the secretary of the Department suggested to his Minister, Frank Aiken, that they could tell McQuaid the number was an 'official secret'.[2]

In fact, the true number of 'illegitimate' children sent across the Atlantic may never be known. No one was counting before American businessman Rollie McDowell's visit in July 1949. From then onwards the American embassy in Dublin kept a record of entry visas issued to such children[3] and from the end of 1950 onwards the Department of External Affairs kept a tally of adoption passports issued. These official figures suggest that around 2,100 children were sent to America between July 1949 and the end of 1973, but there is no record of the numbers before 1949. The earliest post-war reference to a child going to America for adoption is November 1947, but there may have been many before that.[4] Nor is there any way of knowing how many children were taken or sent illegally. What newspaper reports there are from the time certainly put the number of children being dispatched across the Atlantic at a much higher level than is acknowledged in the official figures. *The Irish Times*, for example, reported in October 1951 that 'almost 500 babies were flown from Shannon for adoption' in 1950, while already, it said, in the first nine months of 1951, 'that number is believed to have been exceeded'.[5] The same report referred to 18 *parties* of children leaving Shannon in *one week* in October 1951, yet official figures reveal just nine adoption passports issued for the whole month of October, and just 122 for the whole year of 1951, a small fraction of the 'almost 500' reported by the newspaper.[6] *The Irish Times'* article was read with interest – but with no apparent surprise or explicit disagreement – by the officials in the Department of External Affairs who were issuing the passports. Their sole response was a brief internal memo: 'It would be interesting to know how *The Irish Times* obtained the figure.'[7]

Whatever the numbers, the easy availability of Irish children for removal abroad, particularly when it was prominently reported as in the McDowell and Perry cases, helped paint a picture of Ireland abroad not unlike the image the Irish themselves would come to hold of Romania, China, Russia, Vietnam and other countries where they went in search of babies to adopt in later years: a pathetic and brutal country, teeming with abandoned and desperate children just waiting to be scooped up by more enlightened and kindly souls, and removed from their misery with a minimum of fuss. Regrettably, such an image of Ireland was not entirely unjustified.

The decade after World War Two was probably the most desolate and gloomy period in modern Irish history. As a wartime neutral, the country was cut off from progressive post-war developments in Europe, and isolation simply made the country more conservative than it already was. Ireland was a solidly Catholic country and the Church's authority was unquestioned, at least in public. It was still a predominantly rural society as well. Church and State were as one in their determination to enforce a deeply traditional moral code, and in the process they displayed what many would see today as an unhealthy obsession with matters sexual, seeking to extend their authority into the bedrooms of the nation. Artificial birth control was outlawed and chastity was demanded of everyone who wasn't married.

Today almost a quarter of all families in Ireland are headed by a single parent – most of them unmarried mothers – but in the 1940s, '50s and '60s, single parent families, other than those headed by widows or widowers, were virtually unknown. Unmarried couples did not live together, with or without children. 'Illegitimate' children, with few exceptions, were consigned to 'orphanages'. And the orphanages were bursting at the seams, for despite the confining Puritanism of the times, premarital and extramarital sex were far from uncommon. Nowadays, when around 25,000 children are born each year to unmarried women in Ireland (amounting to 34% of all births in 2010), the figures from years past may seem small, at between one and two thousand annually. But it all added up, and the fact that more than 100,000 Irish children were born outside marriage between 1920 and the mid-1970s – when the stigma lessened – seems adequate enough testimony to the hypocrisy of the times.[8] Countless thousands more 'illegitimate' children were born to young, unmarried women who fled to England to hide their shame. They were so numerous they earned the nickname 'PFI' – Pregnant From Ireland.

There was scarcely a family in 1940s, '50s or '60s Ireland that didn't have a relative, friend or acquaintance who either got pregnant out of wedlock or fathered an 'illegitimate' child. Yet it was a taboo subject, never discussed in polite company and if mentioned at all then only in hushed tones of holy indignation. An appalling stigma attached to 'illegitimacy'. Having a child outside marriage was regarded as an unspeakably scandalous act. The mother was seen as a wicked sinner and her child a tainted outcast. Father Cecil Barrett, head of the Catholic Social Welfare Bureau, and Archbishop McQuaid's closest adviser on such matters, described single mothers as 'fallen women' and 'grave sinners' with severe 'moral problems'. Their children were the victims of 'wickedness'.[9] Humanitarian or material assistance, Barrett maintained, 'may be of no avail, unless the rents in the mother's spiritual fabric have been repaired'.[10] Another Catholic writer described 'natural' children as 'rebels' who 'suffer from complexes analogous to those of certain invalids'. They were 'destined for suffering and often for failure', while 'the girl who gives birth to one of them takes upon herself the responsibility for these evils'.[11]

Men, on the other hand, who fathered children out of wedlock, faced no such stigmatisation. They may have feared retribution from a girl's family (if family members knew), but by and large the attitude was that it was the 'fallen' woman who tempted the hapless man into a sinful relationship. Men were just men and women had to control the male's 'natural urges' by acting modestly. The idea that women, too, might have natural urges was anathema. Female sexuality was denied in a repressive regime designed to exercise maximum control by the male dominated Catholic Church over women, their bodies, and their reproductive capabilities.

Given such attitudes, it was hardly surprising that a girl who became pregnant outside marriage was unlikely to tell her own parents of her predicament, or if she told her mother, the father was kept in the dark. And whoever in the immediate family knew, certainly the neighbours would never be allowed to find out. Many young women who got pregnant were thrown out of the family home and completely disowned by their parents, so great was the shame.

If they were allowed to return it was only after they had got rid of their babies, the visible proof of their mortal sin.

Before the early 1970s, when an allowance for unmarried mothers was first introduced, the Irish State offered no help. Rather than provide an adequate means of life to so many mothers and their children, the State, in effect, closed its eyes to the reality of thousands of births outside marriage. Successive governments ignored the constitutional undertaking to cherish all the children of the nation equally, and simply abandoned all responsibility in this area – as in so many others – to the Catholic Church and its religious orders.

For most of the unfortunate young women caught up in this world of exclusion and deceit, the only option was to turn to the nuns for help. Religious orders such as the Sisters of the Sacred Heart of Jesus and Mary, the Irish Sisters of Charity and the Daughters of Charity of St Vincent de Paul ran maternity hospitals and mother and baby homes that catered exclusively for single women. There were also religious-run 'orphanages' for older children, and beyond them the industrial schools. Most of these homes received income from their local authority which had a statutory responsibility to provide the bare necessities for those who could not provide for themselves, and that included 'destitute' children. But the Sisters also received bequests and donations, and many boosted their income further by running farms, bakeries and laundries, all staffed by 'fallen women' who were compelled to work for their own and their children's keep. Yet, as with so much else, the full extent of the financial dealings of these religious-run institutions – who were in effect being paid twice for the service they provided – remains shrouded in mystery.

As for the unmarried mothers, even if they had the means, they were unlikely to have the inclination in conservative Catholic Ireland to set up home as single parents.

The overwhelming majority of them had no real alternative but to give their babies away as soon as possible after birth. The stigma attached to their condition meant their first objective was to hide the fact that they had had a child at all, a process that involved concealment, deception and denial, with unquantified consequences in terms of long-term psychological damage. Again, it was the nuns who ran the fostering and adoption societies who arranged to have the children of these single mothers taken from them. And in most cases, it seems, they not only made the arrangements but took all the critical decisions as well, assuming control in the belief that they knew best. So convinced were they of their right to decide that they frequently disposed of children without consulting or informing the mother beforehand. Their assumed moral (whatever about legal) authority to do so was simply not questioned. And, again, this was a further source of income for the sisters, for although they appear not to have charged directly for providing children to adoptive parents (which would have been illegal after 1952), they certainly knew how to maximise the 'donations' that flowed into their coffers from the grateful recipients of children for adoption.

For the children themselves there were few options. In the absence of legal adoption in Ireland before 1953, many were 'boarded out' to foster parents, with the possibility of being informally adopted, in so-called *de facto* adoptions. But for some – barely old enough to work – fostering was a euphemism for child labour, mostly on farms, and not infrequently with bachelor farmers. The fate of these children has never been recorded. The alternative, of course, was to remain in institutional care with the nuns.

For the nuns this whole business was something of a paradox. On the one hand they were virtually the only people prepared to offer any kind of help or relief to women who were shunned by the rest of society. But on the other hand they were part and parcel of the established Church, the sole arbiter of society's moral values. As such, the nuns themselves helped enforce and perpetuate the ethical code that rejected unmarried mothers and banished their hapless offspring. It was a vicious circle.

Entering a mother and baby home run by the Sisters was, more often than not, a last resort for a pregnant woman, a move that was undertaken with great trepidation for these homes had frightening reputations as places of retribution and punishment as much as places of confinement. They most certainly were not places where the bringing forth of new life was celebrated. The nuns provided secrecy, but they exacted a price. Girls and young women entering these institutions, unless they had independent means, had to 'work their passage' with hard manual labour, scrubbing and cleaning indoors, working the land outdoors. Many women whose children were not fostered or adopted immediately had to work in the convents for as much as two years after their babies were born before the nuns would agree to take charge of their children. Indeed, some of these unfortunate young mothers became so dependent they remained for the rest of their lives working in the institutions where their children had been born.

This, then, was the world that Rollie McDowell, Eugene Perry and hundreds like them visited so cursorily in their quest for children. They, of course, came from a very different world: the world of wealthy, powerful, self-assured, middle class, white America. They were the victors of the Second World War. Whatever they wanted seemed to be theirs for the asking, Irish babies included. Unlike the mothers of the children, the Americans had everything going for them. Regardless of individual attitudes, it was a grossly unequal relationship, a form of cultural and economic exploitation. At the outset it was not the nuns but the Americans who set the ball rolling, for white middle class America had always experienced a shortage of 'suitable' babies for adoption. It was estimated that 20 American couples were chasing after every available white American child. Inevitably in such circumstances a black market developed within America with unscrupulous doctors and lawyers, among others, running 'baby farms' – obtaining babies from unmarried women and selling them to childless couples for thousands of dollars.

In the mid-1940s, hopeful American adopters were presented with a new source of children among the hundreds of thousands of displaced orphans in post-war Europe. Many such children were acquired by American military and government personnel stationed in US-occupied territories such as Italy and West Germany. Others were shipped to the States in groups to be offered for adoption there. Thousands of American servicemen were also stationed in Britain and remained there long after the war ended, but in 1948 the UK forbade foreign nationals from taking British children out of the country.[12] As a result, many of the US military personnel stationed in Britain turned to Ireland, just a short flight away. As a wartime neutral, Ireland had no war orphans, but it had a superabundance of 'illegitimate' children. As in the rest of Europe, the dislocated years of the Second World War saw a huge increase in the number of births outside marriage in Ireland – up by an average of 23% a year – putting the nation's 'orphanages' under even greater strain and providing opportunities for childless Americans like McDowell and Perry to take their pick. And, as these gentlemen had discovered, Ireland had no laws prohibiting the removal of such children. Nor were there restrictions on their entry into America since Ireland's US immigration quota of 18,000 a year was under-subscribed.

The attraction of Ireland as a potential source of babies for well-to-do white Americans was heightened when other European countries moved, as Britain had done, to protect their children. By July 1948 the Children's Bureau of the US Social Security Administration was reporting that many European countries who had suffered huge population losses as a result of the war were now 'anxious to keep all children who are their citizens', and as a result had 'set up regulations which prevent children being taken out of the country for purposes of adoption'. By 1950, according to the Geneva-based International Union for Child Welfare, there were approximately 10 qualified European couples willing to adopt each available European child, a complete turnaround from the situation at the end of the war when children could, literally, be picked up in the streets. The Union's secretary, Mrs J. M. Small, told a conference of the Child Welfare League of America in New York in November 1950 that it was now futile for American couples to go to mainland Europe in the hope of finding children for adoption.[13]

Ireland, by comparison, had become a happy hunting ground for would-be American adopters. The powers that be in Ireland, clerical and lay, had decided that 'illegitimate' Irish children were dispensable. Their removal from the country would not be banned, even though it was a period of mass adult emigration resulting in a declining population. The fact that Americans wanted these children was quite fortuitous for it meant they could be disposed of in a way that seemed beneficial for all concerned: the natural mothers were relieved of their offspring; the Americans found the children they craved, and the children themselves went off to a better life. That, at least, was the theory, but theory and reality were not always the same.

When American Catholics came looking for children to take away to the United States, the nuns who ran the orphanages must have been delighted. For one thing, they had more babies in their care than they could adequately cope with, and it seemed a natural match to pair them off with willing American couples. It also meant fewer mouths to feed, and, as an additional bonus, satisfied wealthy Americans were a potential source of generous donations.

America, of course, had always been seen as the land of opportunity by Irish people seeking a better life. There was nothing at all unusual about crossing the Atlantic to escape the confines and miseries of life in Ireland, and in the postwar era Irish people were again flocking abroad in ever increasing numbers. The nuns no doubt believed America would provide a wonderful chance to children who otherwise would spend many years of their lives in religious-run institutions, and it seemed self-evident that life with a loving family would be preferable to life with the nuns. But at the same time there had to be something fundamentally awry in a society that tried to solve its 'illegitimacy problem' by banishing thousands of children to a foreign country, while at the same time doing nothing to address the underlying fears and prejudices that made such banishment both possible and necessary. And unlike adult emigrants, of course, these children had no say whatever in where they ended up. What is more, despite all the efforts to find 'good Catholic homes' for them, there is an abundance of evidence that many of the children sent to America faced an uncertain future in the hands of people whose suitability as adoptive parents was seriously in question.

When we add in the plight of the natural mothers who were left behind with their dark, destructive secrets and their numbing pain, it is easy to understand why this is a story Church and State would prefer had not been told.

2. McQuaid's Rules, OK?

'We shall have to be careful not to do anything which would embarrass the Archbishop.'

Department of External Affairs
internal memo, 1950

It was Eamon de Valera, self-styled father figure of the Irish nation, who opened Ireland up to America's child-seekers. De Valera – who had himself been born in America to an unmarried mother – was not only Taoiseach when the baby exodus began, he was also Minister for External Affairs and, as such, responsible for issuing the first children's 'adoption passports'. Yet there is no record of de Valera's thinking on the matter and no record either of how many passports were authorised in his name. What is clear, however, is that he took no steps to stop the departures, although, in an era when tens of thousands of Irish people were leaving the country in a desperate search for work and a decent life, it was his Government's policy to stem the emigrant tide, not add to it. It was not until after the change of Government in 1948, when Sean MacBride, of the small, radical republican party Clann na Poblachta, was Minister for External Affairs in the country's first inter-party Government, that steps were taken to regulate – but not stop – the practice of dispatching 'illegitimate' children to America.

In the wake of the publicity given to the McDowell and Perry cases in the United States, demand there for Irish babies was rocketing. The McDowells themselves had been inundated with enquiries from other American couples wanting to know how they got their children.[1] At the same time, various American Catholic welfare bodies were being bombarded with requests from childless couples across the States for assistance in obtaining Irish children. When the Perry story broke a few months after McDowell's widely publicised coup, the Irish Consul in San Francisco, Patrick Hughes, wrote to the Department of External Affairs in Dublin seeking advice on the current law relating to such cases. He needed to know, he said, because 'I receive many inquiries by callers, by telephone and by mail from persons who wish to adopt Irish children.'[2]

This was the first time an Irish government department had been asked to explain its position regarding the American adoptions, and its reply to Hughes showed the matter had not provoked any deep thought. Hughes was told simply that as there was no law prohibiting the removal of Irish children from the State, the Department of External Affairs was prepared to issue passports to such children provided their mother or guardian had consented to their removal and that there was satisfactory evidence of the suitability of the would-be adopters.[3] On the surface these may have seemed reasonable safeguards for both the natural mother and her child, but no one was really concerned about the circumstances in which the mothers – mostly young, vulnerable and frightened women – were 'consenting' to the permanent removal of their children from the State. This issue was never seriously addressed during the lifetime of the American adoptions. What was more, in the early years at least, there were no established criteria for determining the 'suitability' of applicants for Irish children. And these were certainly matters that should not have been left to civil servants who had no training or expertise in adoption matters and whose function was merely to issue passports, not make critical decisions affecting the future welfare of hundreds, if not thousands of infants and their mothers.

From the very start the whole business had been handled in a haphazard manner, without thought or preparation, and without rules or regulations. And there was evidence that the civil servants who decided whether or not a child would be allowed to go abroad for adoption had little knowledge of adoption policy. In one case officials gave permission for a 57-year-old woman to take a two-year-old child abroad for adoption. In the many letters and memos generated by this particular application, the woman's advanced age was never once mentioned as a negative factor even though it was generally accepted in adoption practice that 40 was the maximum age at which a woman should adopt a two-year-old.[4]

Elsewhere, however, concern for the welfare of the infants in question was slowly beginning to surface. In December 1949, within weeks of the Perry case, Health Minister Dr Noel Browne expressed his 'uneasiness' to the Department of External Affairs over the growing number of foreign adoptions. As a member of Clann na Poblachta, Browne in effect was questioning his party leader, the Minister for External Affairs, Sean MacBride, in whose name the 'adoption passports' were now being issued. Browne had two principal concerns: first, that the applicants for Irish children 'may be persons turned down as adopters in their own country', and second, that 'there is no means of knowing or ensuring that children placed in the care of applicants will be adopted legally in their new country or even that they will remain in the care of the original applicants'.[5] The Minister for Health clearly feared that unsuitable people were obtaining Irish children with a view to trading them on, and given America's notorious black market in babies, Browne's fears were far from imaginary. His suspicion that people who had been rejected in the States were now getting children from Ireland was borne out when an American journalist, following up the Rollie McDowell story, casually informed the Department of External Affairs that American 'rejectees' were indeed turning to Ireland where they encountered no obstacles.[6] The Department, however, does not appear to have responded in any way to the warning (which is precisely how it reacted when the same issue arose time after time in the future).

Noel Browne, however, was not proposing that the export of Irish babies be halted. Rather he was urging that it be better regulated so as to safeguard the interests of the children involved. 'The children so adopted are, in the main, illegitimate children with an uncertain future in this country,' his officials wrote, and Dr Browne 'would be diffident in suggesting that obstacles should be placed in the way of their acquiring a new permanent home.' But would-be foreign adopters, Browne urged, 'should be obliged to produce evidence of character, suitability and religion, supported by a recommendation from the Diplomatic Representative in this country.'[7]

The Health Minister's intervention was the first time anyone in authority in Ireland had asked questions about the safety and welfare of Irish infants who were being sent abroad in ever growing – but still unrecorded – numbers. Distressingly, the Department of External Affairs, which was facilitating the children's removal, had no reply to give. Instead, the consular officials at Iveagh House asked their embassies in London and Washington what the British and American authorities did to protect Irish children once they

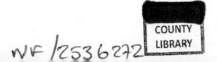

had come to *their* countries for adoption. It looked very much like they were passing the buck.

Noel Browne's protestations had no immediate impact, and his officials were still pressing External Affairs for a response three months later – by which time another interested party, whose influence was greater than that of a mere cabinet minister, had begun to mobilise – the Catholic Church.

* * * * *

The Reverend Robert Brown, assistant secretary of America's largest non-governmental welfare organisation, the National Conference of Catholic Charities, was an extremely busy man. He had to keep an eye on a sprawling network of local agencies, all linked under the Catholic Charities umbrella, but each one working independently of the organisation's Washington head office. Brown's boss was an Irishman, Monsignor John O'Grady, a native of Roscrea in County Tipperary, where his sister was a nun. After 30 years of involvement with Catholic Charities, O'Grady was now the organisation's national secretary. He was to play a critical role in the transatlantic adoption business over the next number of years.

O'Grady and Brown were becoming concerned with the ever-growing number of enquiries to local Catholic Charities branches about how to get a baby from Ireland. Each story that appeared in the newspapers about another American couple's acquisition of an Irish 'orphan' simply encouraged more and more childless American couples to come knocking on their door.

Although overworked already, Brown decided to make some enquiries of his own, and on 8 March 1950 he wrote an anxious letter to the St Vincent de Paul Society in Dublin, drawing its attention to the American newspaper articles. The Rev Brown was worried at the apparent lack of regulation in the growing baby export trade, and what concerned him most of all was the danger of Catholic Irish children falling into the hands of non-Catholic American adopters. Brown elaborated on his concerns. He knew of one woman, he said, a non-Catholic who had received a letter from an Irish nun saying she would be 'very glad to send her a baby'. Although the woman's husband was a Catholic, Brown went on, they had married outside the Church. 'One of the basic concerns should certainly be to preserve the faith of these youngsters', Father Brown concluded. He offered the collaboration of Catholic Charities 'in any way possible to this end'.[8] With this letter, Brown had set the pattern for all future interventions by both Church and State: religion came first.

As they had no experience in this area, the Society of St Vincent de Paul forwarded Brown's letter to Father Cecil Barrett, head of the Catholic Social Welfare Bureau in Dublin. The CSWB was an organisation set up by Archbishop McQuaid in the mid-1940s to provide for the welfare of Catholics, and Barrett was the acknowledged clerical expert on child fostering and adoption. He was also head of the Catholic Protection and Rescue Society (CPRS), a militant anti-proselytising organisation that spent much of its time bringing Catholic 'Pregnant From Ireland' young women back from England in an effort to ensure their babies did not fall into non-Catholic hands. In its annual report for 1950, the CPRS noted that many of the children that it had 'taken over' in the preceding year 'were in grave danger of being handed over to Protestants'. This was precisely the thinking that shaped the Church's attitude to the American adoptions as well: it was better that Irish children be dispatched to Catholic couples thousands of miles across the Atlantic – even if their suitability as adoptive parents could not always be guaranteed – than that they fall into the hands of Protestants closer to home.

Before advising St Vincent de Paul on how to reply to Father Brown in America, Cecil Barrett took the precaution of consulting Archbishop McQuaid's secretary, Father Chris Mangan. It was as well he did, for when McQuaid heard of what was happening, and of the danger that non-Catholics could acquire Catholic infants, he ordered that no more babies be sent to America until all the circumstances were fully investigated.[9]

At the time, children were being taken or sent to America from religious-run institutions all around the country. McQuaid's writ, however, did not extend beyond the two religious-run agencies that came within his Dublin diocese – St Patrick's Guild in Abbey Street and St Patrick's Home on the Navan Road. Provincial homes that were actively sending babies to America, such as those run by the Sacred Heart Sisters in Castlepollard, Roscrea and Cork, were unaffected by the McQuaid ban. Over the years the Roscrea nuns sent around 450 children, those at Castlepollard 300, and the nuns in Cork, 100. But, as the Dublin ban took effect, Father Brown was informed that the 'problem' was under investigation and reassured that the clerical authorities in Ireland 'would not be a party to any arrangements unless we were assured of the absolute preservation of the faith of the children involved'.[10]

McQuaid's instant and firm response once the matter of faith was called into question threw into even sharper relief the State's dithering when Health Minister Noel Browne had raised his concerns about the legal status and general welfare of departing children. While the State abdicated responsibility, the Church was gaining the upper hand and in the future would be calling all the shots. What was more, this seemed to be the outcome desired by the Department of External Affairs. A senior official in the Department told the departmental secretary that he had not dealt with Dr Browne's query, several months after receiving it, 'because... I am not aware whether the Archbishop has yet arrived at any policy'.[11] A vital matter concerning child welfare had been put on hold until the Archbishop made his position clear.

McQuaid's insistence that the removal of babies be halted until matters of faith could be guaranteed was relayed immediately to Sister Frances Elizabeth, head of St Patrick's Guild, and to Sister Monica Farrelly, in charge at St Patrick's Home. Despite their similar names, these institutions were quite distinct. St Patrick's Home on the Navan Road – known as St Pat's – was run by the Daughters of Charity of St Vincent de Paul. It was a home where unmarried women lived before and after their babies were born. It came under the Dublin Board of Assistance and was maintained on the Dublin rates. It took in single women from all over the country, and it was known as the only home of its kind that would take in a woman who became pregnant out of marriage a second time – 'second offenders' as Cecil Barrett labelled them.[12] Nuns elsewhere simply turned such women away. But St Pat's also had a reputation for exceptional harshness towards the 'offenders'. In total, St Pat's sent more than 250 children to the United States.

St Patrick's Guild, on the other hand – with offices at Middle Abbey Street in Dublin – was run by the Irish Sisters of Charity. By comparison with St Pat's, it had little direct contact with the mothers of the children it dealt with. It was not a mother and children's home as such but a fostering, and later an adoption, society, connected with the infants' home at Temple Hill in Blackrock, the source of most of the children it sent to America. Temple Hill, in turn, took in babies that had been born elsewhere. It did not take their mothers. The Guild had been founded in 1910 by Miss Mary Cruice, who wanted to provide the first Catholic alternative to Dublin's Protestant fostering services. Later Miss Cruice linked up with the Sisters of Charity and in 1942 the Guild was placed 'under Diocesan control subject to such conditions as His Grace the Archbishop of Dublin may approve'. The Sisters of Charity were by then in day-to-day control and were to the forefront in organising the dispatch of babies to America. The Guild sent its first 'illegitimate' child to the States for adoption on 18 November 1947.[13] By 1950 it had sent 57 children and before it ended the practice in 1967 the Guild had dispatched a total of 572 infants across the Atlantic, more than any other single adoption society.[14]

This was how Sister Frances Elizabeth, the nun in charge of St Patrick's Guild, described one of the children in her care to an American couple who were hoping to adopt him, sight unseen:

'All our children are born out of wedlock of respectable parents and no child is given for adoption unless the background is excellent. Anthony has a particularly good background... His mother was a very superior type of girl. She lived at home with her people. The family are very respectable. They know nothing of her misfortune. It is because of Anthony's excellent background that we are anxious to get a good home for him. He is a very gentle lovable little boy. He has made his First Communion and is getting on very nicely at school. He is perfectly healthy. We are enclosing a little snap of him. He has fair hair, blue eyes and reflects the gentleness and culture of his mother.'[15]

This seems typical of the sort of information that was made available to adopting Americans – minimal, non-specific and of little real value, if not totally inadequate, as the basis of any adoption. The couple in this case were told that if they did not accept the child immediately he would be offered elsewhere. They accepted. The whole business, from first postal enquiry to dispatch of child, was completed within two months.

This was the sort of rapid-fire adoption that archbishop McQuaid wanted to bring under control – and Sister Frances Elizabeth was none too pleased at the Archbishop's letter enforcing a no-warning ban on her entire operation. She penned a frantic letter in reply to the Archbishop. 'We have seven adoptions already arranged for the USA,' she wrote. 'Three of the children have been issued with visas and four have their passports. All transport has been arranged. In one case the adopter is on his way over to take the baby back with him. One of these intending adopters is a personal friend of His Eminence, Cardinal Spellman and His Lordship, Dr O'Leary, both of whom have recommended him.' She went on: 'I beg His Grace to allow us to send these little children. It would be such a bitter blow to the adopters to be denied their little child just when their hopes were about to be realised. Also, I would be very grateful if you would advise me what to say to the many others whose applications I have already received. All are vouched for as excellent Catholics and they have beautiful homes.'[16]

Even in 1950, being the friend of a Cardinal, an excellent Catholic, and having a beautiful home could not have been considered even remotely adequate qualifications for adopting a child, yet the Archbishop agreed that Sister Frances Elizabeth's seven adoptions could go ahead once he had sight of legal agreements signed by the prospective adopters 'to the effect that they undertake to rear the children in the Catholic faith'. When the transatlantic adoptions eventually recommenced, this was to be the fundamental condition applied to all applicants, and in these cases it seems to have been sufficient for the Department of External Affairs to issue passports. Sister Frances was also told there was to be no publicity for any of these adoptions and that she must make no more arrangements until permitted to do so by the Archbishop.[17]

Over at St Pat's on the Navan Road, Sister Monica was equally put out. She had nine children ready to go to America, and scheduled to travel in a week's time. What was more, the prospective adopters had already parted with considerable sums of money to pay for the children's and their escorts' air fares, and for clothes and legal fees. Again, Archbishop McQuaid gave the go-ahead for all nine children to be sent off to the States as soon as Sister Monica produced the requisite religious proofs.[18]

Archbishop McQuaid was clearly concerned over the publicity given to earlier baby shipments, and he now moved to halt publicity altogether. In the most recent case, photographs had been published of six children departing for America from the Navan Road. The *New York Times* carried a detailed report of the children's arrival in the States:

> Six orphans from St Patrick's Home in Dublin, Ireland, arrived yesterday – by coincidence – on St Patrick's Day at New York International Airport, Idlewild, Queens, to meet their foster parents.
>
> The youngsters, wearing sprigs of shamrock, were accompanied on the trip aboard an American Clipper by Miss Nora O'Sullivan, 26 years old, a nurse from the orphanage. When greeted by their 'new' parents, it was difficult to tell whether the children of the adults were more excited.

Francis Bergin, five years old, handed over a box of shamrocks and sang 'Hail, Glorious, St Patrick,' when he and Bernadette Smith, three, were introduced to Mr and Mrs John Halloran of Jamaica, Queens.

Not all of the foster parents were of Irish descent. Philip Golletta of Astoria, Queens, and his wife, Lillian, were there to take charge of Joseph Maloney, three, and Mary Purcell, 10 months, the youngest child in the group.

Mr and Mrs Albert Rees of the Bronx, adopted Angela Kane, three. Mr and Mrs William J. Gooth of Bayville, Long Island, will make a home for Patrick John Coll, five.[19]

Following these much-publicised cases, McQuaid's secretary, Father Mangan, intervened directly with Pan American Airlines, whose public relations officer at Shannon was instructed to 'close down on publicity'. Pan Am not only acceded to the order themselves but, if Mangan was right, also seem to have persuaded the main press agencies, Reuters, Associated Press and United Press to do likewise.[20] It proved an effective ban since the American babies were scarcely mentioned again. The Archbishop did not like publicity because it made matters more difficult for him to control. Civil servants too, for their own reasons, were anxious to keep the whole business secret. As one official was to put it: 'in this section we rather dislike publicity in these adoption cases for obvious reasons, e.g., a question in the Dáil.'[21]

In the meantime, Father Cecil Barrett, on behalf of the Archbishop, had taken up the offer of help from Father Robert Brown and proceeded to open negotiations with US Catholic Charities' boss, Monsignor John O'Grady, to see what could be done at the American end to safeguard the faith of Irish children.[22] The matter was on the agenda when the Directors of Catholic Charities met in Washington DC on 19 May 1950. These eminent American churchmen were of the view that the policy of sending 'illegitimate' children abroad was being 'fostered by the Irish Government'. They also noted the possibility of using Irish children 'as a means of supplementing the dearth of children for adoption in the United States', but postponed their decision on becoming officially involved.[23]

* * * * *

While Archbishop McQuaid and Cecil Barrett looked for the best arrangements to safeguard the faith, and Catholic Charities pondered the possibilities presented to them by an abundance of 'illegitimate' Irish children, the civil authorities back in Ireland were letting slip an opportunity to develop a professional, child-centred scheme for regulating and monitoring the American adoptions. This turned out to be a critical lapse since – with disastrous consequences for unknown numbers of Irish infants – Catholic Charities could not in many cases (as we shall see) guarantee the children's welfare, whatever about their religion.

On 23 May 1950, just days after the indecisive Catholic Charities conference, the Irish embassy in Washington sent a set of proposals to the Department of External Affairs in Dublin for the secular management of the American adoptions.[24] In effect, this was a belated response to the concerns and proposals that had been raised by Health Minister Noel Browne almost six months earlier. What the Washington embassy suggested was a link-up between the Irish authorities and the American Children's Bureau, the professional non-denominational welfare agency that investigated the suitability of most US couples before they could adopt American children. The Children's Bureau had also vetted many of the couples who adopted European war orphans. What was more, the Bureau was part of the federal social security administration, covering the entire United States and applying uniform regulations and procedures – something that could not be said of the decentralised and irregular Catholic Charities branches.

But for the religious, like Father Brown, the Children's Bureau was totally unacceptable. Brown had complained to the Irish embassy in Washington that while Bureau staff had the 'power to enquire into the religious background' of adopters, 'in practice they often tend to disregard this aspect.'[25] Brown continued to push Catholic Charities as a better option, but the Irish diplomats in Washington still kept their lines open to the Children's Bureau. With the active involvement of the US State Department, a senior Irish diplomat held a top level meeting with a consultant from the Children's Bureau in June 1950. The consultant told him that the Bureau 'would be able and willing to afford every assistance in investigating candidates wishing to adopt children, and making reports on all the relevant aspects including that of religious background.'[26]

It was the clearest offer yet of a full and proper adoption vetting service for ensuring decent homes and suitable parents for the hundreds of Irish children being sent by the nuns to America. Given that no one was proposing to put a permanent stop to the business, this was as much as could be hoped for. But the Department of External Affairs back in Dublin was wary of getting involved at this level. 'Our policy should be to keep out of the adoption procedure as much as possible,' one official advised.[27] Another concurred: 'We would lay ourselves open to criticism were we to assist foreigners to remove children from this country.'[28] Nothing further was done with the offer from the Children's Bureau. The same thinking prevented the Department from dealing directly with Catholic Charities but that didn't mean the State was neutral between the two organisations, one secular, the other religious.

Catholic Charities' national secretary, Monsignor John O'Grady, had sought Department sponsorship for a high level meeting in Dublin in August 1950 on 'processing' the Irish-US adoptions. O'Grady's proposal, however, was turned down. Joe Horan, the official then initiating Department policy on foreign adoptions (and a future senior diplomat), was of the view that they couldn't sponsor such a meeting as it 'would be an overt act on our part, giving recognition to this so-called processing of orphans for export.'[29] O'Grady's request was described as 'very delicate' because there was 'considerable danger of public criticism if official backing seemed to be available for this traffic.'[30] Civil servants like Horan feared that their Minister, and through him the Government, would be censured for encouraging emigration in general and the export of 'illegitimate' children in particular.

Consequently, O'Grady's request for a Department-sponsored conference was politely refused on the grounds that 'the Irish Government cannot see its way to take part in arrangements designed to facilitate the removal of Irish children from this country,'[31] but unlike the secular American Children's Bureau, which was simply given the cold shoulder, O'Grady was encouraged to take the matter up with Archbishop McQuaid. The Department of External Affairs clearly felt they could not agree to any course of action on the American adoption issue without McQuaid's prior approval. As Assistant Secretary Brendan Gallagher put it: 'We shall have to be careful not to do anything which would embarrass the Archbishop.'[32] The way things were going there wasn't much danger of that happening.

* * * * *

As the summer of 1950 drew to a close, McQuaid's ban on baby exports was still in force. Father Cecil Barrett, his main adviser, later admitted to having reservations about lifting it. 'I have never been in favour of sending Irish children to America for adoption,' Barrett wrote to McQuaid's secretary, Father Chris Mangan. 'In my view, public opinion would be aroused against any large scale extra-territorial placement of children.'[33] Barrett and McQuaid would have preferred an Irish solution through fostering and informal adoptions, but there simply were not enough families willing to provide Catholic homes for all the country's 'illegitimate' children. And the numbers of children in care of the nuns was constantly growing. As a result, the nuns began to pressurise McQuaid to lift the American ban.

Sister Frances Elizabeth at St Patrick's Guild gave a graphic account of the effects of the ban in a letter to McQuaid's secretary, Mangan. She pointed out that the Guild was overwhelmed with unmarried mothers seeking homes for their children, but they had run out of foster parents, and a huge backlog was building up. 'Girls are flocking here daily,' Sister Frances wrote, 'some of them in great distress... Many of them will become disheartened, no doubt, and who can be sure the children will be safe... Our work is practically at a standstill and many babies, born or expected, are in grave danger.' The Archbishop would be in no doubt as to want she meant by 'danger', and it had nothing to do with the state of the babies' health. Unmarried Catholic mothers, desperate to find homes for their children, might resort to one of the Protestant fostering societies for help. That was the danger. To frustrate the proselytisers, Sister Frances begged the Archbishop to reopen the American outlet immediately. 'The Americans have been a sad loss to our children,' she wrote, 'and we think with longing of those grand Catholic homes which offered such love and security to our little babes.'[34]

Had there been legal adoption in Ireland greater numbers of Irish Catholic couples might have been encouraged to take children from the 'orphanages', but McQuaid himself had frustrated all attempts to bring in legal adoption. It wasn't that he opposed such a measure in principle. He was just unconvinced that the law could guarantee the future faith of adopted Catholic children.[35] With no legal adoption in sight and with a permanent shortage of foster parents, the pressure to find new outlets for 'illegitimate' children was becoming unbearable.

McQuaid and O'Grady finally got together in Dublin in September 1950. O'Grady told McQuaid that he personally 'was not in favour of these American adoptions of Irish children' but he agreed that if certain conditions, as laid down by McQuaid, were fulfilled, then Catholic Charities might co-operate by vetting American applicants for Irish children.[36] To satisfy McQuaid, would-be American adopters had to fulfil certain conditions and these were reproduced as a one-page leaflet which would be sent to all Americans seeking an Irish baby. The leaflet read:

1. The prospective adopting parents must have a written recommendation from the director of Catholic Charities of the Diocese in which they live.
2. The prospective adopting parents must supply for inspection their Baptismal certificates and their Marriage certificates.
3. The prospective adopting parents must have a written recommendation from the Parish Priest of their Parish.
4. The prospective adopting parents must submit a statement of their material circumstances, with a guarantee as to their income, so as to ensure a good home and good prospects in life for the adopted child.
5. The prospective adopting parents must submit medical certificates stating their ages, that they are in good health, physical and mental, and that they are not deliberately shirking natural parenthood.
6. The prospective adopting parents must swear an affidavit to the effect that they are Catholics, that they guarantee to rear the adopted child as a Catholic, that they undertake to educate the adopted child, during the whole course of its schooling, in Catholic schools, that, if in the future the child is sent to a University, it will be sent to a Catholic University, that they undertake to keep the adopted child

permanently and not to hand it over to any other party or parties.[37]

The conditions set by the Archbishop, with minor variations, were to regulate the American adoptions for the foreseeable future. They are notable for their almost single-minded concentration on matters of faith, on the provision of proofs of Catholicism and undertakings regarding the future religious upbringing of the child. Even the medical proofs required by the Archbishop included certification that the couple were not 'shirking natural parenthood' – a euphemism for using contraceptives. Mixed marriage adoptions, of course, were so completely out of the question that they did not even need to be mentioned.

The Church's overwhelming concern for preserving the faith was no more nor less than was to be expected, particularly in the pre-Vatican II era, when Catholicism was held to be the only true Christian doctrine, the 'one true faith', and when it was believed that a child 'lost to Protestants' was doomed. The affidavit swearing to bring the child up a Catholic was the key document in the McQuaid package, yet it is difficult to imagine that it could carry much legal force. Persuading an American court to hear a case on such a matter would have been difficult enough, even if the Archbishop were in a position to discover that the terms of such an affidavit had been broken in the first place. And if he did so discover, it is hard to imagine that he would take the errant parents to court and seek the child's return to the nuns in Ireland, possibly years down the road.

In comparison to the minutely detailed religious and financial proofs required by McQuaid, the method of establishing a couple's suitability *as parents* was somewhat imprecise. What McQuaid asked for was a 'recommendation' from Catholic Charities, but he laid down no standards of his own in this regard, content, it seems, to trust the entire process to the Americans. But when the Diocesan Directors of Catholic Charities met for their national conference in November 1950, they expressed great reluctance to get involved. They did not favour the transatlantic adoptions at all, and only agreed to co-operate because nothing could be done to stop the importations. O'Grady told the conference, 'I should make it clear once more that we are not trying to encourage people to bring Irish children into this country. We are simply trying to do what we can to protect the faith of the children when people insist on bringing them in.'[38] A couple approved by Catholic Charities would be approved primarily as good Catholics. But was a two-paragraph letter from a priest an adequate recommendation, or was a full social worker's report required? These matters were left vague.

And there was another problem, for while Catholic Charities might recommend a couple as 'suitable' adopters on the basis of their religion and material wealth, they had no way of recommending them as parents for a particular Irish child about whom they knew nothing and in whose selection they would play no part. McQuaid cannot have been ignorant of the pitfalls of his scheme since his closest adviser, Cecil Barrett, knew precisely what contemporary adoption theory said was required for a successful adoption – including very close matching of child and parents, something that was totally impossible in the Irish-American mail-order adoption scenario.

Nevertheless, the half-hearted agreement from Catholic Charities made it possible to reopen the door for Americans to again take children from the two main Dublin 'orphanages'. From now on the standard procedure required the American couple to write to the orphanage of their choice, enclosing all the religious and financial proofs. The nuns would then forward the papers to Chris Mangan, McQuaid's secretary, who might consult Cecil Barrett if there were any obvious peculiarities, such as if the applicant were a single male, an elderly couple, or a couple with very many children already. When Mangan was satisfied all was in order, he put the papers before the Archbishop for formal approval, and if McQuaid said yes, the nuns proceeded to apply for a passport for the child they had selected for the successful couple. That at least was the theory, but it didn't always work like that. Loopholes were found.

While the Church authorities – on both sides of the Atlantic – had been quick to identify their concerns and take the steps they thought best to protect the faith, the civil authorities in Dublin had simply marked time as they awaited Archbishop McQuaid's final decision. Peter Berry, of the Department of Justice, gave a candid explanation for official inactivity. 'We might', he wrote, 'lay ourselves open to accusations from high places that we were facilitating the adoption of a child by a person not of the religion in which the child was being reared... Very delicate questions might arise and it was felt that Departments of State should keep clear.'[39] But 'keeping clear' meant abdicating civil responsibility for the social welfare of minors, something that could not simply be equated with their religious welfare.

McQuaid had finally laid his cards on the table, putting it up to the State to play its hand, something it did only after the Department of External Affairs received a copy of McQuaid's new requirements from Sister Frances Elizabeth of St Patrick's Guild. 'Very satisfactory' was how McQuaid's scheme was described within the Department.[40] Copies of McQuaid's regulations were sent to Irish diplomats in the United States with a request that they be treated as 'confidential, private and secret, and not... used officially under any circumstances.'[41] At the same time, however, Irish diplomatic staff in America were told that the Department had 'independently' reached the same conclusion as the Archbishop.

In practice this meant passports would be issued only to children whose intending adopters had been endorsed by Catholic Charities; who had sworn affidavits saying they would rear and educate the child a Catholic; who had produced proofs of religious devotion and, ultimately, who had provided 'clear certificates from their doctor that they are not avoiding natural parentage'.[42] In other words, the State's 'independently' crafted conditions mirrored McQuaid's requirements in every detail, right down to precluding people who practiced artificial contraception. Joe Horan, who was now personally handling each application for an 'adoption passport', even took it upon himself to advise the religious superiors of 'various Catholic institutions throughout the country... that the Conference of Catholic Charities is at their disposal.'[43] For an official body that did not want to be seen to be promoting child exports, the Department of External Affairs was certainly doing a great deal behind the scenes to ensure the smoothest possible passage for children whose dispatch across the Atlantic was approved by the Archbishop.

There could be no doubt that the State had simply followed where the Church had led, yet the Department of External Affairs clearly felt it could not be seen to be taking its cue from the Archbishop. And there were good reasons for that, for the new arrangements came into force at the very moment in 1951 when Church interference in the conduct of the affairs of state had led to an unprecedented political crisis that brought down the inter-party government, enabling Fianna Fáil to return to office. The crisis erupted when Minister for Health, Dr Noel Browne, attempted to introduce his 'Mother and Child' scheme, offering free medical treatment to all expectant mothers and all children up to age 16. The Hierarchy was vehemently opposed, fearing, among other things, secular intrusion into matters such as birth control that were considered 'moral' as opposed to simply medical issues. The bishops told the government in no uncertain terms that such legislation was unacceptable to them. The government – including Noel Browne's party leader, External Affairs Minister Sean MacBride – told the Dáil that 'all of us in the Government who are Catholics are… bound to give obedience to the rulings of our Church and our hierarchy.'[44] The whole affair led *The Irish Times* to conclude that 'the Roman Catholic Church would seem to be the effective Government of this country.'[45]

Such a judgment could equally have been applied to the regulation of the transatlantic adoption traffic.

3. Me Tommy, You Jane

'Ireland has become a sort of hunting ground today for foreign million-aires who believe they can acquire children to suit their whims.'
8 Uhr Blatt (German newspaper)
13 December 1951

No sooner had Church and State concluded their supposedly independent but in practice identical arrangements for controlling the flow of 'illegitimate' babies to America when another scandal broke – this time on a much bigger scale than the McDowell case of 1949.

Tommy Kavanagh was 15 months old when he left for America, where he enjoyed a wealthy and privileged lifestyle. But how he came to be in the United States in the first place was an issue that scandalised Ireland, Britain and America, leading to questions in the Dáil, the House of Commons and the American Congress. Tommy Kavanagh's adoption was the most sensational and notorious of all the Irish-American adoptions, yet his name has long been forgotten. The same, however, cannot be said of the woman who adopted him: millionaire Hollywood actress and 1950s pin-up, Jane Russell, whose death in February 2011 inspired obituaries around the world.

In October 1951, Jane Russell, then 32 years old, flew to London to take part in the Royal Command performance. But she had other business to see to as well. As she announced to the media on her arrival, she had come to acquire a little boy for adoption, a brother for the four-month-old baby girl she had already adopted. As one British paper put it, 'Americans like Miss Russell are constantly besieging adoption society offices in this country. They seek British children because of the possible "colour taint" in their own country.'[1]

As a result of all the publicity, Russell was inundated with letters from British mothers offering their children to her. But as she quickly discovered, British adoption law prohibited her, as a foreign national, from taking a child who was not a relation from the UK to the US for adoption. But she was not deterred, and she soon let it be known she would not be going home empty handed. 'I have been advised to try Ireland,' she told reporters. 'If it is possible I would like to fly to Dublin this week to pick out a child and make all the arrangements for bringing him to America.'[2] It was almost half a century later when another US idol, Madonna, created a similar uproar when she swooped not on Ireland but on Malawi in search of children to take back home for adoption. In the event, however, Russell did not have to go to Ireland. The Irish came to her.

Florrie Kavanagh came from Derry and her husband Michael was from Galway.[3] They had both emigrated from Ireland to the UK to get work in the munitions factories during the Second World War. They met at a hostel dance in Coventry and were soon married. Later they moved to Lambeth in south London where they lived in a small council flat. Michael worked on the building sites and earned six pounds ten shillings a week. They had three children of whom Tommy was the youngest.

Florrie claimed to be a big fan of Jane Russell and to have seen all her films. When she heard that Russell was looking for a little boy to adopt she thought Tommy would be ideal for the actress, and would get a great opportunity in life that she and Michael could never provide for him. Shortly afterwards she noticed Tommy kissing a picture in a newspaper and when she looked she saw it was a picture of Jane Russell. Florrie Kavanagh had 'a strange feeling' and resolved to make contact with the American actress so she could offer Tommy to her for adoption.

After finding the name of Jane Russell's London hotel in the newspaper, Florrie bundled up her children, and went out to the telephone box. Russell's mother answered the call and Florrie told her she had a baby boy to give up for adoption. Mrs Russell remarked that there were difficulties in adopting British babies. 'But my baby is an Irish baby,' replied Florrie. That made all the difference. She was invited to bring him to the hotel at 4.30pm that afternoon. It was Saturday, 3 November.

When Florrie arrived with Tommy, Jane Russell was in bed, resting between rehearsals. Tommy crawled up to her and hugged her. That, it seems, was all it took. Florrie was given tea and shown photographs of Russell's Hollywood mansion which made her gasp. Back home in her Lambeth flat that evening, Florrie discussed the matter with Michael. They agreed Tommy would have a 'better life' with Jane Russell. All that was needed now was for the actress to accept the offer.

On the morning of Tuesday 6 November, the Kavanaghs were told to come immediately to Russell's hotel. She wanted Tommy, but there had been a change of plan, to keep on the right side of British adoption law. Instead of taking Tommy for adoption, Russell would take him for 'a three-month holiday.' That afternoon Tommy was issued with an Irish passport and that night he was on the plane, bound for the USA. He never came back. Florrie Kavanagh's last words to Jane Russell were, 'I would like you to have him for always.' Russell squeezed her hand and replied, 'Sure'.

'I don't care what the neighbours are saying,' said Florrie. 'My Tommy has been given a chance in a million. And I know in my heart that Miss Russell is a good woman who will give my baby a mother's love and so much more than I could ever give him.' She denied she had received any money from Jane Russell, but there was no doubt the child was going to the States for something other than a holiday.

Many years later Tommy Kavanagh's elder brother, Michael, gave this account: 'At home… we had an outside toilet and kept things in orange boxes. We didn't even know what a cushion was. All of a sudden, all these decorators arrived with expensive paintings and furniture. Jane Russell had paid a fortune for them to do the house up. As soon as the decorators finished, though, my mum sold the whole lot down Wilcox Street Market. We got our orange boxes back, we were happy, and we all had a big laugh.'[4]

When news of Jane Russell's easy acquisition of young Tommy Kavanagh became public, it sparked an international controversy. One British newspaper wondered if it really was a good thing 'for a child who was born perhaps from a stock accustomed and inured to hardship and struggle', to be 'transplanted to a life of comparative ease.'[5] Others asked how it was possible for a mother and father to just give away one of their children. But questions were also asked about the legality of it all.

Had Tommy's parents applied for a British passport to enable him to travel to America for adoption, their application would have been turned down automatically. British law prohibited the adoption of British children by foreign nationals unless the foreigners were resident in Britain or related to the child in question. That was why Russell decided on an Irish child. Tommy Kavanagh, of course, was an Irish citizen, and left Britain on an Irish passport. But British adoption law also prohibited the removal for adoption abroad of children who were citizens of the Irish Republic resident in Britain, a clause presumably designed primarily to protect Catholic children in Northern Ireland who had availed of Irish citizenship. The law, of course, applied not only to Florrie and Michael Kavanagh, but to Jane Russell and the consular staff at the Irish embassy in London as well. Yet an Irish passport was issued without difficulty allowing Tommy Kavanagh to leave the country with Jane Russell.

The issuing of the passport in London was a cause of deep embarrassment because it could have been inter-preted as condoning, encouraging, and even committing a criminal offence under a law that was designed to protect the interests of vulnerable children. Anyone guilty of assisting in the removal of a child for adoption abroad faced up to six months in prison and a £50 fine, a substan-tial amount in the early 1950s – around €4,800 today.

As the scandal unfolded, the British authorities came under pressure to explain how a wealthy and flamboyant Hollywood actress could so easily procure a child in broad daylight, as it were, and in the middle of London. The British police even followed Tommy's father, Michael Snr, around London – surreptitiously but fruitlessly – to see if he would collect money from Jane Russell's agents in return for his son. By contrast, the only question asked of Frank Aiken, Minister for External Affairs in the Irish Parliament concerned whether he seen the newspaper reports, and 'what precautions were taken to protect the religious life of the infant?'[6] The questioner was Waterford Labour TD and future party chairman Tom Kyne, and his curious question was no doubt prompted by the fact that Russell was a devout and practising Protestant while Tommy Kavanagh was, by birth if not by choice, a Catholic.

Aiken sidestepped the religious issue but did tell the Dáil that newspaper reports of the case 'were not correct in stating that the passport was granted to enable the child to be adopted in the United States.' It had been granted, he said, so the child could go to America on holiday with his new friend, Jane Russell. But Aiken knew the explanation he had given was a fiction, and if opposition deputies had known the full background to the case they might have accused the Minister of deliberately misleading the Dáil.

A detailed memo had been prepared for Mr Aiken before he answered Kyne's question.[7] It gave the complete background to the case, from the point of view of the passport staff in the Irish embassy in London. In so doing it left no doubt at all that Tommy Kavanagh was given a passport so he could travel to the States to be adopted. Had this come out, of course, it could have caused a diplomatic incident and could have led to the prosecution of Irish embassy staff.

On 5 November 1951, the day before the passport was issued, one of Russell's London agents, George Routledge, telephoned the Irish embassy in London to enquire about passport regulations. In the course of his conversation with embassy staff Routledge referred to Russell's intention of adopting an Irish child – an intention that had been widely reported in the newspapers, including *The Irish Times*. The consular staff explained the legal position to Routledge – it would be unlawful to remove an Irish child from the UK for adoption in the US. On the next day, Routledge came in person to the embassy along with Michael Kavanagh, Tommy's father. They completed the application form, giving 'holiday' as the reason for the child's visit to America. They were issued there and then with a passport for the infant.

Although the application form made no mention of adoption, the Irish officials clearly knew this was the real intention behind the request for a passport, and just two days after the passport was issued, the embassy telexed the Department of External Affairs in Dublin to inform them that 'a passport had been granted to enable an Irish child to travel abroad for adoption.' The telex didn't name the child or the adopters, but when Dublin asked for particulars, the embassy replied that the passport had been for the child in 'the Jane Russell baby case'.

This exchange of correspondence was quoted in the memo to Frank Aiken, to inform him fully of the position before he spoke in the Dáil. It made it absolutely clear the embassy staff in London knew Tommy Kavanagh was to be taken to America for adoption, regardless of what was said on the passport application about a 'holiday'. Officials in the Department of External Affairs were also very clear on the significance of the deception. Had it been 'admitted that adoption was contemplated', an internal memo noted with considerable emphasis, *'our passport officer would be liable for 6 months!!*[8]

The Irish denial of culpability was helped a little when the British Home Secretary, Maxwell Fyfe, in reply to questions in the British Parliament, repeated the formula that Mr and Mrs Kavanagh had officially consented only to Tommy travelling to America for a three-month holiday, not for adoption.[9] But the British authorities later showed that they themselves were not convinced when they charged the Kavanaghs with the offence of 'unlawfully permitting the care and possession of the said infant to be transferred to one Jane Russell Waterfield, a person resident abroad, namely in the United States of America.'[10]

The Irish authorities were also clearly unconvinced by their own public pronouncements. Just the day before Aiken spoke in the Dáil, instructions were rushed to Irish embassies and legations around the world that no passports were to be issued to children under the age of 18 without prior clearance from the head of mission. It was an excessive measure if all they were concerned with was Irish children having innocent holidays abroad with friends approved by their parents.

Back in Hollywood, Jane Russell soon let it be known that she had every intention of adopting Tommy Kavanagh, once the 'fuss' had died down.[11] But when the Kavanaghs were subsequently brought before the courts, they were reported as accusing Jane Russell of 'keeping in the background' while they took all the blame.[12] The Kavanaghs pleaded guilty at Bow Street Court and were each given a twelve month conditional discharge. As they left the court they were jeered and jostled by a hostile crowd. They had told the court they received photographs and regular letters from Russell, and when the Magistrate read these he remarked that Russell 'must be a very very nice woman'. Eventually the adoption went ahead.

In fact, Jane Russell's interest in adoption went far beyond Tommy Kavanagh. With her American-football star husband, Robert Waterfield, Russell set up a full-scale professional adoption service – WAIF – which subsequently handled around 40,000 American adoptions.[13] But Russell's activities were not always welcomed by Catholic agencies in America. The National Catholic Welfare Conference, which handled scores of requests from Americans looking for Irish babies to adopt, wrote to Archbishop McQuaid's adoption advisor, Father Cecil Barrett, in 1958 warning him that 'there will be trouble' should Ms Russell and her associates 'engage in bringing over Catholic orphans' from Ireland, for despite their claims to be 'non-sectarian', they were in fact connected to the Young Women's Christian Association – a wholly Protestant outfit.[14]

The Russell/Kavanagh affair also had a more immediate sequel when a mass-circulation German evening newspaper, *8 Uhr Blatt*, published a long article on December 13, 1951 under the heading '1,000 children disappear from Ireland'.

'A wave of resentment sweeps Ireland at present,' the paper stated, 'after American film-star Jane Russell flew to the USA with 16-month old Tommy Kavanagh, because she wanted so much to have a child.' The case simply highlighted 'a regular export in children to the USA' which had reached such a pitch, the paper said, that the government in Dublin was planning a new law 'to put an end to the traffic'.

An Irish child welfare organisation was quoted by the German paper as saying that Ireland 'has become a sort of hunting ground today for foreign millionaires who believe they can acquire children to suit their whims just in the same way as they could get valuable pedigree animals. In the last few months more than one hundred children have left Ireland without any official organisation being in a position to make any enquiries as to their future habitat.'

The article quoted examples of children being sent to the USA with no further news of what became of them. It claimed that 'altogether almost a thousand children have been taken abroad from the Green Isle during the course of the past year.' And with 80,000 couples queuing up to adopt children in the United States, there was plenty of scope for this traffic to grow. But where demand outstripped supply to such an extent, people would inevitably pay to get a baby, thus ensuring 'a regular black market' in babies in the USA.

The German paper pointed out that baby-selling enterprises had recently been broken up in New York, Maryland and Massachusetts and the operators arrested. One lawyer alone had already sold 100 children at the lucrative rate of $3,000 apiece before he was caught. $300,000 in 1951 is the equivalent of a business with a turnover well in excess of €10m today.

This was a hard-hitting article that made Ireland look like a pathetically backward Third World country where stray or unwanted children could be acquired at will. Not surprisingly, the *Chargé d'Affaires* at the Irish legation in Bonn, Aedan O'Beirne, read the *8 Uhr Blatt* article – which he described as 'sordid' – with a growing sense of anger. His immediate reaction was to seek permission from the secretary of the Department of External Affairs to demand of the paper's editor that he 'publish a rebuttal of the story'.[15]

O'Beirne's request for 'speedy counter action' was circulated among senior officials in Dublin, but the unanimous view there was that no action should or could be taken. As one official noted: 'No action is required, especially as the article is largely correct.'[16] Joe Horan replied to O'Beirne by saying they could only demand a rebuttal if they could 'put matters in truer perspective'. This they were unable to do, Horan pointed out, for the article was 'largely not incorrect.' It was better to say nothing at all since to complain would be to attract 'more adverse publicity'.[17] This was an astonishing admission by a very senior Irish State official that the American adoption business was riddled with uncertainty, to put it at its mildest. The only fact that was disputed was the figure of 1,000 children exported to the US in the course of a year. This was far in excess of *The Irish Times*' estimate of '500 plus' for the first nine months of 1951[18] and completely out of line with the official figure of 122 'adoption passports' for the whole year. But Horan seemed to accept that the number of children exported from Ireland exceeded the official tally to a considerable degree.

Joe Horan was the civil servant with the greatest hands-on experience of the American adoption scene. All passport applications passed through his hands. Not surprisingly, he was well aware of the realities of adoption in the American context, and when he said that such a damning article was 'largely not incorrect', he knew what he was talking about. Horan had serious reservations about the effectiveness of official controls. The Department, he noted, was only aware of adoption cases where intending adopters actually applied for passports for the children they wanted but, as he pointed out, they did not need a passport to get the child out of Ireland. 'Once they have the child,' Horan wrote, 'there is nothing to stop them getting on the boat at Dun Laoghaire or the plane at Collinstown' and going first to Britain.[19] Once they were out of the Irish jurisdiction, the authorities in Dublin would simply lose track of them. International travel without a valid passport was no easy matter of course, but there was a black market in forged and stolen passports. What was more, American embassies around the world had the authority, under US federal law, to issue entry visas to people without passports, and that included babies and children. The main requirement for getting a visa for a child was simply that the American 'sponsor' gave an undertaking that the child would not become a 'public charge' after entering the United States. But as the ever-perceptive Joe Horan noted, 'such an undertaking is worthless since… there is no danger that such a child would become a public charge after entering the United States; it would simply be sold to another couple.'[20] Knowing what he did about the loopholes in the official system, it was little wonder Horan felt unable, in honesty, to refute newspaper claims that there was a significant black-market trade going on in Irish babies.

As much as a year before the Jane Russell case, Horan had expressed his deep-seated fears about this 'veritable trade in orphans'. 'There is a market for children in the USA,' Horan wrote. It flourished because 'demand exceeds supply,' and as a result, 'there are in some states shady institutions known as "baby farms" which specialise in collecting children and giving them to adopting parents for a consideration'. There was an obvious concern that Irish children might be procured by these baby farms since among certain Americans, Horan noted, Ireland 'enjoys quite a reputation... as a place where one can get children for adoption without much difficulty.'[21] In further writings, Horan again drew attention to the 'many private institutions' in America that 'do a business in children for adoption,' and he described Ireland as 'a happy hunting ground' for people looking for children – the same phrase used by the German paper, *8 Uhr Blatt.*[22]

Following the outcry surrounding the Jane Russell case, and clearly worried by the amount of media attention it attracted, Horan again recorded his concerns about dispatching children to America. 'Supposing it happened,' he wrote, 'that the child was surrendered to persons who, on arrival in the USA, proceeded to sell it off to the highest bidder, with consequent press publicity etc. It is we who would be held responsible as it is we who would have to answer parliamentary questions, face a press campaign here, and so on.'[23] This overwhelming concern with adverse publicity was reflected in another of Horan's revealing papers. 'One always has the horrible fear,' he wrote, 'that some of the proposed adopters may wish to get their hands on a child for the purpose of making money by selling it to another couple anxious to adopt a child... with for us, all sorts of undesirable prospects such as letters to the newspapers, parliamentary questions and so on... We must be alive to the possibility that the name of this country might one day figure in one of those "exposures" they have from time to time in the USA.'[24] The fate of the children seemed of much less concern than the prospect of 'bad publicity'.

Another issue that Horan drew attention to was the 'race' factor. He was a sharp-witted man and could see clearly why Irish babies were so popular for Americans – indeed why they might carry a premium price. 'Americans,' he wrote, 'are colour-conscious and people adopting a child from an American institution could never really be free from the fear that one fine day it might transpire that the child had negro blood, while of course they can be sure that a child got from Ireland would be 100% white.'[25]

Horan also noted that the practice of sending children to American couples who had never been to Ireland and who had never met the children in question increased the danger of the infants falling into the wrong hands. This, he observed, was a problem peculiar to Catholic children dispatched by the nuns, since the Protestant adoption societies 'insist on the adopting parents seeing the child before they will even consider surrendering the child to them'. This policy also meant the Protestant agencies in Ireland had an opportunity to interview and assess all prospective adopting couples, something the nuns rarely did as their US adoptions were becoming more and more of the 'mail order' variety with everything done by letters and photographs. (Only 24 of the 2,000 American adoptions involved Protestant children.)

What is perhaps most disturbing about Horan's observations is that they were made long after Catholic Charities had taken on the role of 'proving' the suitability of Catholic American adopters. If Horan still feared that children could be sent to people in the States who might sell them, he must have had serious reservations about the American vetting procedures, the procedures that underpinned the entire system and justified the issuing of Irish passports.

Horan's fears about Irish babies changing hands in America for money could not be dismissed as imaginary. He had evidence of what he called 'a little racket' operating in Co. Louth where a woman, known to the authorities, was engaged in sending children to Chicago for adoption. The woman had relatives in Chicago who were involved in selecting the children before their dispatch. This led Horan to conclude that they were running some sort of family business and 'earning a bit on the side by finding children for childless couples'. Ireland, he said, 'is a "gift" from their point of view,' because 'there is nothing to stop anyone coming into this country and taking away children for adoption'. He related his suspicions to a local Garda Chief Superintendent, with a request that the police investigate the family concerned. 'We know there really is a market for children in the USA,' he said.[26]

Unfortunately the results of the police chief's inquiry are not available, but whatever effect his investigation had on the family 'racket', it failed to put an end to the traffic in Irish babies in Chicago. In the summer of 1952, for instance, a number of Irish priests travelled to Chicago and made 'private arrangements' for the placement of children there. The children in question were placed without any prior investigation into the background of the people to whom they were given – a fact that led the Rev Bernard Brogan, Associate Director of Catholic Charities in Chicago, to declare himself 'fearful of the ultimate outcome of these placements,' since 'visiting priests are not in any position to judge the acceptability of an adoptive home'.[27] And it wasn't just Chicago. During a visit to Ireland at the end of 1951, a senior social worker from Catholic Charities told an official in the Department of External Affairs that she had investigated cases in the Cleveland area of Ohio where Irish children had been sent to unsuitable and uninspected homes.[28] And their unsuitability had nothing to do with the religious pedigree of the adopters.

What these cases make clear is that there was a gaping loophole in the official monitoring system as well as in McQuaid's controls. The Department of External Affairs had announced in early 1951 that passports would only be issued to children after approval of the adoptive parents by Catholic Charities. Yet here were cases over a year later – the priests taking children to Chicago – where a number of children had obtained passports to leave Ireland although the Americans who were adopting them had not been vetted by anyone.

The Department of External Affairs expressed shock at Father Brogan's revelations from Chicago and asked for a list of the children's names so a check could be made to see how they managed to get passports in breach of the Department's own regulations. If Brogan replied, his response is not on file. Nor is there any evidence on file to suggest the Department carried out an investigation of its own. The same has to be said about the revelations from Cleveland. The matter was noted on file, but no attempt seems to have been made to find out who the children were or what became of them – an appalling indictment of official hypocrisy. While the people involved in promoting and processing the export of Irish children to the United States may once have assumed that those they dispatched were going to a better life, by 1952 they had abundant evidence that it was a very hit-and-miss affair. No one knew – or seemed to want to find out – how many vulnerable Irish children had been sold on the thriving American black market, possibly into a life of exploitation, physical and/or sexual abuse, or worse – their fates unrecorded and, sadly, unknowable.

One case, however, can be reported in some detail since the child at its centre survived and resurfaced to tell her story. Mary Theresa Monaghan was born on 7 October 1950 to an unmarried mother at the Sacred Heart convent in Castlepollard. Her mother, in line with standard practice and with no meaningful alternative available to her, surrendered Mary Theresa to Sister Rosamonde McCarthy, the head nun at Castlepollard, and on 13 September 1952. Sister Rosamonde, following Archbishop McQuaid's requirements to the letter, surrendered the infant to her would-be American adopters, well-to-do Catholics, William and Marguerite O'Brien of Huntington Park, California who already had an adopted son, Patrick. On 22 September

1952, an Irish passport was issued under the authority of the Minister for External Affairs, Frank Aitken, so Mary Theresa could be dispatched to her new life in the United States. Mary Theresa's US entry visa shows she arrived in California on 2 October 1952, and within two years her legal adoption by the O'Briens was completed. On paper, at least, everything looked normal and above board. The adoption had proceeded in line with all the legal and administrative rules set down by the Irish State and Catholic Church to supposedly protect children and preserve their faith. But Mary Theresa's story shows how totally inadequate those rules and regulations were, for although she wasn't sold on the black market, she suffered terribly in her new home.

Four and a half decades after her arrival in America, Mary Theresa imagined herself back in 1952 and began writing about how she had experienced her new life from the outset. 'Today I am two years old,' she wrote. 'I hide. I fear. I cry. I cannot eat. I sense consternation. I sense anger. I sense that I am no longer safe. Where is this place of danger? I cry. I hide. Why can I not find safety or protection? I crawl into every dark place that I fit. I must find a place to be away from the noise and the screams of ridicule. What have I done? Why is everyone so angry?'[29]

Bill O'Brien, her adoptive father, was a violent and dangerous man who beat his wife and sexually abused Mary Theresa throughout her childhood and into her late teens when she finally escaped the family home to attend university.[30] At an early age she had discovered that her adopted brother, Patrick, was actually Bill O'Brien's natural son, one of twins born to a woman with whom he had had an extramarital affair. Mrs O'Brien, who was unable to have children of her own, had gone along with the subterfuge in the hope that it would make Mr O'Brien a less violent and abusive partner. It didn't. He would regularly taunt

Mary Theresa, 'Your real parents didn't want you', which increased her sense of abandonment and isolation and robbed her of whatever self-esteem remained.

When Mr O'Brien died in 1977, Mary Theresa obtained a file of her adoption papers from her adoptive mother. They gave the first clues as to how her life had taken such a dreadful course. Among the documents was a letter to Sister Rosemonde McCarthy at the Sacred Heart convent, Castlepollard, from the Right Reverend Monsignor Raymond J. O'Flaherty of the Californian Catholic Welfare Bureau, the body charged with conducting a Home Study and verifying the suitability of Mr and Mrs O'Brien as adoptive parents. The letter was dated 8 September, 1952, five days before Sister Rosemonde signed legal documents surrendering Mary Theresa to the O'Briens. 'You realise, of course', O'Flaherty wrote, 'that our Home Study cannot be considered complete since Mr O'Brien could not be interviewed.' They couldn't interview him because he had already travelled to Ireland to collect Mary Theresa. Pressures of time took precedence over producing a comprehensive report. 'Our Home Study is not as complete as it would have been were it not for the time element,' O'Flaherty acknowledged. 'It is our understanding that Mr O'Brien will soon leave Ireland to return to his employment and must complete plans for the little girl to accompany him to California.' O'Brien, it seemed, was dictating the terms.

'However', O'Flaherty added rather pointedly, 'you have had the benefit of interviews with Mr O'Brien and so have made an evaluation and a decision, feeling secure that Mary Teresa (*sic*) would be given a good home.' It was evident that Bill O'Brien had been to Castlepollard to see the nuns and had been interviewed in person by Sister Rosemonde, who clearly had no qualms about releasing the infant Mary Theresa to him. With this disclaimer, O'Flaherty proceeded to recommend the adoption based on the 'excellent reference' provided by the O'Briens' priest, Father Thomas Morris, who had known the couple for 14 years, together with a letter from Bill O'Brien's work associates at the Studebaker Corporation, and another from the couple's GP.

O'Flaherty wrote of the 'seemingly good relationship' between Mrs O'Brien and her adopted son Patrick, and the 'fine relationship' that existed between Mr and Mrs O'Brien, and he referred to their 'apparently genuine' wish to adopt a second child. O'Flaherty's otherwise sparse and somewhat qualified letter ended with a thoroughly detailed account of the O'Briens' finances: Mr O'Brien's salary was $350 a month (equivalent to €12,000 a month today), and they had deposits of $750 in two banks, a further $875 in US Savings Bonds, $1,540 in the Credit Union, $4,000 worth of shares in retail giant Sears and Roebuck, and real estate in San Gabriel, near Los Angeles. They owned their own home and furnishings as well as two cars, and they had no debt. The letter of recommendation that O'Flaherty enclosed from the O'Briens' doctor, Bernard Corren, stated: 'From our observations of both Mr and Mrs O'Brien over a period of time, we feel that they have the necessary qualities for parenthood.' They weren't 'shirking natural parenthood' either: Mrs O'Brien had had a hysterectomy a year previously. The other note O'Flaherty enclosed was from Doug Gittins, Personnel Director of the Studebaker Corporation where Mr O'Brien worked. It wasn't a recommendation of any sort and was actually addressed to Mr O'Brien. All it said was, 'we are all very anxious to see the little colleen which we trust you will be able to bring back to the States with you.'

This, it seems, was the sum total of what it took for an abusive (but devout) Catholic to obtain an Irish child for adoption in 1952: a seriously incomplete Home Study report, a sugary note from an employer, a misjudged letter from a doctor, an unknowing priest's recommendation, the nod from a nun sorely lacking in professional qualifications, and a very fat bank balance.

Reflecting on her years of brutal sexual abuse Mary Theresa said, 'Perhaps if a pre-adoption interview with Mr O'Brien had taken place by a trained person I would not have been placed in the home of a very violent paedophile.' Describing her life with the O'Briens simply as 'painful', Mary Theresa pondered, 'I can't help but wonder who I might be now if there hadn't been so much abuse to overcome.' Therapy, and good friends, helped. So too did her search for her natural mother, although it took twenty years to complete. In the course of her search she had written to Father P.J. Reagan, parish priest at Castlepollard, asking for her baptismal certificate. In his reply, and in blithe ignorance of the reality of Mary Theresa's life as an adopted person, Father Reagan, who was himself closely enmeshed in the American adoption business, asked about the only subject that really mattered: 'I do hope your Irish Catholic Faith continues to mean a lot for you?' But whatever Faith there had been, it had long since evaporated.

While Tommy Kavanagh's life with Jane Russell in Beverly Hills certainly did not mirror in any way that of Mary Theresa, even his story was not, in the end, a happy one. 'My parents got divorced in 1965, when I was 15', he said in a revealing 1998 interview.[31] 'That was when things got pretty stressed for me. When it's your Mum and Dad in the papers every day, it's tough.' After the divorce, Tommy wanted to know more about his natural parents, so Jane Russell brought him back to London to meet them. The reunion was conducted in the full glare of the media. 'I was told, "The cameras are rolling, now you walk in and sit over on the couch and you meet your real mum." The whole thing was staged. It was really confusing. I wasn't sure if I should feel guilty because they lived so humbly.' Tommy went on to say that the 'confusion' he faced in his life 'became too much' for him. He left home, 'became a tearaway', used drugs, fathered a child out of wedlock, and sorely disappointed Jane Russell by failing to go to college. Approaching the age of 50, he said he had got himself together again after an unsuccessful marriage that ended in divorce. 'I'm just a working guy struggling to pay the bills,' he said. 'I make leather belts for a living and at weekends play in a band called Russell in honour of my mother.' Meanwhile, his brother Michael revealed that when Tommy wrote to him from his adopted home, 'it was obvious from the letters that he wasn't always happy... Being adopted had its effect on Tommy... If Tommy had stayed with us, he wouldn't have had a bad life. Dad brought us up, worked hard and gave us everything... I would never change places with Tommy, never.'[32]

Tommy Kavanagh and Mary Theresa Monaghan spent their troubled childhoods in California, but for much of the 1950s, the real locus of questionable adoptions remained Chicago. A couple of years after Father Brogan's revelations concerning Irish children being handed over to unvetted adopters in the city by visiting Irish priests, Chicago was back in the limelight when the city was at the centre of a full-scale US Senate inquiry into an international baby adoption racket where infants were changing hands for $3,000 each (€100,000 today). According to one report, adoption law in the state of Illinois was so lax that people came to Chicago from all over the United States to procure babies without any investigation of their suitability.[33] The report did not say if any of the children in question had originated in Ireland. But it is known that almost 300 Irish children were sent to Illinois during the course of the American adoption programme, making it second only to New York as a favoured destination.

With stories like these now surfacing fairly regularly, it was little wonder that Joe Horan in the Department of External Affairs was so obsessed with protecting the Department from prying journalists and questioning politicians. But Horan was certain that his dilemma would soon be resolved by the introduction of an Adoption Act which he believed would 'put an end to the taking of illegitimates and orphans out of the State by non-nationals'.[34]

He was wrong.

4. A Hard Act to Follow

'The Episcopal Committee had in mind the danger of proselytism in the six counties if there were no restrictions on sending children across the Border'

Department of Justice letter, 1952

At a time when the Catholic Church seemed to have no difficulty permitting children to be sent abroad for adoption, it had vehemently opposed the introduction of adoption law within Ireland. This seeming contradiction, however, had a simple explanation. The Church was in a position to exercise control over the foreign adoption programme, but the hierarchy feared they might not enjoy such untrammelled power if adoption law were introduced at home. They were not opposed to adoption in principle, only to an adoption system that might result in the children of Catholic mothers falling into the hands of non-Catholics, and particularly of Northern Irish Protestants. But in January 1952, in the immediate aftermath of the Jane Russell affair and under some pressure from a multi-denominational lobby group called the 'Legal Adoption Society', the Irish bishops announced their willingness to countenance adoption legislation provided the 'faith and morals' of the children involved could be safeguarded.

Shortly after the bishops had given this green light, Joe Horan of the Department of External Affairs noted that the officials of the Department of Justice, whose job was drawing up new legislation, had been 'working day and night' to 'bring their draft Bill into line' with the bishops' new position.[1] But it was not simply a matter of state functionaries doing their best to draft a law that would meet the approval of the Church. The Church – in the person of Archbishop John Charles McQuaid – was playing a direct role in shaping the legislation. Horan recorded that 'the AB called twice on the M for Justice', while two of the Minister's senior officials 'went twice or more to the AB in connection with the whole business.' Horan's source for this revealing piece of information was the Secretary General, Peter Berry, right at the heart of the Department of Justice. Indeed, Archbishop McQuaid himself was to reveal in later years that, along with Father Cecil Barrett, he 'went over every clause' in the Bill.[2] What this meant was that when the Adoption Act was eventually published, the Archbishop's imprimatur was firmly stamped upon it.

Joe Horan mistakenly believed the new legislation was being designed to put an end to the transatlantic baby shipments and he was not the only one. This was a view that was held widely and aired publicly. The German paper *8 Uhr Blatt*, for example, had made the same claim in the midst of its exposé of Ireland's adoption rackets, and no one had seen fit to contradict it. Even in distant Australia, Ireland's decision to legislate for adoption was seen as essential for bringing the American adoptions – and particularly the more dubious ones – to an end. An article in the *Sydney Sun* stated: 'The Government of Eire is rushing through a Bill to curb an extensive baby black market. Irish babies are allegedly sold to childless American couples for about £900 each...' (or close to €86,000 in today's money). The *Adelaide Mail*, under a headline 'Eire to end Baby Sales,' quoted an official of the Legal Adoption Society as saying Irish babies were selling in the United States for $2,000 each (nearly €70,000). The new law, it was stated, would prohibit non-nationals from adopting Irish children, just as the law in Britain did.

The same point of view prevailed in the Department of Justice where the Bill was being drafted. An assistant secretary there had been asked to check and authorise a letter to the Irish ambassador in Washington explaining to him the thinking behind the forthcoming adoption legislation. The approved text stated: 'There has been a demand in certain quarters for the enactment of such legislation during the last few years, particularly as a result of the activities of certain aliens who wish to adopt Irish children and held out the inducement of large sums of money to induce Irish parents to allow their children to be taken away by these people.' It was precisely 'to deal with this situation' that the Government decided to legislate.[3]

What is more, it seems the nuns who were sending the children abroad also believed the new law would put an end to their entire lucrative business, for there was an apparent rush to dispatch as many children as possible before the door closed. The number of children legally sent abroad for adoption in 1952, the last year before the Adoption Act came into force, was 193, an increase of nearly 60% on the previous year, and the highest figure recorded for any year.

Although there seemed to be near unanimity, not only on the need to end the American traffic but also on the belief that the forthcoming Adoption Act would do so, Archbishop McQuaid had different ideas. When the new Bill was finally published it fell far short of a ban on the export of Irish children. What was outlawed, under section 39 of the Bill (becoming section 40 of the final Act), was the export of *legitimate* children, but it remained perfectly legal to dispatch 'illegitimate' children overseas for adoption

– precisely the children under Church control.[4] The only other restriction related to age: children earmarked for export would in future have to be at least one year old and no more than seven, where previously they could be of any age. The Adoption Act also required the child's mother or legal guardian to consent to the sending of the child abroad for adoption. In addition, it made it an offence generally to charge fees for arranging an adoption but it did not preclude adopters from making 'donations' to adoption societies. Nor did it prohibit the religious orders who ran the societies from soliciting 'donations'.

The clauses in the Act relating to child exports were extremely hard to follow. They were written in such convoluted language that anyone reading the relevant section might not immediately grasp the fact that it was there to regulate the practice of exporting 'illegitimate' children. Whether that was the intention or not, it is equally hard to know. (The Act's distinction between legitimate and illegitimate was eventually found to be unconstitutional.)

The main thrust of the Adoption Act, however, had nothing whatever to do with foreign adoptions. The Act was brought in primarily to establish legal adoption within Ireland. To this end it set up an Adoption Board to oversee the whole business and, in particular, to approve each individual adoption. In line with the hierarchy's requirements, the Act prohibited inter-denominational adoptions: only Catholic couples could adopt Catholic children, a child's religion being defined as that of its parents, or of its mother if she was unmarried. Mixed-marriage couples were not allowed to adopt at all, nor could orphaned children of mixed marriages ever be offered for adoption. Believing Catholicism to be the only true religion, the Catholic Church would have had no problems in allowing Catholic couples to adopt Protestant children, but permitting this while prohibiting the reverse would have been too blatantly sectarian, even in the early 1950s.

The Adoption Act also required all organisations and societies engaged in placing children for adoption to be registered with the Adoption Board, but the law laid down no conditions that had to be met by such societies before or after registration. Any individual or any group of people could constitute themselves as an adoption society, register under the Act, and engage in acquiring and disposing of babies. There was no requirement that the nuns, who continued to dominate the Irish adoption business, should have any qualifications, professional or otherwise.

One other aspect of the Act deserves mention. It instituted a regime of 'closed' adoptions: the natural parents of the child surrendered for adoption were expected to never want contact with their child again, and they were told nothing of the identity of the adopters, while children given up for adoption were denied any legal entitlement to their birth certificate (even though it is a public document) where their pre-adoption Christian name and their mother's full name (and possibly address), would be recorded. Instead, if they asked for their birth certificate, they would be given an adoption certificate instead, recording only their adopted name and adopted parents' details. (Ironically, if they knew their actual date and place of birth, they had a very good chance of finding their birth certificate in the public register, and with it, their natural mother's name.) In years to come, when many natural mothers would try to trace their adopted children, and those children when grown would likewise look for their natural mothers, the 'closed adoption' dogma, and the denial of information or meaningful assistance in tracing and reuniting would become an issue of enormous controversy, and source of deep anguish for a great many people.

As for the failure of the Adoption Act to outlaw the transatlantic baby traffic, this can be attributed directly to the influence of the Church. The relevant part of the Bill,

Section 39, was shaped by the hierarchy, a fact that was acknowledged by the Department of Justice. 'Section 39,' the Department stated in a contemporary paper, 'was inserted in the Bill as one of the safeguards suggested by the Episcopal Committee in a memorandum that was handed to the Minister for Justice by his Grace the Archbishop on the 3rd of January this year (1952)'.[5] But Section 39 was not a safeguard against transatlantic adoptions. The bishops' concerns lay closer to home. 'There is little doubt that in suggesting this safeguard,' the Department of Justice revealed, 'the Episcopal Committee had in mind the danger of proselytism in the six counties [i.e. Northern Ireland] if there were no restrictions on sending children across the Border'.[6]

Even though there were far fewer would-be adopters in the Irish Republic than there were babies in 'orphanages', McQuaid and his fellow bishops, in effect, wanted to stop Catholic babies from being taken across the border and placed with Northern Irish Protestant families. Section 39 was aimed against Protestant adoption societies in the Republic who were believed to be engaged in this sort of 'proselytising' practice. Under Section 39 of the new Bill, no child could be dispatched in this way without the prior approval of its mother. McQuaid assumed the unmarried Catholic mothers of Ireland, for all their sinfulness, would still have sufficient faith in the 'one true church' to refuse to allow their offspring to fall into the hands of Six County Protestants. But at the same time he clearly intended that these mothers should continue to consent to the shipment of their children thousands of miles across the sea to American Catholics.

The ban on the removal from the State of children under one year of age was also aimed at the Protestant adoption societies. They did not have the same resources as Catholic institutions to house women and their babies for a full year before the children would be old enough to be exported from the Republic, and if they could not provide such places, they would not be able to get their hands on the babies. But of course one potentially very damaging consequence of this was that the children who were destined for America would have bonded with their natural mothers for at least a year before they were separated and shipped off to new parents. Severing this bond at such a late stage in its evolution would do incalculable damage to both mothers and children.[7]

So while Section 39 of the Adoption Act sought to close off the cross-border route and further curtail proselytising Protestants, it did nothing whatever to close the route across the Atlantic. Joe Horan, and everyone else who thought the legislators would put an end to the American traffic, must have been sorely disappointed that the new law left the door wide open for it to continue. All they had to fall back on now was Catholic Charities: in its hands lay the future well-being and happiness of hundreds, even thousands, of Irish children. But those who placed their trust in Catholic Charities were in for a shock. And what was more, the 'little rackets' that Horan had described with such concern continued to flourish, uninhibited by the new law or those charged with enforcing it.

5. A Major Inquisition

'50 American couples buy Irish babies through international adoption ring.'

New Haven and Connecticut Register,
2nd February 1955

'There was some basis for the allegation in question.'

Peter Berry, Department of Justice

Confidential memo 325, dated 8 June 1954 from the US embassy contained an unusual request to the Department of External Affairs: assistance in investigating eight mysterious births in Dublin. The eight babies in question had been born in 1952 and 1953, ostensibly to the wives of American servicemen stationed in Britain who came to Ireland to give birth.[1] To the American consular officials it seemed strange that so many military wives should have travelled from the UK to Dublin to have their babies, and they wanted to know what lay behind it. Before the matter was finally resolved, the Minister for External Affairs, and future Taoiseach, Liam Cosgrave, was to become personally involved.

'It is suspected,' the embassy noted, 'that the persons who reported the births of these children and, presumably, registered them with the local authorities are not the mothers of the children, but obtained them from the real mothers.' In other words, there was some sort of racket going on whereby Irish babies were being passed to American servicemen and their wives and registered as the Americans' natural children. If so, it would be highly irregular and illegal.

As we have seen, American servicemen stationed in the United Kingdom had been among the first to spot the opportunities presented by Ireland's bulging 'orphanages'. Commenting on their great interest in acquiring Irish babies, one official in the Department of External Affairs had noted a 'higher than average level of sterility' among American airmen. But he cited no scientific evidence for this sweeping assertion.

Joe Horan in the passport section of the Department recorded an early meeting he had held with an American airman's wife who told him Ireland enjoyed 'quite a reputation among the personnel of the US airbases in Britain as a place where one can get children for adoption without much difficulty'.[2] The woman described Ireland as 'a happy hunting ground', a phrase that seems to have been in common use.

In the early days, before any sort of regulations were introduced, the airmen would come armed with little more than a reference from a superior officer which was usually enough to secure a child. Major Randal Cole of the United States Air Force supplied such a reference to one of his Staff Sergeants. It makes interesting, if somewhat garbled reading. 'From my personal association with this airman,' Cole wrote, 'I find him of the greatest character, morally and mentally which, in its self (*sic*) is a pleasure to have a person of this calibar (*sic*) in your command. These qualities are an asset to the United States Airforce (*sic*) and a credit to the individual concerned. I take great pride and pleasure to recommend this airman to you.'[3] It isn't clear if this particular airman obtained a baby or not, but certainly others did with even less to go on.

Someone who had direct experience with members of the US armed forces on their adoption trips to Ireland was Anne Phelan, who worked for Aer Lingus in the 1950s. She recalled sitting beside an American Colonel on a flight to Britain. 'He had a child on his knee and he was very nervous and sweating,' she said. 'He asked me to hold the child, which I did of course. We got chatting and then he told me he had bought the baby from an orphanage. I am in no doubt at all that he used the word "bought", it has stuck in my mind ever since.' Some time later Anne was working in the Aer Lingus office on Dublin's O'Connell Street when a different American officer came in with his wife. 'They informed the Aer Lingus staff that they had come to buy a second Irish baby, because the first one had proved so successful,' Anne said. Again, she was in no doubt that they referred openly and unashamedly to buying babies.[4] Whether the officers Anne Phelan encountered were among the ones now being investigated by the American embassy, it is impossible to tell.

The scam that had been uncovered by the American authorities would certainly have had many 'benefits'. By registering the birth of an Irish child to an American couple, which is what the embassy knew had happened, the natural mother's – and father's – anonymity could be permanently guaranteed since their identities would be completely obliterated, with no reference even to their existence appearing on official documents of any kind. Pretending the child had been born to American citizens also disposed of the need for an Irish passport or American entry visa. Such illegally registered children could simply be entered on the Americans' own passports. In addition, the American couple could acquire a child (or children in some cases) without having to formally adopt them, thereby avoiding a lot of procedural and legal red tape – an ideal system for couples who, for whatever reason, had been refused permission to adopt a child legally. And for those running such an illegal racket, there was the obvious prospect of making big money, since desperate couples would go a long way to secure a child. And, relative to the Irish, the Americans certainly had the money. Children removed from the country in this way, of course, would not show up in the official statistics – which is why the official figures grossly understate the true extent of the baby export business.

In helping the American embassy with its investigation into the eight suspicious cases in 1954, the Department of External Affairs accepted the request for confidentiality. Some of the servicemen involved were high ranking officers in the US Air Force. Scandal had to be avoided. By chance, in that very month of June 1954, the Department had acquired a new (Fine Gael) Minister, Liam Cosgrave.

Although it was clear the law had been broken – and broken in many places – the main concern of the authorities was less to apprehend the wrongdoers than to 'regularise the position as soon as possible' by getting the paperwork in order.[5] The police were asked to help and Garda Chief Superintendent Carroll of the Special Branch obliged, advising the Department that 'the necessary enquiries can be made without attracting undue publicity'.[6]

The task of finding out about the eight babies was given to Detective Inspector John Flaherty of the Special Branch. Flaherty soon reported that seven of the children had been born at St Rita's Nursing Home, in Ranelagh, South Dublin, a private institution run by an enterprising midwife called Mary Keating. The eighth child would have been born at St Rita's too but because of antenatal complications, the mother had been referred to the Rotunda maternity hospital.[7]

Mary Keating, who will feature again in this story in later years, was a capable and ambitious woman with a growing family of her own. As a midwife in 1940s Dublin, she had responded eagerly to a suggestion from one of the city's leading gynaecologists, Dr Cross, that she should open a private maternity home and go into business for herself. It was 1947, and the American adoptions were already underway. For £1,200 Mrs Keating bought a large, terraced house at 68 Sandford Road, Ranelagh, which she soon opened as St Rita's Nursing Home. Business was brisk, and not only among the respectably married ladies of the south city suburbs, for Mrs Keating catered also for unmarried girls and women – from city or country. Most of her clients, married or not, were reasonably well-to-do, with enough money behind them to pay the private confinement fees. But Mrs Keating could always find space for a few girls who couldn't pay, taking them in in return for cleaning and cooking and attending to the needs of her paying clients.

Yet Mrs Keating wasn't just a hard-headed business-woman. She also had a reputation for kind-heartedness and an open, non-judgmental approach to the unmarried women and girls in her care. It would have surprised, indeed shocked, her neighbours to know that the Special Branch were interested in the goings-on behind St Rita's respectable red brick facade.

Detective Inspector Flaherty soon discovered that the eight infants of concern to the American embassy were 'illegitimate'. But each one, he claimed, had been 'handed over with the mother's consent.' In fact, the only real job the Gardai were asked to perform was to establish whether the mother of each child had consented to their being given to an American for removal from the country. There was no question of discovering who falsified the birth records – a serious offence in itself – or if the Americans had been asked for money in return for the children – also a criminal offence under the recent Adoption Act – and if so who benefited financially. Nor was there any consideration given to prosecuting the American couples for removing children under one year of age from the country. All the babies had been taken to the UK when just days old, again a fundamental breach of the law.

Although a whole string of potentially serious offences had been committed, Detective Inspector Flaherty, quite incredibly, made no mention whatever of illegality in his report. What he did establish was that while all of the unmarried mothers in question were Irish, several of them had been living in England and had been brought back to St Rita's to have their babies. There was evidence that at least one British anti-proselytising organisation was involved: the Crusade of Rescue and Homes for Destitute Catholic Children.[8]

Flaherty had indicated that all of the mothers had consented to the surrender of their children, yet when it came to substantiating this claim it turned out that he had been able to obtain signed consent papers in respect of three of the children only. In the other five cases he had no evidence of consent other than the word of Mrs Keating. Indeed, it transpired that Flaherty did not even know the true identity of four of the seven mothers concerned (one of them had twins) since false names had been used throughout their stay at St Rita's. It was clear that the Special Branch were totally out of their depth in handling such matters.

Despite the law-breaking involved, and Flaherty's acknowledgement that many of those interviewed by him had been uncooperative for 'fear of exposure', the Special Branch man ended his report by assuring his superiors that he had conducted his enquiries on a strictly personal and confidential basis, 'as instructed'.[9] No one would be embarrassed and certainly no one would be prosecuted. Had

Flaherty looked deeper into Mrs Keating's business he would have discovered that falsifying birth records was common practice for 'illegitimate' babies born at St Rita's.

Major Charles Harden and his wife Lucille were one of the air force couples, whose acquisition of not one but two babies from Mrs Keating had been investigated by the Special Branch.[10] The two children Mrs Harden acquired – whom she named David and Lynda – had been born two days apart to separate mothers in December 1952, but Mrs Keating registered them as having been born on the same day to Mrs Harden herself. Mrs Harden had already been turned down when she tried to adopt a child in California before she and her husband moved to a US Air Force base in Britain. It may have been just her age that was against her – she was 40 – but such matters were of no concern to Mrs Keating. Mrs Harden recalled in later life how cold she had felt while staying at St Rita's waiting for 'her' babies to be born. And in later life too, Lynda's natural mother, Vivian, who was Welsh rather than Irish, told of how she had been directed to St Rita's by an Irish priest who in turn had been contacted by a family priest in Wales. Vivian recalled how devastated and heartbroken she had been when her eight-day-old baby was removed from her side while she slept, allowing her no opportunity to say goodbye. Vivian had no idea she had been sucked into an illegal baby black market until the Special Branch came knocking on her door three years after she had given birth. It was something that would haunt her through all the years to come. One thing she could – and did – do, however, was attempt to correct the birth registry. When Lynda came to Ireland in later life looking for her birth certificate, it still incorrectly recorded the Major and Mrs Harden as her birth parents, but in the margin was a note to say Vivian had reported this as false and had given her name as the real mother. (This enabled Lynda to find Vivian in later life.)

As for the Hardens, they had already returned to the United States with their babies when the Special Branch investigation got under way, but as their illegal acquisition of the children had been discovered, they had no alternative but to proceed with a legal adoption in the United States, something they had hoped wouldn't be necessary. To avoid another adoption 'no' from child welfare agencies, Mrs Harden this time lied about her age, claiming to be 28 when she was by then well over 40. Somehow she got away with it and their acquisition of the children was finally legalised. David found out at an early age that he was adopted but Lynda only discovered the fact by accident when she was 13. But she was in her late 30s before she found out, through a conversation with David, that they were not twins. These were enormous shocks that she had to cope with in her life – a life already made difficult by profound deafness from birth. The deception in which her adoptive parents had engaged with Mrs Keating had prevented them from ever talking openly or honestly with Lynda about her origins, and this meant relationships were always challenging, imposing great strain on everyone.

'After learning that I was adopted at age 13,' Lynda said, 'I tried to pursue more information from my parents, but they refused to explain what really took place in my birth mother's life. But I do remember pretty vivid things like my dad saying, "It was very unpleasant and she was very young." And that was all I could get out of my dad, which really made me angry because I really thought he would tell me since I was closer to him than I was to my mom. From then on I knew they were hiding things from me. I strongly believe what my dad was referring to when he said "it was very unpleasant" was this illegal stuff, this Catholic mess. My parents did not have a good marriage because I remember sensing strong frictions between them when I was growing up without understanding why, and it probably started with all the "illegal mess." They eventually divorced after David and I became adults. I grew up angry because I hated secrets and I just simply wanted to know what happened and who I was. Later, in my middle twenties, I tried to get some information from mom. She got very defensive and basically told me that I was not old enough to know, which deeply hurt me. After that I never questioned her again because I saw how terrified she was. Sadly both of my parents took their secrets to their graves.'

Another couple who learned about Mrs Keating's illicit baby business from the Hardens – and subsequently found themselves in the sights of the Special Branch – were Master Sergeant Wesley Autry and his wife Mary.[11] It was on Mrs Harden's advice that Mrs Autry contacted Mary Keating to ask if she could find her a baby. Mrs Keating took her details, and a series of telephone conversations and letters ensued. On 13 March 1953, after Mrs Keating become unwell and had gone into hospital, her daughter, Marie Keating, wrote to Mrs Autry, 'The girl whoes (*sic*) baby you are to get is not so very well... The doctor thinks he may have to send her into hospital yet.'

Marie Keating went on to explain what this could mean. 'Of course if that happens,' she wrote, 'we will not be able to get the baby as in the hospital she would be under the authorities, the same as in England as we now have an adoption law here. In our home we would register the baby in your name, but in the hospital the babies are registered in their Mothers (*sic*) name.' This was a clear and unambiguous acknowledgement that St Rita's operated outside the law by falsely registering the details of children born there. Marie Keating also revealed the utterly haphazard nature of matching children with would-be adopters: 'Mammy said to tell you,' she assured Mrs Autry, 'if you do not get this Baby, that the very next one you shall have, and when she comes out of hospital she will see about it for you... we will get you one very soon.'[12] And so they did.

Before the end of the month Mrs Keating called Mrs Autry and told her to come immediately: a baby had become available, a boy whose unmarried mother, Mrs Keating said, was a singer, and whose natural father was a policeman. But when Mrs Autry arrived it turned out that 'her' baby was too sick to travel. She had to spend the next week residing at St Rita's while the baby, whom she named Eugene (Gene), was kept in a box next to a heater. In the meantime, Mrs Keating registered the baby's birth, giving Wesley and Mary Autry as his parents' names. And to make it appear that Gene was born after Mrs Autry entered Ireland – which was essential if the deception were to work – Mrs Keating also falsified Gene's birth date, entering 24 March 1953 in the register when, as the Garda investigation later discovered, he had actually been born on 7 March. In later years Mrs Autry told Gene she paid nothing to Mrs Keating other than the fees associated with her own and the natural mother's stay at St Rita's.

When baby Gene was well enough he was baptised at the Sacred Heart Church in Donnybrook as though he were the natural child of the Autrys – just as the Harden babies had been before him – but whether or not the Parish Priest, the Very Reverend Timothy Condon, was party to the deception is unclear. During Reverend Condon's time at the Donnybrook Church (1950-1962), virtually all the falsely registered babies from St Rita's were baptised there. And in 1954, the year of the (first) Garda investigation into St Rita's, Donnybrook Sacred Heart Church had got a new Sacristan, Joe Doyle, then just 18 years old but in later life a Fine Gael TD, Senator, and Lord Mayor of Dublin. Joe Doyle remained as Sacristan in Donnybrook for 28 years, relinquishing the post only when he was elected to the Dáil in 1982. Mr Doyle developed a close friendship with Mrs Keating but, when approached by this author, he angrily refused to discuss what he knew of her illegal business.

Although they had baptised baby Gene a Catholic, neither Wesley nor Mary Autry were Catholics and, according to the Garda investigation, both were divorcees from previous marriages. The Garda investigation also revealed that baby Gene Autry's natural mother used a false name – Power – during her stay at St Rita's, and although they quickly discovered her real name, no one in authority saw fit to correct the false information in the Register of Births where, by law, the natural mother's name must appear. Instead, the name 'Autry' has been allowed to remain indefinitely on the public record. And this was done not just in the Autry case but in all eight cases investigated by the Gardai in 1954.

Within days of baby Gene's false birth registration and baptism, Mrs Autry took him back to the UK, where she and her husband were subsequently interviewed by officers from the Irish Special Branch. They lived in constant fear that their baby would be taken from them and sent back to Ireland, and they spent the next two and a half years in the UK desperately trying to resolve the mess their association with Mrs Keating had got them into. Although the Irish authorities never issued a passport so Gene could be taken legally to the United States, as we will see, the Autrys – along with the other Air Force couples involved in the Garda investigation – found a way around this obstacle, to the great annoyance of Irish officialdom.

Another of the cases that Detective Inspector Flaherty investigated involved a Major Burns of the US Air Force. Major and Mrs Burns had acquired no less than three children from St Rita's, a boy and twin girls. The American couple appear to have met the expectant Irish mothers of these children in England, through the Crusade of Rescue and Homes for Destitute Catholic Children. An English priest attached to this organisation provided them with an introduction to another priest in Dublin, and he in turn put

Mrs Burns in touch with Mrs Keating at St Rita's. Mrs Burns then arranged the repatriation and confinement of the unmarried women concerned and paid all their expenses, including Mrs Keating's bills. The whole operation had the appearance of a well worked-out system based on an intricate network of contacts in Ireland and Britain. Major and Mrs Burns acquired their three children on two separate visits to St Rita's – in October 1952 and November 1953. As with baby Gene Autry and Lynda and David Harden, all three children were registered as the Burns' own natural children, eliminating the real mothers from the record. They took the children back to the American Air Force base at Ruislip in West London where Major Burns was stationed.

Once the conspiracy was uncovered by the American embassy in Dublin, and when the Special Branch had completed their investigation, Major and Mrs Burns, like all the other couples involved, were told not that they faced prosecution for potentially serious criminal offences, but that they had to apply in the normal way for Irish passports for their illegally acquired children. It was the beginning of a long and sometimes bizarre religious inquisition for the Major and his wife in which the Irish State acted – aggressively and with seeming relish – as the thought-police of the Catholic Church.

The Irish natural mothers of the three Burns children were Catholics, and so the Department of External Affairs undertook to satisfy itself that the Burns couple would bring the children up in the Catholic faith. The new Adoption Act made no reference whatever to such conditions being met by intending foreign adopters before passports would be issued to their selected children. This was a condition inserted entirely by the Department. But the manner in which the Department dealt with the Burns' application for passports indicated that the Irish civil servants, and their Minister, Liam Cosgrave, were determined to apply Archbishop McQuaid's religious tests as though they had the force of law – while, bizarrely, ignoring the actual *breaches* of law.

When the Department received the required documents from the Major and his wife in support of their passport applications, the officials immediately rejected their marriage certificate because it was a civil document, not a Church one. They also demanded Major Burns' baptismal certificate and a reference from the couple's Catholic pastor in America recommending the adoption of the three children 'from the religious point of view'.[13] The 'problem' was that Major and Mrs Burns were a mixed-marriage couple. She was a Catholic, he a non-Catholic. And there was another obstacle: Mrs Burns had been married previously and had failed to produce evidence of how her first marriage ended, leaving open the possibility that she had been divorced. What relevance this had for the future well-being of the children was not specified, but it was seen by Department officials as a fundamental obstacle in the way of the Burns' application.

With so many obstacles in their path, the Burns couple had become deeply frustrated. So much so, they engaged a barrister, William Fitzgerald SC (a future Irish Chief Justice), who contacted the Minister for External Affairs, Liam Cosgrave, in person.[14] Cosgrave, in turn, demanded to know from his civil servants what was going on. They explained the background: that the children had been obtained illegally, that the law had been broken by Major and Mrs Burns as well as by the children's natural parents, and 'very probably also' by St Rita's Nursing Home. They confirmed that the Department of Justice had decided not to prosecute because it had been the American authorities who brought the matter to their attention, and, as we have seen, the American embassy wanted the entire affair hushed up.[15]

But it was the religious issue that was the real drawback, the Minister was told. 'We must feel morally certain that these children will receive a proper upbringing in… the Catholic religion,' his officials said. 'It is true that Major and Mrs Burns have submitted a sworn declaration to the effect that they will bring up the children in the Catholic Faith,' they went on, 'but this is, of course, not sufficient for our purposes.' The word of the American couple could not be relied on. By obtaining children illegally, Major and Mrs Burns had already proved themselves to be untrustworthy, raising doubts about their suitability 'for the adoption of Irish Catholic children'.[16]

Mr Cosgrave's private secretary, however, took a different point of view and strongly recommended to his Minister that he issue passports for the three children involved, even though the Major wasn't a Catholic and had married in a registry office. Referring to the Burns' own oath-bound undertakings to bring the children up Catholics, and to their seemingly excellent character references, the secretary concluded, somewhat philosophically: 'It would be impossible to obtain more satisfactory evidence… To adopt any other standard would be to pursue an impossible perfectionism and to seek for criteria unobtainable in this imperfect world…' And more prosaically, '… moreover, it would be to place an impossible burden on the limited staff of our consular section…' As for worries that because of their civil marriage Major and Mrs Burns could some day divorce, the private secretary pointed out they could just as easily be killed in an accident or die young, and so 'we should not concern ourselves with unnecessary and futile speculation about a future which no man can control.' He ended by reminding his minister of something that no one else had given any thought to: as the children had been in the Burns' care since birth, one and two years ago, 'a strong bond of affection' had been formed and it would be 'an unbearable hardship' to break the family up at this point by refusing passports to the children.[17]

Mr Cosgrave remained unconvinced and ruled that unless the Major and his wife could produce all the religious proofs demanded, no passports would be issued.[18] In the event, they could not produce a Church marriage certificate as they had only had a civil wedding. Nor could the Major turn up a Catholic baptismal certificate since he wasn't a Catholic. However, Mrs Burns did produce sworn declarations to the effect that her first marriage ended with the death of her husband, and not with divorce. 'This removes one of the main anxieties which we had,' noted a Department official.[19] But the Burns couple were still far from being in the clear.

Unable to obtain a recommendation from a Catholic pastor who knew them in America, they produced instead a reference from a London priest, Father Keane. But when this arrived in the Department of External Affairs early in January 1955, on unheaded notepaper, the officials became so suspicious they asked the Irish embassy in London to check out the priest's credentials. There followed a series of 'urgent' and totally bizarre telexes between Dublin and London, desperately trying to confirm that Father Keane actually existed and that his reference was genuine.[20] The London embassy found a full entry for Father Keane in the Catholic Directory, but Dublin was still unhappy. 'The main point,' they emphasised to their London staff, 'is that Major Burns is not – repeat not – a Catholic.' As the whole business had become 'red hot', the Irish diplomats in London were told to track down Father Keane as a matter of 'top priority' and contact him in person. If they found he really did exist, they were told to avoid implying that they ever doubted the authenticity of his letter and to 'throw the blame' for their intrusion 'on the regulations'. But 'the main thing' was 'we must be absolutely sure that Father Keane recommends these adoptions from the religious point of view'.

Father Keane may have been surprised to find himself confronted by professional diplomats from a supposedly modern democracy conducting a religious inquisition into the private beliefs of an American citizen, but Keane had no hesitation in standing over his 'spiritual' recommendation, expressing himself 'fully satisfied about the future of the children in that respect'. He had known the Burns couple for three years; Mrs Burns was a regular church attender; the Major was an upstanding man, taking an interest in Catholicism and wishing to start instruction. What was more – although to the Irish inquisitors this was apparently irrelevant – the children were dearly loved and extremely well cared-for.[21]

After a six-month-long investigation of the Major and Mrs Burns' spiritual suitability (and nothing else) it was time to close the file. 'We have now reached the point where we must decide these applications on the basis of the information and references available to us,' one official wrote.[22] The strong recommendation from Father Keane had encouraged the Department to look at the case more favourably. It hadn't been mentioned before, but now it helped enormously that the 'Catholic party' in the marriage was the mother since 'in the nature of things a mother is always more closely connected with the religious education of children than a father'. The couple's apparent dishonesty, once a barrier to adopting, was now a factor demanding sympathy. They had both told their families back in America that during their British posting Mrs Burns had given birth to three children. To deny passports to these children now would cause the couple severe embarrassment with their relatives. And, as a final seal of approval, it was noted that 'the Archbishop of Dublin has approved the adoption of a Catholic child by parents of whom one was not a Catholic'. If the Archbishop could do it, why not a mere government minister? Finally, it was noted that a denial of passports would deprive the children of 'their comfortable home,' and by splitting up the family, impose 'a great hardship' on them.[23]

The arguments had all been reassessed in the Burns' favour and the civil servants concluded that passports should be issued after all. Liam Cosgrave concurred, instructing, 'please have this done as soon as possible.'[24] But, regrettably for the Burns couple, the matter did not quite end there, for before the Minister's instructions could be acted on, the Department was thrown into turmoil when a startling story found its way into the newspapers.

Under the headline, '50 American Couples Buy Irish Babies Through International Adoption Ring,' one American paper, quoting a senior Irish police source, said Americans were paying between $600 and $2000 to obtain a child in Dublin (€20,000 to €70,000 at today's prices). The anonymous Garda officer was quoted as saying that 'upwards of 100 illegitimate children passed through bogus and other nursing homes in this country and in no case was the birth recorded. At least half of them, we are convinced, are now in the United States'.[25] The newspaper report described how American couples first made contact with the baby-sellers' agents in London, Frankfurt or Paris – each the location of large numbers of US military personnel – and how they were referred from there to Ireland. It also reported, accurately, that no prosecutions were to be taken against either Irish or American citizens.

'At least five nursing homes in Dublin are involved,' the report said, and two midwives had been questioned and warned by police. One of them, although not named, was Mrs Keating, owner of St Rita's. 'To adopt a baby,' the report went on, 'the American soldier and his wife would travel to Dublin, where the wife checked in at the nursing home as an expectant mother. An Irish woman would actually bear the child, but the birth would be registered in the name of the American.' This was exactly what had been happening repeatedly at St Rita's nursing home. In an interesting aside, the newspaper quoted an Irish nun's explanation for the popularity of Irish children among Americans: 'Irish children are pure-blooded,' she had said.

Copies of this newspaper article were forwarded to the Special Branch who responded: 'Certain highly confidential investigations were already made in this matter... and the results communicated to the Department of Justice. In view of this position it was not considered desirable that further investigations should be made at this stage'.[26] Significantly, the only aspect of the American newspaper article the Special Branch called into question was the claim that the story had come from a high-ranking police officer. The Branch claimed that the real source was a private investigator, whom they named as James Ryan of Mountjoy Square, who had stumbled upon the 'illegal adoption ring' while inquiring into the completely unrelated theft of a baby, Pauline Ashmore, from her pram on Dublin's Lower Camden Street. But the police did not dispute in any way the accuracy of the claim that large numbers of babies were being sold to Americans in the manner described.

When Peter Berry at the Department of Justice was asked by External Affairs to comment on the allegation that 'an illegal international adoption agency with its headquarters in Dublin is arranging for the removal of children from this country',[27] Berry replied 'there was some basis for the allegation in question,' and the story 'could not truthfully be refuted in full.'[28] The Department of External Affairs decided that any attempt at a public refutation 'would be ill-advised'.[29] This was another implicit admission on the part of the State that there was an illegal traffic in Irish babies to the United States. But what is most astonishing and disturbing about the entire business is that while the civil authorities expended huge effort and resources chasing down proofs of religious conformity, they came up with no proposals whatever for putting a stop to the illegal traffic or bringing the traffickers to justice.

But one thing the authorities could, and did, do, was reopen Major and Mrs Burns' passport applications. In the circumstances of such adverse international publicity it was going to be much more difficult for the couple to obtain passports for children acquired illegally. Yet, as their alleged criminal behaviour had never been offered to them in the past as a reason for being refused passports, it could hardly be used at this late stage. The documents in the case were given another meticulous going over to find a way out and, ironically, it was something the London priest, Father Keane, had said that provided the answer. Notes taken by Irish embassy staff of their interview with Keane had referred somewhat cryptically to the Major and his wife having to 'sort out their own matrimonial entanglement' which, the priest had remarked, would 'take some time'. With this ammunition in hand, senior officials consulted Cosgrave again before giving a final verdict on the Burns' case to the American embassy in Dublin.

'I pointed out,' one of the officials recorded, 'that we could never be satisfied with vague references to "matrimonial entanglements" and "regularisation of marriage" and that these had never been satisfactorily explained... I said that where there was a background of divorce or an impediment to conversion or marriage in a Catholic Church – or even in the case of a mixed marriage – the Department's view was that they would not be satisfied that there existed a reasonable chance of the child receiving a proper Catholic education and upbringing'.[30]

Liam Cosgrave immediately withdrew his consent to passports for the three children[31] and went on to formally ban any future issue of passports to children whose would-be adopters were in a mixed marriage, thereby bringing the regulations on American adoptions more fully into line with domestic adoption law, as dictated by Archbishop McQuaid.[32] The Burns case illustrated clearly that the State was perfectly capable of acting on its own initiative when it came to enforcing religious tests. Archbishop McQuaid had not been involved in any way. Almost a year after Major and Mrs Burns had first come to the Department's attention, their application was rejected,[33] notwithstanding the Department's own previously stated view that this would result in serious hardship for the children.

In the meantime, Master Sergeant Wesley Autry and his wife Mary had also been refused a passport to take baby Gene to America, and the grounds of refusal were the same as in the Burns case: the Autrys weren't Catholics. The Hardens, too were refused passports for their 'twins' on the same grounds, as were another (un-named) Air Force couple who had acquired one of the St Rita's babies. But although passports were refused, all the children in question had long since left Ireland for US Air Force bases in the UK, and the Hardens had already returned to the US.[34] If the law was complied with the children should have been returned to Ireland, to take up residence in some religious-run institution. But this simply didn't happen and all the children were able to travel to the United States without passports. When the Department of External Affairs investigated how this was done, they discovered that American law permitted passport requirements to be waived in certain circumstances and allowed the US immigration service to issue entry visas for people without passports. A minor diplomatic row ensued in which the Irish authorities let it be known how angry they were, especially since the US embassy staff in Dublin had been fully appraised on the goings on at St Rita's and their counterparts in London were also aware of the illegalities in the manner of the children's original acquisition and registration.[35]

These cases also raise doubts about the value of official passport statistics as an accurate indicator of the number of Irish children taken to America for adoption, since a passport was clearly not always necessary. It is impossible to know how many other cases passed undetected by the Department of External Affairs. But given the growing file of uncontradicted newspaper reports, the numbers must have been considerable.

For baby Gene Autry there was to be a further complication. Because his parents' efforts to avoid the need for a formal adoption in the US by having him registered as their natural child in Dublin had been frustrated by the Garda investigation, the Autrys – like the Hardens – had to go through the legal process of adoption once they got Gene back to America – a move that was triggered when the Autrys received another overseas posting and discovered they couldn't take Gene with them unless he was adopted first. But to make this possible, the Autrys required proof that Gene's natural mother had consented to his adoption. At one point Mrs Autry herself returned to Ireland – along with Major Burns' wife – to look for the natural mothers of their acquired children, but without success. The Gardai, of course, had obtained the necessary consents from the mothers in the course of their investigation, but when asked by the Autrys to submit proof to the adoption court in Fort Worth, Texas, the Irish authorities refused to do so. Yet, somehow, the adoption went ahead which meant the US court allowed the Autrys to adopt a child whose birth certificate showed he was their natural son, and in the absence of any proof of consent to the adoption from the child's actual mother. As Gene himself remarked, 'It's hard to believe that the courts allowed this to be processed in this manner. How they were able to pull this off is beyond comprehension.'

As it happens, Gene Autry had a happy childhood in a loving family, although Archbishop McQuaid's rules, as implemented by the Irish State, decreed that he should never have fallen into the hands of people like Wesley and Mary Autry, who were regarded as 'unsuitable' simply because of their religious beliefs. Whatever problems or difficulties there were in Gene's and his adoptive parents' future lives, they were related to Mrs Keating's web of deceit rather than to matters of religion. Mrs Autry suffered stress related illnesses that she later admitted arose from keeping the illegalities around Gene's acquisition secret from him. In later years Gene also discovered that Mary Keating had added another layer of deception to the entire process: his natural mother had never been a singer, nor his father a policeman, as Mrs Keating had told Mrs Autry back in 1953.

The shady goings-on at St Rita's and its links to the wider illegal adoption black market may have fallen outside the official child export scheme as regulated by Archbishop McQuaid and facilitated by the Department of External Affairs, but the official system, too, as we shall now see, was full of disturbing ambiguities and serious lapses that meant no one in authority really knew – or seemingly cared – what fate befell the children dispatched to America under their auspices.

6. From Cock-Up...

'If Catholic Charities recommend the couple, we can be quite satisfied that the recommendation is sound.'

T. J. Horan
Department of External Affairs, 1952

'I am more and more convinced that many of the homes in which children were placed are undesirable.'

Monsignor John O'Grady,
Head of Catholic Charities, 1955

The Angel Guardian Home in Brooklyn, New York, is a vast redbrick institution set in its own high-fenced grounds, and surrounded by flower beds and holy statues. In years gone by this imposing orphanage was the most active branch of the Catholic Charities organisation involved in placing Irish babies with American adopters, accounting for almost 300, or one in seven, of all the children officially sent to the USA. But a quarter of a century after the adoption trade ended, other than confirming the numbers, the nuns who ran the home were refusing to discuss their past involvement in organising Irish adoptions. The most basic questions were treated with suspicion, even hostility, and the nuns offered no explanation for their unwillingness to talk.

The placement of Irish children in Brooklyn was not always satisfactory. The fact that there were problems was first revealed in May 1954 – by which time 700 children in total had already been officially shipped out from Ireland to the States. Sister Mary Augusta, director of adoption services at the Angel Guardian Home, wrote with her concerns to the three head nuns at Sean Ross Abbey in Tipperary, St Patrick's Home in Dublin, and Castlepollard in Westmeath. These three adoption societies, together with St Patrick's Guild in Dublin, St Clare's in Stamullen, County Meath, and the Sacred Heart adoption society in Cork, were responsible for most of the children sent to America. Sister Mary Augusta in Brooklyn told the sisters in Ireland that because of overworking and understaffing the Angel Guardian home was having difficulty in adequately vetting Catholic American couples who wanted to adopt Irish babies. Consequently they were now giving priority to placing their own, American orphans. Sister Mary Augusta also pointed out, ominously, that would-be American adopters who had already been 'rejected for serious reasons' by Catholic Charities were now turning directly to the Irish adoption societies for their babies.[1]

The Department of External Affairs had been alerted to this danger as early as 1949 by the then Health Minister, Dr Noel Browne, and had received confirmation from an American journalist the following year that people deemed unsuitable as adoptive parents in the US were obtaining children from Ireland. But when someone with Sister Mary Augusta's direct knowledge spoke about it, it was clear that the deep-seated cracks – that until now had remained largely hidden – were at last reaching the surface of the official baby export system. Within nine months of Sister Mary Augusta's first warning, the Brooklyn Director of Catholic Charities, Monsignor J.J. Reddy, acknowledged in a letter to Father Cecil Barrett, head of Archbishop

McQuaid's Social Welfare Bureau in Dublin, that the problems were now 'acute'. The Angel Guardian Home, he admitted, simply wasn't up to the job of properly assessing would-be adoptive parents. It just didn't have sufficient qualified staff. As a result, Brooklyn Catholic Charities and the Angel Guardian Home were pulling out completely from the Irish adoption programme.[2]

The available records don't indicate how many Irish children had already been dispatched to Brooklyn on the strength of home study reports produced by overworked and under-qualified Catholic Charities staff, but given the length of time the problem had been in existence, and the key importance of New York as a destination for Irish children, it seems reasonable to assume that the number must have been considerable. The home study report – or lack of it, as described in the earlier case of Mary Theresa Monaghan and her adoption by a paedophile in California – was *the* critical document. It was the only one among the many required by Church and State in Ireland that went beyond the issues of faith and wealth and actually dealt with the suitability of would-be adopters as actual parents as opposed to spiritual minders and material providers. In fact, as far as religion and wealth were concerned, American applicants for Irish babies were largely a self-selecting group. Religious and financial references would not be difficult for them to supply. It was all the other matters relevant to adoption that required the greatest investigation, but such investigation appeared to be dispensable when resources were stretched.

Father Cecil Barrett immediately sent a copy of Monsignor Reddy's letter to St Patrick's Guild to 'keep them out of trouble'. He also sent a copy to the Department of External Affairs, so they were made aware of the problem. The withdrawal of such a key institution as the Angel Guardian Home from the Irish adoption programme should have sounded alarm bells among the authorities back in Dublin, yet almost another year was to pass before the true extent of the problem was discovered. What was at stake was the safety and well-being of hundreds of Irish children. But even that seems not to have motivated anyone to act with any degree of urgency.

Catholic Charities, of course, had been chosen by both Archbishop McQuaid and the Department of External Affairs to vet American adopters in preference to the secular, state-run Children's Bureau, who had offered to provide home studies for would-be adopters of Irish children. Catholic Charities was the biggest non-governmental welfare organisation in the United States, and as such carried a lot of weight, but it still had serious shortcomings, particularly in the sensitive and critical area of placing children in adoptive homes, a task that required considerable expertise and the commitment of long-term resources. Catholic Charities' coverage of America's 50 States was always extremely uneven which meant that some branches were expected to cope with huge geographical areas with few, and frequently untrained staff. What was more, other Catholic Charities branches turned out to have no legal authority whatever for placing children in adoption, a matter that only came to the attention of the Department of External Affairs at the end of 1955. Yet it was on the strength of reports presented by Catholic Charities branches like these that Irish children were being assigned to individual adopters. And if all of this wasn't bad enough, it soon emerged that Catholic Charities even had shady characters operating within its own ranks, selling babies on the side.

In short, by the mid-1950s it was becoming obvious that the Church and State's agreed formula for establishing the suitability of adoptive American parents was far from foolproof. It was not simply an academic matter, but potentially one of life and death. And things were set to get even worse.

In July 1955 the national secretary of Catholic Charities, Monsignor John O'Grady, made an astonishing and disturbing admission. In a letter to Father Cecil Barrett he revealed that he was 'more and more convinced that many of the homes in which children were placed are undesirable'.[3] It was clear their 'undesirability' arose from factors other than religion: the 'unsuitable' homes were Catholic homes, and O'Grady's use of the word 'many' indicated that the problem was potentially huge. There was also evidence of children being placed with American couples who simply had not been vetted at all. In August 1955 Barrett received another unsettling letter, this time from the Director of Child Welfare for the state of Kansas, telling him that St Patrick's Guild were placing Irish children for adoption in Western Kansas 'without any agency approval of the placement or of the plan which has been made'. The Guild hadn't even sought the assistance of the Catholic Social Services in Kansas, even though they had expressed a willingness to help.[4]

This was extremely unsettling news, and all the more so since the Kansas welfare agency failed to give any indication as to what had happened to the children in question. Nor did anyone in authority in Ireland seem concerned enough to try to find out. What is not clear is how the children involved in these cases managed to get Irish passports in the first instance since, under the Department of External Affairs' written rules, passports were supposed to be issued only after Catholic Charities had verified the adopting parents as suitable. Yet here were clear, documented cases – and not for the first time either – of children being placed in homes that had never been vetted by any agency. Over the years around 40 Irish children were sent to Kansas.

One possible way of getting around the rules was outlined in a brochure that was circulating at this time among American couples who wanted to adopt an Irish child. The three-page circular, produced by Father Michael Quealy, Administrator of Ennis Cathedral in County Clare, explained that the Department of External Affairs usually required a Catholic Charities home study report together with a priest's testimonial. But it went on to say that if Catholic Charities didn't operate in their area (as they didn't in Western Kansas), and the couple had a letter saying this was the case from Catholic Charities head office in Washington, they could still qualify for an Irish child on the basis of personal testimonials from two priests instead of just one. 'The passport office in Ireland,' Quealy's leaflet said, 'will accept these as alternatives for a Catholic Charities Report.' Father Quealy had sent a copy of his brochure to the Department of External Affairs, specifically seeking their approval for its contents, and there appears to be no record of anyone in the Department dissenting or asking him to change it in any way.[5] A recommendation from a priest, of course, was no substitute at all for a professional social worker's investigation into the adoptive couple and their home, especially since priests could be subjected to all kinds of pressures and inducements by parishioners who were desperate to obtain a baby. Archbishop McQuaid's own requirements were somewhat vague in this matter, and it was not until July 1955 that McQuaid explicitly demanded a Catholic Charities report as distinct from a recommendation.[6]

On the other hand, there is evidence that the Department of External Affairs could turn down passport requests where a detailed home study report from Catholic Charities was missing. In one case a Catholic couple from Rhode Island had been promised a baby by the nuns in Ireland after supplying all the required affidavits and references except the Catholic Charities home study report. In its place they had furnished only a two-paragraph recommendation from the priest who was their Diocesan

Director. When the couple then applied for a passport, submitting the same documentation, they were turned down.[7] Cases such as this were a cause of considerable friction between the Department and the nuns, as they both appeared to be applying different rules, and couples could incur great expense in arranging to get a baby before falling at the final hurdle of the passport office.

Yet the disturbing revelations from Kansas indicated that the Department was not always as rigorous as it appeared to be in the Rhode Island case. The Kansas affair still left unanswered the critical question of how children were able to travel from Ireland to unapproved homes. Even by their own flimsy standards, the authorities were failing. Unbelievably, this was still not the end of it.

American law required that all organisations engaged in placing children for adoption be legally registered, and it had always been assumed within the Department of External Affairs that all branches of Catholic Charities met these criteria and were entitled to handle adoption arrangements for Irish children. But towards the end of 1955 – more than four years after Catholic Charities was chosen for the job and by which time the number of children officially dispatched to the United States had reached the 1,000 mark – the civil servants back in Dublin discovered that some branches of Catholic Charities with which they had been dealing had no legal status whatever when it came to placing children for adoption.[8] In practice this meant that home study reports, produced to secure passports from the Irish authorities, had no standing in American courts when it came to legalising the adoption.

In the absence of a home study report by an approved agency, the proposed adoption could not proceed, and the child's future would remain undecided until the mess was sorted out. This could all be going on without anyone in authority back in Dublin knowing about it, as there was no monitoring of children once they had left the country. Yet until they were legally adopted and naturalised as Americans, these children were still Irish citizens and the responsibility of the Irish State. The Department's blind faith in Catholic Charities had resulted in an abdication of responsibility for the welfare of the Irish children they had so trustingly, but carelessly, dispatched across the Atlantic.

The practice of sending children to America was turning out like a game of Russian roulette. Things might work out, but then again they might not. It was a case of give them a passport, put them on a plane, and hope for the best. Even if most of the cases worked out well, or at least reasonably well (and that's a big 'if'), all the evidence indicates that a great many individual Irish babies ended up with people who were regarded – before they got their hands on the children – as totally unfit to become adoptive parents.

When the authorities back in Ireland learned the sad truth about Catholic Charities and its inadequacies, Sean Morrissey from the Department wrote to the organisation's national secretary, Monsignor John O'Grady, requesting a list of registered branches. If they knew which branches had the legal right to place children, they could ensure that no more children were sent to areas where the branches were not registered.[9] But instead of sending the list as requested, O'Grady got on a plane and flew directly to Dublin to confront the Department face to face. The meeting that resulted was to reveal yet more serious problems.

On 16 January 1956, O'Grady spent four hours in heated debate with three senior officials at the Department of External Affairs in Iveagh House. Sean Morrissey, who attended the meeting, described it subsequently as 'disturbing,' stating that O'Grady 'made a very poor impression'; that he was 'very old and rather senile at times', and that 'it beats us how he can hold down such a job'. Morrissey recorded that he and the other two officials who met

O'Grady were 'thoroughly exhausted and exasperated after the meeting,' but 'we kept hammering at him and extracted eventually the revelation that all the branches of his organisation were not reliable as we had been led to believe'. This, he added, 'was a blow to us because... all our adoption arrangements centred around the recommendations of the branches'. Morrissey was unaware of 'mass irregularities', but he said it was 'disturbing for us to find that any loophole existed,' because 'there is persistent public criticism in this country of these adoptions, most of it admittedly emanating from "wild" reports in the cheap English Sunday papers'.[10] Once again, the need to avoid adverse publicity came before the need to avert the potentially dire consequences for children of officialdom's glaring errors.

The meeting with O'Grady had got off to an awkward start. Sean Morrissey told him that the Department of External Affairs now realised that not all branches of Catholic Charities were legally registered to handle adoptions. O'Grady defiantly denied the charge and asserted 'there was no such thing as an unregistered branch.' This was a claim he repeated 'a number of times,' but the Department officials already knew otherwise. Trying to evade their questions, O'Grady engaged in a long and irrelevant monologue on the wonders of the American judiciary.[11]

But suddenly the American priest changed tack. The minutes of the meeting record that he 'began to speak about certain "irregular" adoptions' which had recently taken place in the states of Texas and Wisconsin. The person behind these adoptions was described by O'Grady as a 'commercial operator' who 'had made money from these operations', causing Catholic Charities 'grave embarrassment'. Eventually O'Grady got to the point: the children involved 'were coming from Ireland,' and their passport applications had been 'cleared through the Department of External Affairs'.

These revelations came as 'a complete shock' to the Department officials who believed they had taken precautions 'which appeared to be foolproof in their security,' especially their 'inflexible rule' of dealing only with Catholic Charities. So how, they asked, did the Wisconsin 'operator' get his hands on Irish children to sell, unless he himself was part of the Catholic Charities organisation? At first Monsignor O'Grady 'avoided a direct reply to this question,' but when pressed by Morrissey he agreed that the Department was 'being deceived by persons on the American side'.

The precise details of how the Wisconsin scam operated were not recorded, but it would seem that someone within Catholic Charities in the Wisconsin area was producing home study reports making it possible for Irish children to be dispatched to people within Wisconsin who were unfit to adopt children but who were prepared to pay for the privilege. This was precisely the nightmare scenario predicted a few years earlier by Department official Joe Horan. Presumably something similar had been happening in Texas, which O'Grady had mentioned in similar tones. In addition to these astonishing lapses, O'Grady revealed that in certain areas it was 'impossible to maintain thriving branches,' while there was also 'a lack of funds which restricted employment of specialised personnel,' an admission which led the Irish officials to conclude that the organisation was simply 'not equipped at all its branches to deal satisfactorily with adoptions'.

O'Grady proposed a remedy to this series of problems. In place of individual Irish children being sent to individual adoptive couples, he wanted Irish children shipped to America *en bloc*, under the auspices of the head office of Catholic Charities in Washington. The children would be held in orphanages and homes in those areas that had sufficient funds and trained staff to arrange proper adoptions. When asked which areas he had in mind, O'Grady could name just six: Chicago, St Louis, Milwaukee, Newark, Albany and Syracuse. At a time when Catholic Charities had several hundred branches throughout the United States, and was placing Irish children across the country, this was a staggering admission of inadequacy. O'Grady was told that his proposal was a non-starter primarily because it would deprive the Irish authorities of control, but fears were also expressed about hostile publicity.[12] Single 'illegitimate' children could be dispatched discreetly, but bulk exports would attract unwanted attention. There was a third, and even more compelling reason for rejecting O'Grady's 'group plan,' as it came to be dubbed: Archbishop McQuaid disapproved.[13]

Shortly after O'Grady's visit to Dublin, the Department received the first small piece of concrete evidence of the Wisconsin problem. A pointed letter from the Welfare Department at Madison, Wisconsin, revealed that an Irish child had been given to a highly unsuitable family in the area, even though the home and the adoptive parents had been recommended by Catholic Charities.[14] This, presumably, was one of the children handled by the Wisconsin 'operator'. As with all previous revelations of unsuitable adoptions, the Irish authorities showed no inclination to investigate the subsequent fate of the children involved. Instead, they comforted themselves with the belief that the problem was localised rather than general. And when Department officials made discreet inquiries about O'Grady himself, they were told he was held in low esteem by many of his own colleagues.[15] But this was scarcely an adequate answer to the problems that had been revealed. The Department of External Affairs had to respond, and it did so by insisting that all future adoption arrangements for Irish children in America be made by legally registered branches of Catholic Charities. This was a vital improvement, but for an unknown number of Irish children, dispatched to America under a wholly inadequate regime, the new rules came five years too late. And even then, unsuitable people continued to obtain Irish children.

It might be argued, of course, that the Irish authorities could not be held responsible for blunders and failings on the other side of the Atlantic, but it must be remembered that Catholic Charities was chosen to do the job in preference to the federal Children's Bureau, which had offered a full and comprehensive adoption vetting, placing and monitoring service long before the job was entrusted to Catholic Charities. And Catholic Charities was chosen, not because it offered greater protection for the overall interests of the Irish children involved, but because it alone could be trusted to put matters of religion at the top of the agenda. It was more likely to deliver fervent Catholic couples as adoptive parents than any secular organisation could do.

Given the importance of O'Grady's revelations, and the potential damage they could do, Sean Morrissey took the prudent step of sending a copy of the minutes of the meeting with O'Grady to his Minister, Liam Cosgrave.[16] Cosgrave in turn decided that it was time the whole business of the American adoptions was discussed at the Cabinet table, where until now not a word of it had been uttered.

7. ... To Cover-Up

'It is wrong to suggest that there is anything in the nature of a traffic in the adoption of children.'
Liam Cosgrave, Minister for External Affairs,
Dáil Éireann 1956

'There are certain aspects of this traffic in adoption children over which the Department has no control.'
Department of External Affairs, Draft Statement to
Government on American Adoptions 1956

When the Irish Government met on 23 March 1956, Liam Cosgrave, the Minister for External Affairs, initiated the first ever cabinet discussion on Ireland's booming baby exports. The disturbing revelations from America could not be swept under the carpet indefinitely, and Cosgrave also wanted to ensure that his colleagues were not taken by surprise by parliamentary questions on the subject, questions that were already in the pipeline from an opposition TD. It was going to be hard to keep everything under control.

The total number of children officially sent abroad for adoption had just topped the 1,000 mark. It seemed rather late in the day for the government to start thinking about a matter that up to now it had conveniently ignored. But the absence of a distinct policy did not absolve the government of responsibility. It alone was accountable for the fate of so many hundreds of its infant citizens. There was no question of civil servants, or maverick ministers, running a policy that was not strictly official.

The cabinet discussion of March 1956, as was customary, was not recorded, but Cosgrave was instructed to produce a statement of principles by which the Department of External Affairs would be guided in the matter.[1] His officials got to work and had soon produced a substantial draft document. This was followed by another, then another, and another.[2] What these successive draft statements reveal is how the deep concerns of at least some civil servants about the whole business of shipping babies across the Atlantic were progressively sanitised prior to the submission of the proposed document to government.

The first draft statement was completely candid about the serious problems that had arisen in the past, mentioning the scandal of Catholic Charities in Wisconsin where Irish children had been obtained under false pretences. 'There are certain aspects of this traffic in adoption children over which the Department has no control, and in respect of which it is not entirely happy,' the earliest draft statement said. 'The distance separating the two countries is such as to prevent any interested authority in Ireland making independent inspection or assessment of the American adoptive parents and their home,' it went on. Consequently the Department was left dependent on Catholic Charities, but their 'efficiency and reliability' had now been found to be 'not quite uniform throughout America'. In other words, no one could really guarantee the safety and well-being of over 1,000 Irish children sent to America by Church and State during the past decade.

The shortage of babies for adoption in America, the statement went on, 'creates opportunities for unscrupulous operators and agents to intervene in adoption arrangements for the purpose of commercial profit'. Scarcity also meant the Department came under 'a certain pressure... to make children available,' and overall they would 'prefer that the adoptions should not be subjected to these dangers'. The language was restrained, but this was still a clear admission that there had been serious shortcomings and problems with the American adoptions. This honest account of the system's deficiencies, however, was diluted when the second draft was produced. Now, all references to the sale of Irish children by the crook in Wisconsin were dropped; the term 'traffic' was abandoned; references to 'commercial profit' were erased, and the fact that the Department came under (Church) pressure to keep things moving was omitted.

By censoring their own report to the Government, the civil servants might have hoped to keep political concern to a minimum. But there was a limit to their cosseting capabilities, and as the cabinet waited for an opportunity to discuss the business, one of the greatest fears of the officials in the Department of External Affairs became a reality: deputies began asking questions in the Dáil about children being taken to America. A newspaper picked up the scent, leading to more questions and more pressure on the Department to explain, in a public arena, just exactly what was going on – the very last thing they wanted to do.

The first parliamentary question was asked by opposition Fianna Fáil TD Donagh O'Malley on 10 April 1956.[3] He wanted to know whether children who had been temporary inmates of the County Hospital at Croom, County Limerick, had been adopted by American citizens, and if so, what the circumstances surrounding the adoption were. O'Malley gave no background information that might have put the question in context. This was to come later. But the fact that he addressed his question to the Minister for Justice, James Everett, whose responsibilities related only to adoptions within Ireland, was one indication of how little was known or understood, even among public representatives, about the practice of exporting Irish children to the USA. O'Malley's question really should have been addressed to the Minister for External Affairs, Liam Cosgrave. Everett's answer gave away as little as possible. 'Some such children have been taken out of the country for adoption,' he said, but 'there was nothing irregular or unlawful about this'.[4] As far as Everett was concerned, his brief Dáil answer should have been the end of the matter, and probably would have been had not a mass circulation British newspaper followed up the story.

On 10 June 1956 the *Empire News* published a front-page article under the banner headline 'Babies "Sold" to US in Secret,' with a subheading, 'Nun says – It's quite legal'. The story's opening sentence may seem unremarkable: 'Babies born to Irish girls who are unable to make homes for them are being flown from Shannon Airport to the United States to be adopted by American families,' but this was the first time the American adoption issue had been given front-page headline treatment in any popular newspaper circulating in Ireland. Before now, references to the American adoptions in the Irish papers had been few and far between, especially since Archbishop McQuaid's office had ordered a news blackout some five years earlier. The British Sunday paper went on to say that 'solicitors, doctors and hospitals are involved in the teeming traffic, which is conducted in conditions of secrecy.' Investigations in Dublin, Cork and Limerick, the paper said, revealed that 'payments are made for the children,' but it gave no further details of the financial transactions.

The *Empire News* story was about two specific children who had been sent to America directly from the Croom

Hospital in Limerick: Anthony Barron, who was two-and-a-half, and three-year-old Mary Clancy. Both children were born in Croom hospital to unmarried mothers, Kathleen Barron and Bridget Clancy, and both had been fostered out to Kathleen's sister-in-law, Mrs Joan Barron. Joan Barron told the *Empire News* the two infants had been taken from her 'on various pretexts' and returned to the hospital, which was run by nuns. Soon after that they were dispatched to America. Joan Barron said she had been willing to adopt the little boy herself, but when she tried to do so she found she was too late: he had been seen travelling through Croom in a motor car along with a nun from the hospital, on his way to Shannon Airport.

The fate of the other child, Mary Clancy, was recounted by Joan Barron's fifteen-year-old daughter. She told of going to visit three-year-old Mary at Croom Hospital. 'She had only a small cut from a piece of glass and I could not understand what was going on,' the daughter said. 'She was in bed and strapped to the bed with the strap around her middle. She had a vaccination bandage on her arm... Next time I saw her she was up and prettily dressed. A week later I went to Croom again, to Dr Mullins' dispensary, and asked how Mary was. He said, "She is gone away since last night in an aeroplane."' Dr Mullins, Assistant Registrar at the hospital, told the *Empire News*, 'There is nothing wrong with them when the babies go into the hospital. The idea is to civilise them after life in a cottage. They are taught to eat and to wear their clothes properly. They are built up a bit in the three weeks before their American journey.' Dr Mullins' comments certainly made it sound like a well-organised operation involving many more children than Anthony Barron and Mary Clancy.

Flight arrangements for the children were made by a nun, Sister Christopher, who told the *Empire News* that 'the Irish Government know and approve of what we are doing. It is quite legal and we think it better for the children than the poverty of living, for instance, in Mrs Barron's home. We shall continue to send babies to America until the law is changed. Mrs Barron cannot bring up these children. She is too poor to do so.' Three-year-old Mary Clancy's grandmother said that neither she nor the child's mother, Bridget, who was in London, had received any payment for the infant. 'All I got,' she said, 'was ten shillings from the Sister to buy sweets and odd things for Mary when we went to Dublin to see the American consul.' In Dublin they had seen 'a lot of people' and the very next day Mary Clancy, along with a little boy called Billy, had been flown out to the United States. Mary Clancy's adoptive parents lived in Wisconsin.

When he was asked in the Dáil on 19 June, by Cork Labour TD Dan Desmond, what he proposed to do about the claims in the *Empire News*, Justice Minister James Everett repeated the earlier formula that 'there was nothing irregular or unlawful about this'. Faced with what could have become a national scandal, Everett responded with a promise of firm action. The Government, he said, would 'take steps to deal with such newspapers'.[5]

Although there was nothing in the Minister for Justice's comments in the Dáil that indicated the slightest concern about the goings-on at the Croom Hospital, never mind Wisconsin, his Department had been sufficiently worried to order a Garda investigation as soon as it got wind of the fact that Deputy O'Malley was proposing to ask questions. Reporting back that Anthony Barron's mother and Mary Clancy's grandmother had consented to the removal of the two children from the State, the police declared themselves satisfied that all was in order.[6] They do not appear to have enquired at all into the allegation that the children were 'sold'. Nor was there any indication as to who vetted the American adopting parents in Wisconsin, the very state where a Catholic Charities worker had been selling Irish babies.

James Everett's minimalist replies failed to satisfy another Labour TD, Maureen O'Carroll from North Dublin, who demanded to know the basic facts of the case. Everett's reply, 'I have already given that information,' was simply untrue. He had revealed nothing.[7] Not one to be deterred so easily, Mrs O'Carroll returned to the same matter a month later with a series of questions, this time to the proper authority, the Minister for External Affairs, and future Taoiseach, Liam Cosgrave. She wanted to know how many passports had been issued to 'illegitimate' children over one year of age so they could travel to America for adoption, and she wanted to know specifically how many had come from Croom Hospital in Limerick. Mrs O'Carroll also asked for the names and ages of all children removed from the State since the Adoption Act came into force, the dates of their removal and the institutions from which the removals were made.[8] Her questions brought more information into the public domain than had been available before.

Liam Cosgrave said that in the period between the enactment of legal adoption on 1 January 1953 and the end of June 1956, 543 passports had been issued to 'illegitimate' children for travel to the United States. This, of course, was a very partial answer to the question that had been asked. The Minister could have added, had he wished to give a fuller picture, that his department knew of another 500 or so official child export cases preceding the legalisation of adoption, and was also aware of an extensive black market in babies, proceeding outside the official scheme. As was to be expected, he refused to name any of the children. But, quite arbitrarily, he also refused to name the institutions that had sent them overseas. He did, however, reveal that in the period in question, 26 children (almost 5% of the total) had been inmates of the Croom Hospital in Limerick.[9] This seemed to confirm the impression given by Dr Mullins at the hospital, that what was going on there was a very substantial operation. The adverse publicity, however, seems to have brought the Croom operation to an end since the total number of children sent from there to America stopped short of 30.

It is revealing to note that those TDs who questioned the Government's bona fides in this whole matter were in no way critical of the overriding fixation on matters of religion. Quite the reverse, in fact: they sought to challenge the Government on the grounds that it might not have been doing enough to protect the faith. Labour's Dan Desmond, for example, wanted to know was the Minister satisfied 'that these unfortunate little children are being better catered for in religious homes' than they would be if they ended up 'in the hands of... some nests in this country that in the past laid their hands on these unfortunate children?'[10] The word 'nests' was a pejorative term used at the time to describe Protestant-run orphanages. The name came from a mother and baby home in Dublin called the Bird's Nest which was suspected of proselytising. Cosgrave, of course, had no difficulty in putting Deputy Desmond's concerns at rest: preserving the faith was top of the agenda.

Maureen O'Carroll also let it be known that she had 'no objection to the transfer of these children to America as such,' and went on to say that it was 'quite probable that many of these children are getting an opportunity in life they could not and would not get here, that they can start a new life... [without] the stigma they normally have to bear.' But it would be preferable, she said, if the American adopters had to reside for a time in Ireland 'so that their whole moral character and religious outlook and ideas could be examined'.[11]

Donagh O'Malley, the Fianna Fáil TD from Limerick who had started the ball rolling, was concerned that their misgivings about foreign adoptions would be 'splashed across many a paper, not only in Britain but in other countries, to the detriment of this nation'. But he went on to add his own sharp criticisms of the system. 'I know, as everyone connected with Shannon Airport knows, that these children are going to very wealthy homes,' he said. 'The parents of these adopted children can afford to pay the passage of an employee... to take the child, or children, over there. Her first class return air fare is paid. Evidently these children are going to very good families.' But, he added, 'there are two sides to that'. The other side was, 'Who is at the back of these arrangements? Who is the negotiating body? Who is carrying out the deals for these millionaires and semi-millionaires and very high Catholic Americans? Who is the liaison officer between America and this country? No one can find that out.' Well, Liam Cosgrave certainly wasn't going to reveal the controlling hand of John Charles McQuaid. And O'Malley left no one in any doubt that there was a racket in progress. 'Money,' he said, 'is passing to the very close relatives of these children, in certain cases to the unfortunate mother... It is a temptation to such a mother if she is offered £100 or £150 in order to get her to consent.' (Equivalent to €9,600 and €14,400 today. It is unlikely, however, that the unfortunate mothers were ever the main financial beneficiaries) O'Malley ended by calling for a 'reinvestigation' of 'the whole system of adoption of children'.[12]

But Liam Cosgrave was having none of it. 'I deprecate the type of publicity which this debate will attract,' he retorted, adding, 'it is wrong to suggest that there is anything in the nature of a traffic in the adoption of children.' He went on to defend in vigorous terms the 'very stringent' rules and regulations imposed by his Department before passports were issued to children travelling abroad for adoption. Every case, he said, was subject to 'very careful study' and was investigated by 'appropriate religious organisations in the adopting countries.' He went on to say that 'great care is taken to see that... the prospective adopting parents are suitable and proper people to be granted the custody of a child'[13] – a claim that was flatly contradicted by a huge volume of evidence in Cosgrave's own department. At the very moment when Cosgrave was pacifying the Dáil, his own officials were drafting their report for the Government, on Cosgrave's own instructions, about the disturbing reality of the American adoptions. Not only did the officials themselves refer to a 'baby traffic', they admitted they were neither fully in control nor entirely happy with what was going on.

Cosgrave, of course, was determined to avoid bad publicity as his concluding remarks to the Dáil made clear. 'It is significant,' he said, 'that the only comments on this have appeared in what we here call the yellow English Sunday newspapers, who avail of every, and any, opportunity to smear the name of this country. I do not propose to be a party to any such campaign and I hope that no Deputies in this House will lend themselves to it either.'[14] The opposition was silenced and the matter was never again discussed in the Dáil.

* * * * *

In the meantime another line of opposition had developed, this time from within the ranks of the Government itself, in the person of Health Minister, and future Chief Justice, Tom O'Higgins.

Under the 1953 Health Act, the Minister for Health was responsible for the welfare of orphaned, deserted, and destitute 'illegitimate' children who were accommodated at the expense of the health authorities in institutional homes. One such institution was the County Home in Longford, and in the summer of 1955 five of its young inmates had been sent to America for adoption. The matter came to light when the Longford County Manager was called upon to explain to county councillors why he had spent £10 (€960) on an outfit for one of the children. He told the council that sending the infants to America was 'a great break'. The *Longford News* reported the story under the headline, 'New Export Enterprise'.[15] But when Health Minister O'Higgins found out, he was furious.

On 23 March 1956 – the very day Cosgrave raised the American adoption business at cabinet – O'Higgins wrote to the secretary of the Longford County Council telling him that local authorities had no business making arrangements for sending children in public care out of the state for adoption. His letter eventually found its way to Cosgrave's Department where, for years past, the officials had been happily issuing adoption passports to children from local authority homes such as St Pat's in Dublin and three provincial orphanages run by the Sacred Heart nuns. (Between them these four public institutions accounted for well over 1,000 of the children dispatched to the United States, or over half the total). So if O'Higgins was now taking exception to this practice, a fundamental conflict seemed unavoidable.

Sean Morrissey of the Department of External Affairs, took up the cudgels, and in a rather snooty letter to his opposite number at the Department of Health he complained about them breaking ranks and creating the impression of inconsistency and confusion on the part of the State. 'As you are aware,' Morrissey wrote, 'the question of permitting Irish children to be taken abroad for adoption is one on which strong and divergent opinions are held and it would appear to be desirable that insofar as possible, Departmental action should be consistent'.[16]

But O'Higgins wasn't to be put off so easily. His position was spelled out in a reply to Morrissey. 'The Minister,' the reply stated, 'considers that public authorities should not place themselves in the position of agents for the sending of children abroad as such activities must inevitably damage the status of the public services, and are open to criticism on social and political grounds since they aggravate the decline of the population...'

'It may be argued,' the reply went on, 'that the children sent abroad benefit materially and socially, but the expectation of betterment in another country must be presumed to apply to all emigration and it would be clearly indefensible that public authorities should engage, even in a small way, in organised emigration of children while public policy is directed towards a reduction of emigration generally.'

These were among the strongest and most critical words written on the subject by anyone in authority with any knowledge of what was happening. And the Minister for Health had more to say.

'The correct course to be followed by public authorities who have custody of children is to increase their endeavours towards the improvement of the opportunities of such children to make a normal living in this country. The Minister... considers that such improvements would be much more desirable than any participation in arrangements for sending the children out of the country.'[17]

It was clear from the tone of these letters that there was considerable friction between Health and External Affairs, with Health adopting the moral and social high ground and suggesting that External Affairs was facilitating organised child emigration. And to rub it in, the letter from O'Higgins' officials concluded by asking if the Minister for External Affairs had 'considered the matter from the point of view of its effect on this country's standing with the countries to which children are sent.' In other words, the image of Ireland abroad was being tarnished by the policy of exporting 'illegitimate' children, and the Minister for External Affairs was responsible.

The mandarins at Iveagh House were clearly annoyed at Tom O'Higgins' criticisms, but he was a cabinet minister and they had to respond. They introduced a new rule in the summer of 1956 which appeared to make concessions to his sensibilities: all future passport applications on behalf of children in public authority care intending to travel abroad for adoption would be directed to the Minister for Health so he could personally approve or disapprove each case as it arose. This seemed to put O'Higgins in the driving seat, but it was a move that would give the Health Minister a few headaches – and some experience of the intense pressure that could be brought to bear by the religious orders who ran the local authority homes and who were fuelling the overseas adoption traffic.

In a matter of months O'Higgins found himself overwhelmed with requests for passport clearances, and as the backlog grew, religious pressure mounted. It didn't take long before O'Higgins' officials were looking for a way of disengaging from the whole business.[18] It was a humiliating climb-down, and as his officials made clear, it had been brought about entirely by O'Higgins being 'placed in an embarrassing position *vis-à-vis* voluntary bodies and ecclesiastical authorities'. As a consequence, his officials now asked External Affairs to drop 'the practice of referring these applications for the Minister's consent'.[19]

The Minister for Health, for all his principled opposition to the export of Irish children, had not taken on the 'ecclesiastical authorities' or the 'voluntary bodies' – Archbishop McQuaid and the nuns. The Department of External Affairs agreed to let the Department of Health 'escape from the position into which they have engineered themselves,'[20] but only on the understanding that

O'Higgins had 'modified his previous attitude'[21], which in reality meant abandoning his criticisms.

* * * * *

After the ill-informed and inconsequential Dáil debate of March 1956, and the effective gutting of Tom O'Higgins a year later, the last remaining hope for a serious review of the American adoption issue was that the cabinet would receive the long-awaited policy statement from the Department of External Affairs. But it waited in vain. In March 1957, a full year after the statement was requested, a general election returned Fianna Fáil to power. O'Higgins was out of office. Cosgrave was succeeded by Frank Aiken. Work on various drafts of the statement continued but without urgency, and Father Cecil Barrett was even drafted in to assist in the writing of the document 'on behalf of the Catholic Archbishop of Dublin'.[22] As the matter dragged on into the 1960s, department officials came to the view that there was no longer any need to involve the Government since everything by then seemed to be running smoothly.[23] The cabinet never discussed the matter; no government was ever officially aware of the numerous and serious problems that had been encountered.

The policy of exporting the country's 'illegitimate' children had survived a sustained period of scrutiny and criticism, but only because the truth had been suppressed. McQuaid's six-year-old domestic news blackout was still in force, so the public at large remained ignorant of the baby traffic. The threatening clamour in the Dáil had been stilled by a combination of partial answers, unjustified assurances and bullying assertions that questions on the subject were 'anti-national'. Tom O'Higgins, the only critical voice in cabinet, had been silenced and chastened. The disturbing revelations in the draft statement to the Government about what was really going on had been spiked.

But the staff in the passport section of the Department of External Affairs could at least hope that, in the future, overseas adoptions would be safer under the new rules, which required all child placements in America to be handled by legally registered agencies. The Department of External Affairs had introduced this tougher regulation early in 1956 in response to Monsignor John O'Grady's revelations about the inadequacies of Catholic Charities. But it was not until July 1957, 18 months later, that Archbishop McQuaid followed suit.

The Archbishop's delay in tightening up his requirements seemed inexcusable, especially since the risks facing Irish infants sent to America under the old regime had been made abundantly clear. It seems the reason for his hesitation was that he was trying to bring all the religious-run adoption societies into line so there could be a uniform approach to the issue. The fear now, as always, was that if they were left to their own devices, the nuns would be inclined to accept American applicants at face value and offer babies without asking too many hard questions, so as to keep the babies moving and the donations flowing. But in the wake of O'Grady's revelations, McQuaid wanted procedures standardised. The bishops were contacted with a view to getting them to persuade the nuns in their dioceses to agree common practices for handling future American adoptions. It proved a long slow process, and it was not until early 1958 that Cecil Barrett was in a position to report that McQuaid's requirements for would-be American adopters 'have now been accepted and are being enforced by all the members of the Irish hierarchy'.[24]

This should have marked a turning point in the whole affair. In theory it meant that all future intending adopters, whoever they were and wherever they came from, would need a thoroughgoing home study report from a professionally qualified social worker, employed by a legally registered child-placing agency, before they could get their hands on an Irish baby. In theory at least, professional standards should now have been uniformly applied to all transatlantic adoptions. But they had been a long time coming and even after their introduction disturbing cases persisted.

By the summer of 1958, when the tougher regulations finally came into force, over 1,300 children had been sent to America, and that represented over 60% of the total that would be sent, so at best only a minority could ever benefit from the new regime. What was more, the vetting system that was put in place so late in the day was little different from what had been offered by the secular and highly professional US Children's Bureau, and turned down, eight years earlier. And one fundamental problem had still not been addressed by anyone in authority in Ireland: Americans could still adopt Irish children without ever having to set foot in the country. The baby export business remained almost entirely mail-order.

Perhaps it was an unlucky coincidence, but one of the hardest hitting reports ever published into mail-order adoptions was released in the United States at the very moment when the Catholic Church in Ireland thought it had cleaned up its act. In June 1958, two prominent and highly regarded organisations, the Child Welfare League of America and the US branch of International Social Service published *A Study of Proxy Adoptions* by Laurin Hyde and Virgina P. Hyde, leading experts in the field. The two organisations used the release of this report to mount a campaign for a change in US Federal law to ban the practice of adopting children from abroad unseen – as happened in the overwhelming majority of adoptions from Ireland. By permitting such adoptions, they said, US law had allowed 'an often tragic mail-order baby business' to develop, adding that the current lax system 'has already produced many tragic consequences, including the death, beating and abandonment of children.'[25] The Hyde study recorded cases of 'physical abuse of children, breakdown of adoptive homes, adoption of children by persons who were unstable or mentally ill and placements of upset or emotionally disturbed children with persons unprepared or unable to help them.' As proof of the laxity in American law governing foreign adoptions, the report cited the bizarre case of an Oregon farmer who had managed to import 600 children whom he placed with families of his own choice. And, regrettably, these concerns were far from academic.

It was October 1958 – three months after Archbishop McQuaid thought he had at last established a regime that would safeguard children sent to the United States – when four-year-old Kieran McNulty was put on a plane at Shannon by the Sacred Heart nuns from the Bessboro home in Cork, and flown to his new adoptive parents in Chicago. On top of adjusting to his new and alien environment, the four-year-old had to adjust quickly to a new name as well, for now he was Kevin Murtaugh. 'I remember bits and pieces of what it was like living at Bessboro,' he said in later years, 'things like the nuns hitting us, being called by a number – I was number 36.'[26] It was hard to imagine how life in the United States could be any worse for Kevin, but it was. 'Things went well for the first few years,' he recalled. 'Years later I would figure that it was because I was a novelty to have around.' Kevin described his Irish-American father as 'a mean drunk'. 'When he grew tired of me, he began to beat me, and one of the most common things he would say to me when he was beating me up and knocking me down was, "Get up you son of a bitch and take it like a man."' Kevin had to pay towards his own education. 'I had to get up at 3.45 every morning, Monday through Friday, and sell newspapers on a street corner.' By comparison, he said, none of his adoptive parents' four natural children had to work. 'I always felt like an unwanted guest in their house, not a son.'

One of the things Kevin's adoptive father seemed to hold against him was the fact that his natural mother had been unmarried, a fallen woman whose offspring would carry her tainted genes. It was the ultimate irony. The Catholic Church insisted on placing all 'its' children with devout and practising Catholics – the very people who were most likely to disparage their adopted children's natural mothers for their supposed moral laxity. As a leading Irish social worker noted in later years: 'Since most children placed for adoption are conceived out of wedlock, attitudes [of adopting parents] to non-marital sex are very important as this has been shown to colour attitudes towards the children.'[27] Professional social workers assessing would-be adopters look for broad-minded, non-judgmental parents, the opposite of what McQuaid seemed to want – and, in Kevin Murtaugh's case, got. Kevin was made pay – physically and psychologically – for his natural mother's supposed sexual sins.

On his seventeenth birthday, for the first and last time, Kevin defended himself from his father's blows, giving – he said – as good as he got. Next day he left home and joined the US Army, never to return to his adoptive parents' home. He subsequently married a woman called Diane Camm, a nurse, but the marriage failed. Drugs were involved and Diane had gone off with another man. 'During a period in which we were trying to reconcile our marriage,' he told me, 'we got into an argument and it turned violent. I ended up choking her to death.' This was as far as Kevin went with his story, but court documents obtained subsequently show that strangling his wife was far from the end of it. After killing Diane, Kevin borrowed a neighbour's chain-saw and dismembered her body. It was January 1977. At the age of 22, Kevin was convicted of murder and sentenced to life in jail. When he first contacted me he had already spent over 20 years in prison, years in which he said he had had extensive counselling. 'The psychologists have all said they believe my problems go all the way back to prior to the adoption. I can see why I ended up in prison. No real stable family life; an abusive relationship with my father; the fear of abandonment; always being told I was unwanted; no one or no place to turn to with my problems; the feeling of being a stranger in a strange land, out of place. It all added up.' In 2002, Kevin's request for parole was rejected and he had to wait until 2007 to apply again. On that occasion he was refused once more and told it would be 2015 before he could re-apply.[28] By then he will have served 38 years in jail.

At this remove it is impossible to say if Kevin Murtaugh is simply engaged in a charade of self-exculpation. Certainly Diane Camm's family think he is a master of deception. Yet research shows a very high over-representation of adopted people among those in trouble, of one sort or another, with the authorities. In one 1980s study from California, between 30 and 40% of people in residential treatment centres, juvenile detention facilities and reform schools were found to have been adopted, yet adopted people comprised less than 3% of the wider population. Symptoms that were described as 'consistent' among adopted people referred for treatment included impulsiveness, aggressiveness and provocativeness.[29] For a very small subset of adopted people – especially in closed adoptions marred by denial and deception – the adoption experience has also been linked with extreme forms of anti-social behaviour in later life, including murder and even serial murder. New York's most notorious serial killers – David Berkowitz, known as 'Son of Sam', and Joel Riflin, 'The Ripper', who between them killed 23 women – were both adopted as infants. Berkowitz's biographer, psychiatrist

David Abrahamsen, concluded that the 'mystery of his origins' and the feeling that he was 'an accident, a mistake, never meant to be born – unwanted', played a crucial role in turning him into a killer of young women.[30] And although there are no official statistics on the subject, one American criminal lawyer, Paul Mones, has estimated that in cases of parricide – murder of one or both parents – adopted people outnumber non-adopted people by a factor of 15 or more.[31] In one famous case in America, expert witnesses called by lawyers representing a 14-year-old adopted child, Patrick DeGelleke, whose parents died when he burned their house down, were allowed to introduce what they called the 'Adopted Child Syndrome' as a defence argument. One of the experts, David Kirschner, who has testified at numerous trials of adopted people charged with murder, argues that adopted people are at particular risk of extreme dissociation under stress, especially the stress of real or perceived rejection by family or friends.[32]

It has to be emphasised, of course, that cases of extreme violence and murder involving adopted people, while seemingly more frequent on a pro rata basis than among non-adopted people, are still extremely rare, and that the vast majority of adopted people have adjusted to the conditions in which they have found themselves, or at least sufficiently so for them to function without serious outward signs of being troubled by their conflicted status.

The sort of psychological research that is available nowadays was unavailable in the days when the nuns were sending children like Kieran McNulty/Kevin Murtaugh to the United States for adoption, and it seemed that no amount of regulations from Church or State could prevent such human tragedies. Nor, for that matter, could they curtail the activities of the even less scrupulous baby traffickers who continued to ply their lucrative trade in the shadows.

8. A Very Grave Offence

On the 19th of January 1965, Mary Keating, midwife and proprietress of St Rita's private nursing home in south Dublin, was convicted in the Dublin District Court for what was described at her trial as a 'very grave' offence. Over 30 years after the event, Dr Karl Mullen, the gynaecologist and celebrated hero of 1950s Irish rugby, recalled that Mrs Keating had been prosecuted for 'selling babies to America'. It was an erroneous, but highly revealing, recollection from someone who was personally close to Mrs Keating and who had attended her trial as a potential character witness. Someone else in court that day was future TD, Senator and Lord Mayor of Dublin, Joe Doyle, who for the past ten years had been Sacristan at Donnybook Catholic Church where Mrs Keating had her falsely registered babies baptised.[1] Mrs Keating had, in fact, been prosecuted for forging the official birth register and uttering forged birth certificates with intent to deceive. Behind the seemingly technical charges, however, lay a much bigger story, for while Mrs Keating may not have been *charged* with selling babies to America, as Karl Mullen thought, it was certainly suspected that that was precisely what she was up to.

Mrs Keating's name and that of St Rita's were, of course, well known to the authorities. Back in the mid 1950s they had figured prominently in a Special Branch investigation into a Babies-for-export racket involving American airmen stationed in Britain. On that occasion the authorities had been more interested in keeping the whole business under wraps than in bringing the culprits to justice. On the second time around Mrs Keating was not so lucky, although the full story still never came out.

In 1959, a year after all the regulations regarding foreign adoptions had been standardised and tightened up, an American couple, Mr and Mrs Wedderburn, travelled to Dublin looking for a child to take back with them to the United States.[2] They were introduced to Mrs Keating as someone who might be able to help. She promised to find them a little girl, as they had requested, and they went home with their hopes raised. But they were in for a long wait. After their return home to the States, the Wedderburns maintained a regular correspondence with Mrs Keating as weeks turned to months, and months to years. It was one indication of how difficult it must have been for the couple to adopt a child in America that they were prepared to wait so long to get one from Ireland. But finally there was good news from Dublin. Halfway through 1962 the Wedderburns received word from Mrs Keating that a baby girl had become available. The baby was born at St Rita's on 16 June. Her mother was unmarried, but of good background, and was prepared to 'disappear' from the official records by not having the birth registered in her own name.

A month after the birth, on 16 July 1962, Mrs Keating forged the official register of births and procured a birth certificate for the baby in the name of 'Jane Wedderburn'. The child was then baptised in this name at Donnybrook Catholic Church. Matters appeared to be proceeding as planned; all that was required now was for the Wedderburns to come and collect 'their' daughter. But there was to be a last minute hitch: suddenly and quite unexpectedly the Wedderburns announced they were unable to travel to Dublin. Instead the baby was to be entrusted to a sister-in-law of Mrs Wedderburn's – a Mrs Woulfe – who would come instead. This complicated matters greatly, for it meant that the 16 July birth certificate in the name of Jane Wedderburn was now useless. Another one was needed in the name of Woulfe if it was to match Mrs Woulfe's passport. Again Mrs Keating obliged by forging another entry in the register of births and obtaining a second birth certificate on 25 July, this time in the name of 'Jane Woulfe'. Mrs Woulfe arrived in Dublin soon after, and she and baby 'Jane Woulfe' then travelled back to America where the baby was handed over to the Wedderburns.

The arrival of baby Jane in the States should have been the end of the affair, but it was, in fact, just the beginning. The Wedderburns were proud of their new baby girl, but a neighbour, knowing something of their personal history, became suspicious and notified the authorities of the new and unexplained arrival. Investigations in the States quickly established an Irish connection and the Department of External Affairs in Dublin was advised. When news of the Wedderburn baby reached the Department, a full scale Garda investigation was set in train. Its focus, however, wasn't just this one baby. It wasn't even Mrs Keating. The authorities had their sights on a man whom they believed to be behind a major baby-selling racket that had gone on undetected for a number of years, and that had involved the illegal dispatch of many babies to America. The man, who had a public profile, was never charged with any offence, although it was always suspected that it was he, and not Mrs Keating, who was the principal beneficiary of the scam.[3]

Several senior police officers were involved in the investigation, but when the file was eventually sent to the

Director of Public Prosecutions, he decided to prosecute only Mrs Keating for her role in forging the official birth register. Given the scope of the operation centred on St Rita's, and the potential profits resulting from over a decade and a half of facilitating illegal adoptions, this was indeed a paltry charge.

When her trial took place before Justice Farrell in the Dublin District Court in January 1965, the prosecution described the offences as 'very grave' but stressed that Mrs Keating was 'a respectable woman' who 'derived no more benefit from the birth and the transaction than the normal accouchement fees'.[4] The prosecution offered no evidence of financial dealings, and there wasn't a hint in court of the bigger picture or of the man who was behind the racket. Had there been evidence of 'bribery and corruption,' Judge Farrell remarked, he would have sent Mrs Keating to jail. But if that had happened, she might have been much less willing to take all the blame herself. As it was, Mrs Keating pleaded guilty and the proceedings ended quickly. Had she denied the charge, and had the State been required to prove her guilt, much more would have come out. Despite the acknowledged gravity of the offence, she was put on probation and the matter ended there. It was a small triumph for Mrs Keating's defence counsel, Declan Costello, then a leading Fine Gael TD, a future Attorney General and President of the High Court. She was clearly well connected.

When Justice Farrell asked if Mrs Keating's nursing home licence was in danger, the Garda officer who had led the investigation, Inspector Tony McMahon, said he had no instructions to investigate that aspect of the case. But someone else in court that day had taken it upon himself to ensure that Mrs Keating did not lose her licence. A priest, who knew her well, had come to the court prepared to appear as a character witness for Mrs Keating, alongside Karl Mullen and Joe Doyle. In the event, none of them were called, but the priest was to go to even greater lengths to help ensure she remained in business.

The priest decided to intervene at the highest level possible to plead on Mrs Keating's behalf: with the Taoiseach himself, Sean Lemass. This led to an interesting encounter, not with Lemass, whom he didn't get to meet, but with a future Fianna Fáil Taoiseach, the then Minister for Agriculture, Charles Haughey, who happened to pass by while the priest was waiting in the hope of seeing Lemass. The priest and the minister got talking and when Haughey learned of the reason for the priest's visit he laughed and told him, 'sure half the children born at St Rita's were fathered by members of the Dáil'.[5] An exaggeration, without a doubt, but if there was any truth in it at all, it might explain why the identities of so many of Mrs Keating's 'girls' were obliterated through the issuing of false birth certificates, why she was so keen to dispatch their children to America, and why she was so willing to plead guilty to a very grave offence, protecting the man who was masterminding the whole business in the process. Mrs Keating kept her licence and remained profitably in business until she retired more than a decade later, the Wedderburns got to keep their baby, and 'Mr Big' lived a long, respectable, and prosperous life.

Mrs Keating's was the first and last prosecution arising out of the entire American adoption saga, although it is quite clear that Mrs Keating was far from the only person who broke the law. Some of the goings-on at the Sacred Heart Convent and adoption society at Sean Ross Abbey in County Tipperary also came to the attention of the authorities. Over the years the nuns in Roscrea sent around 450 children to America, and the Superioress, Sister Hildegarde McNulty, was once regarded by Catholic Charities as one of the three 'most important people in the Irish adoption picture'.[6] But there were some things Sister Hildegarde wanted to keep out of the picture.

In February 1968, Margaret O'Neill, an unmarried teenager from County Clare, gave birth to a baby boy, Paul Anthony, at Sean Ross Abbey. For the next six months Margaret worked in the convent laundry and saw her child every day. She had every intention of keeping him and had made this clear, but the nuns had ideas of their own – although at no point did any of them bother discussing with Margaret what their plans for her child were. When she found out she was dumbfounded. It was one day in August 1968 when one of the girls in the laundry told her Paul Anthony was being taken away for adoption. The last Margaret saw of her child was when he was driven out of the convent gates in a car. She didn't see him again for 22 years.

Like many young and vulnerable girls at the time, Margaret O'Neill lived in fear of the nuns. Whatever self-confidence or esteem she had before she went into Sean Ross Abbey, it had been well and truly knocked out of her after six months of Sister Hildegarde's regime. 'I had no one to turn to, no one to help me,' Margaret said.[7] She left Sean Ross Abbey shortly afterwards, still grieving for her lost son and feeling totally powerless.

Margaret married in 1972. Her husband, Thomas McMahon, knew her story and wanted to help, but all their approaches to the Adoption Board proved futile, and Sister Hildegarde kept silent. It was 1989 before the Adoption Board finally agreed to investigate her case. She met members of the Board in a Limerick hotel, and when she gave a sample signature as requested, it was immediately obvious that the 'signatures' on her adoption consent forms were forgeries. In one 'signature' her name was even misspelt. The culprit had little regard for the law and clearly felt so secure and justified in what she was doing that she hadn't even bothered trying to copy Margaret's actual signature or spell her name correctly.

Yet, as with all such consent documents, these had been witnessed and stamped by a Commissioner for Oaths. When asked to explain how something like this could happen, the lawyer said all he had sworn to was that the document was signed in his presence and that the person signing it was 'known' to Sister Hildegarde. The Adoption Board eventually confirmed to Margaret that her son's adoption had been arranged personally by Sister Hildegarde. The Gardai investigated the case and sent a file to the Director of Public Prosecutions, but he decided not to prosecute.[8] Sister Hildegarde was already in her 80s. Margaret McMahon had her position vindicated in a subsequent civil action in the courts against Sean Ross Abbey. They mounted no defence.

Shortly before her death in 1995, Sister Hildegarde told a social worker that donations coming back from American adopters had constituted the largest single source of income for Sean Ross Abbey in the period when the adoptions were in full swing. She also admitted to removing and destroying documents from individual adoption files which related to these American payments.[9] This was all done at a time when Sister Hildegarde feared a nationwide investigation by the authorities into adoption society practices following a very disturbing case that illustrated just how ramshackle Ireland's adoption system really was. It was 1969, and a Waterford man had just been convicted for the manslaughter of his adopted daughter. The victim, a six-year-old girl, had been given to the man and his wife by their local priest, Father Keane, who ran St John's Adoption Society. There had been no assessment of the couple's suitability to adopt – had there been they would not have qualified. The Waterford scandal had led to the first serious questioning of Ireland's adoption service. The adoption societies – including Father Keane's – were all properly registered, but there was no requirement in law that they be regulated, and awareness was growing that the entire area was inadequately monitored and riddled with abuses. As it happened, Sr Hildegarde needn't have worried: no one ever came to inspect the files.

After its closure as an orphanage in 1970, the files from Sean Ross Abbey (as well as from Castlepollard) were sent to the Sacred Heart Convent at Bessboro in Cork, where for many years they were in the care of senior social worker Sister Sarto Harney. Sister Sarto said that after 'serious allegations' had been made about babies being sold to America, 'we checked it out, we went through the files, and there is no evidence there of any money changing hands'. When asked if that could mean that the files were incomplete (as a result of Sr Hildegarde destroying the vital evidence), Sister Sarto said, 'I don't know. We only have what we have and we cannot comment other than that'.[10]

9. Troublesome Priest

'A practice which… does not appear to have been considered unacceptable.'

Austin Currie, Minister of State for
Children's Policy, Dáil Éireann, 5 March 1996

When news of Ireland's past practice of dispatching 'illegitimate' children to America first broke on an unsuspecting public in 1996, the religious orders involved and other supporters of the scheme were quick to condemn those who criticised 'with the benefit of hindsight'. The implication – voiced more explicitly by Junior Minister Austin Currie, who described it as a practice that was 'not considered unacceptable' – was that when it was happening, everyone approved. This is simply not so.

As we have seen, two Ministers for Health in the 1950s, Noel Browne and Tom O'Higgins – at opposite ends of the political spectrum – voiced strong reservations, although neither followed through on their concerns. It is also clear that those most closely associated with the overall management of the scheme – Archbishop McQuaid and the Department of External Affairs – dreaded publicity, not least because they knew that if attention were focused on the practice, much of it would have been critical.

At various points in contemporary documents it is even made plain that Archbishop McQuaid and his social welfare adviser, Cecil Barrett, were not all that keen on sending children abroad for adoption. They succumbed in the end to pressure from the nuns whose primary interest seems to have been to avoid congestion in the 'orphanages' while turning a useful profit from the abundance of babies for export. And when McQuaid and Barrett took an active hand in servicing the child export scheme, it was not because they thought it was a good idea in itself but because, as determined anti-proselytisers, they dreaded the alternative, where the children of many 'fallen' Irish Catholic mothers might fall in turn into the hands of Irish Protestant adopters, many of them north of the border.

But there were others – admittedly few in number – whose opposition to the scheme was total and complete. Some argued against it consistently and refused – on principle – to assist in any way. Portarlington-born Monsignor Bryan Walsh was among them, and he was a leading figure within the Catholic Charities hierarchy, director of the organisation in Miami and one-time national Vice President. Before his sudden death from a heart attack in 2001, he expressed his views on the Irish baby export business cogently and forcefully.[1]

'There is no question in my mind that there has been a large international business in finding children for adoption and placing them in the United States – and I know there's big money involved in it.' Monsignor Walsh said. 'I have no doubt there was money involved in the Irish adoptions – donations made to the orphanages, that sort of thing. It is accepted practice among Americans: anyone adopting a child in the States expects to have to contribute to the adoption service. The amounts are calculated on a sliding scale – the richer you are, the more you pay. I can't quote figures for Irish adoptions, but I am sure money was involved.'

Quite clearly the American couples who were able to adopt Irish children were privileged. They were jumping ahead of the queues in their homeland and they were getting babies who would be 'guaranteed pure white', something that would have enhanced their appeal and value to middle class white couples who could never be sure of the racial origins of children in American orphanages. 'You have to understand the fundamental fact about adoption in America,' Monsignor Walsh went on. 'Demand has always been much greater than supply. That isn't to say there is anything like a shortage of dependent children – there clearly isn't. There are plenty of children in need of care, but many are of mixed blood, many are black, and white Americans won't adopt them. And there have been many stories of white children who turn out to be carrying black genes which only become evident in the next generation. So the demand in certain quarters has been for white babies and what better place to get them than Ireland?' The interplay of race and scarcity has always ensured a higher premium is placed on white babies.

The idea that an organisation like Catholic Charities should be involved in the business of finding racially pure babies for wealthy couples who wanted them was not one with which Monsignor Bryan Walsh had any sympathy.

Indeed he did not believe the adoption process should be demand-led at all. 'In my view it wasn't our job to respond to the demands of people who wanted children, to go out and find what they wanted. It was our job to find homes for the children already in our care, not to recruit children for adoption. The Irish adoptions, it seems to me, fell into this category. There is no doubt it was a demand-led process.' In other words, it was undertaken in the first instance to meet the needs and requirements of wealthy American adopters, not the Irish children.

This led to further problems down the line. In a country like America, where couples seeking children for adoption outnumbered available children by twenty to one, priests and others associated with Catholic Charities were under constant pressure to find children for demanding parishioners. There were even cases of couples threatening to leave the Church unless they were supplied with a baby, Monsignor Walsh said. Under these circumstances, many clerics within Catholic Charities looked to Ireland for an answer to their own local problems and pressures. And there was an obvious danger that in their desire to keep strident parishioners happy, they would cut corners.

And there were other practical and immediate concerns. The procedure followed by the adoption societies in Ireland, whereby a single mother signed her child over to a named nun, permitting the nun to export the child, was a dubious practice in the eyes of Monsignor Walsh. 'We had no means in an agency like ours of being assured that everything had been done properly and above board in Ireland; that there had been proper surrender papers, freely signed on the basis of informed consent; that the mother – and the father even – knew what they were doing in surrendering their children for adoption by Americans. This was a fundamental concern of mine right from the start.'

And he had good reason to be concerned, for there were often question marks over signatures on consent documents. But even where signatures were not in doubt, other serious questions remained. One official in the Department of External Affairs had described adoption society procedures for handling child exports as having 'no valid foundation in law' because a society had 'no legal right whatever to the custody of an illegitimate child until it is constituted a legal guardian of the child by an Irish court.' But 'in normal cases this does not take place,' because the societies never 'indulge in the expense involved.'[2] In his concerns over this issue at least, Monsignor Walsh was clearly not alone.

But even had the moral and legal basis of many of these adoptions not been in question, Monsignor Walsh still had major reservations. 'I was very concerned how serious a matter it was to pluck a child out of Ireland and place him permanently for adoption in a new culture – cut off his or her roots in Ireland without any consent on the part of that child, saying "you're going to be an American from now on". That was questionable,' he said. 'I never did think that was the solution for Irish children. My argument was that through education and proper social services, the solution should be in Ireland itself.' This was the very argument that had been advanced by Minister Tom O'Higgins in the mid-1950s, but no one had been listening.

Bryan Walsh also knew from those of his colleagues within Catholic Charities who did handle Irish adoptions that they had endless problems in their dealings with the nuns back in Ireland. The single biggest issue concerned 'matching' – the critical process by which a particular child was selected for placement in a particular home. 'Catholic Charities were expected to vet American couples without being given any information at all about the child they were hoping to receive,' Monsignor Walsh said. Another prominent Catholic Charities director put it this way: 'We have to send a complete case history with many documents and in return we get a picture and a birth date!'[3] This meant that while Catholic charities could say in general that a couple would make suitable adoptive parents they could not say they would be suitable parents for the child subsequently picked by the nuns, since they knew nothing of the child in question. This was a symptom of the mail-order nature of the business that had been so roundly criticised by the Child Welfare League of America and the US branch of the International Social Service in 1958. Father Cecil Barrett was well aware of this problem and even brought it to the attention of Archbishop McQuaid's secretary. 'The success of the adoption often depends on the care exercised in selecting a particular child for a definite home,' he noted, but in the American adoptions, elementary matching was impossible because of 'the difficulty of obtaining a full and complete history of each child from the Sisters here.'[4]

But Monsignor Walsh acknowledges that he was 'a fairly lone voice' within Catholic Charities, where his attitudes were seen as 'almost un-American' and where the predominant view was that 'any child from Ireland would be better off in the United States.'

'I simply did not agree with that reasoning. I did not share that opinion,' he said. 'The attitude I took was one of questioning America, questioning the Church in America even. I had some fierce arguments on this point within Catholic Charities, but the opposite view prevailed, that anyone really would be better in America than in Ireland. Now from the point of view of those looking after these children in Ireland I can see the attraction of the nice American couple coming in and offering a nice home to one of their babies. There is no question that to the religious sisters in the orphanages the offer of a home in the United States – where they thought everyone was a millionaire – was marvellous. That was understandable from 3,000 miles away where all the images of America were positive. But those of us who worked in welfare programmes in United States knew differently. Poverty was endemic in the States with two out of every three children growing up in deprivation. Racism was a serious issue and anti-Irish feeling ran very strong in many areas and communities. America was a very violent society. It's not a land of milk and honey for most of the people who live there. But that's what the sisters back in Ireland thought and I'm sure they believed they were doing the best for the children in their care. I saw it very differently, and I think history bears out my view because child welfare in America has been steadily deteriorating for the past 40 years, all the way through from the beginning of the Irish adoption programme, as it happens.'

Monsignor Walsh's opposition to the entire practice of importing Irish children into America for adoption led him to boycott the scheme. Catholic Charities in Miami simply refused to co-operate in any way. It refused to offer advice to parishioners on the procedures involved in obtaining children from Ireland. It refused to do home studies and Monsignor Walsh continued to argue against the whole business at Catholic Charities conferences. The effect of his boycott can be seen in the fact that throughout all the years of the American adoptions, only five Irish children were sent to the state of Florida.

'Now we are seeing some new problems when people try to trace their roots,' he noted. 'In the 1950s and 60s the emphasis was all on confidentiality and complete separation of the adoptive family and the natural family. The mother and her child should never see each other again. That was the theory. Today we know differently – you just can't do that. Tracing and searching are commonplace, but for the Irish adoptees it is made much harder across 3,000 miles of ocean. And having two different legal systems doesn't help. It just makes something that is already difficult and traumatic even worse. But of course nobody thought about that when they were sending Irish babies to the States in the past.'

PART II
Mother and Child

Prologue
The Adoption Triangle

Adoption is a three way process involving the child, the birth parents and the adoptive parents. Everyone's story is different, but the ones told here, which look at the experience from all three sides of the triangle, have been chosen because each of them raises issues and deals with emotions that are common to all.

Jim and Dorothy Rowe were a typical Catholic American couple who turned to Ireland for a baby after many frustrating years of trying to adopt in the States. Their story shows how they went about getting an Irish baby and what they had to do to make it all legal. Their story also raises questions about money...

Maureen, their Irish-born daughter, grew up in comfort, but also in conflict – with her religion and with her adoptive mother. It was not a happy childhood. In later years when Maureen set out to discover her roots, what she found instead was an obstacle course leading to a wall of silence.

Patricia Eyres was one of the unmarried mothers whose children were sent to America. For nearly two years she lived with the nuns before parting with her baby, a blow from which she never recovered. She kept the whole affair secret for thirty-four years. When she finally discovered her son's fate in America, she was devastated.

When Mary Cunningham and Michael Geraghty got married they thought their secret 'love-child', born seven months before the wedding, had already been sent to America. They went on to have six more children. Thirty-four years later they discovered some startling facts about what actually happened to their long-lost son.

10. Jim and Dorothy:
No Price Too High

'We pray for our benefactors every day.'
St Clare's Adoption Society, 1966

Jim and Dorothy Rowe were probably quite typical of the American couples who obtained babies from Ireland.[1] They were natives of New York's Brooklyn district and had married when they were both 30 years old in 1949. But Mrs Rowe was infertile. In 1955 they had adopted a little boy, George, from the nuns at the Angel Guardian Home, their local orphanage in Brooklyn. But all their efforts since then to acquire a sister for George had proved futile. There just were not enough babies to go round, and priority was given to the first-time adopters. It was getting to a point where the nun in charge of adoptions at the Home wasn't even bothering to reply to the Rowes' increasingly desperate letters looking for a little girl: 'Each day we eagerly await the mail to see if there will be something from you, but each day we are disappointed...' 'A year has passed since we applied and we have had no word from you...' 'We were wondering if we were still on your list...' And so it went on.

And Jim and Dorothy weren't getting any younger. Catholic Charities usually applied an upper age limit of 38 to women – Dorothy's age in 1958 when their latest efforts to adopt had come to nothing. But as luck would have it, the Angel Guardian Home, after a period of disengagement from the Irish adoption business, was back on stream when the new standardisation regulations for Irish adoptions came into force in 1958. Under the new rules the Irish authorities, unlike Catholic Charities, would permit American women up to 42 years of age, and men up to 45, to adopt Irish children. When the Rowes got to hear of the Irish babies through a priest in the neighbourhood, they jumped at the chance.

The Rowes were devout and traditional Catholics. They were also comfortably well off. Jim was an engineer on a salary of $7,500 a year. They owned two houses worth $31,000. Their savings amounted to $4,000 and their life policies to $20,000. They also had a new Chevrolet and furs and jewellery worth $5,000. They had no debts. To anyone in Ireland the Rowes would have appeared fabulously wealthy. Mr Rowe's salary was equivalent to around £52 a week at a time when the average wage in Ireland was just £7. His salary was equivalent to around €260,000 a year in today's terms. Likewise, the Rowes' houses, savings and other assets were worth over €2m at today's values.

Immediately they heard of the Irish babies, they wrote to the Angel Guardian Home, this time asking specifically for 'a little girl from Ireland'. The nuns at the home knew how desperate the Rowes were. They were also aware of their advancing years and of their financial status. The mention of Irish babies seemed to have unlocked the door and things suddenly began to happen. On 25 February 1960, Jim and Dorothy were invited to attend the Home to discuss their 'interest in Irish adoptions'. The meeting was brief and matter-of-fact. The Rowes were given the name and address of an Irish adoption agency: St Clare's, at Stamullen in County Meath. The nuns had also given them some useful hints, which they scribbled down on a small piece of paper – when they wrote to St Clare's they should emphasise two things above all: their devotion to the faith, and the size of their bank balance.

St Clare's adoption society was run by the Franciscan Sisters of St Clare under the chairmanship of Father PJ Regan. Father Regan was also parish priest at Castlepollard, about 20 miles away in County Westmeath, where the Sacred Heart nuns ran one of their mother-and-baby homes. During the years of the American adoptions, almost 300 children were dispatched from Castlepollard home and another 130 or so from St Clare's. Many of the children offered for adoption by St Clare's were babies who had been born at Castlepollard, and Father Regan was the link.

On 14 April 1960, the Rowes wrote to St Clare's seeking a little girl, or 'more than one if it is possible'. As advised, much of their letter was taken up with the details of their material circumstances. They enclosed verification of Mr Rowe's salary from his employer, federal income tax returns and assorted bank statements. They also laid great stress on their religious zeal and promised to 'do all in our power to see that our children receive a good sound Catholic education and upbringing'. In line with Archbishop McQuaid's requirements, their doctor also wrote to say they were not 'shirking natural parenthood'. With the letter they sent multiple copies of their Church marriage certificate, Catholic baptismal certificates and personal recommendations from priests and nuns. They also enclosed an assortment of family photographs.

Their letter had been remarkably unrevealing about their personalities, even about the reasons for wanting a second child, other than as 'a sister for George'. The unspoken, but unambiguous, assumption underlying their entire approach was that adoption was a 'cure' for their own childlessness rather than a service to the adopted child. That this assumption went entirely unchallenged by either the St Clare's Adoption Society in Ireland or the Angel Guardian Home in New York simply indicated their acceptance of it. But the critical point in the Rowes' letter to St Clare's was left to the end: Angel Guardian Home, they said, 'mentioned to us the cost involved in getting a child from Ireland and we are perfectly willing and capable of meeting the expense'. And not only of one child, but of two if possible. From then on everything moved at high speed. Within a fortnight a Catholic Charities report on the Rowes had reached Ireland and was approved at diocesan level. One of the nuns at St Clare's wrote to say they hoped 'very soon to be in a position to choose a baby girl for you'. Two weeks later, on 13 May 1960, she wrote again, just a ten line impersonal note: 'I now enclose a photograph of a baby girl who would be available for you if you would like to have her.' The baby's name was Marion. She had been born on 1 June 1959. By the time formalities were completed she would be over one year old and eligible to leave the country for adoption. She had suffered from gastro-enteritis in early infancy but had made a full recovery. Marion's mother was 'unmarried but comes from a respectable family and is well educated'.

That was the sum total of the information available to the Rowes, on which they had to decide whether or not to adopt the infant Marion, whom of course they had never seen. This was strictly babies by mail-order. The description of the mother as 'unmarried but respectable and well educated' was the formula repeated by the nuns in virtually every case. It conveyed no impression whatever of the kind of person the mother was. There was no mention of the child's father. The circumstances in which the baby had been placed for adoption were not mentioned. There was no family medical history. The list of missing information could go on and on, but the Rowes weren't asking questions. After years of fruitless searching for a child in

America they were unlikely at this stage to put obstacles in the way by asking for further information or appearing awkward. They replied by cablegram: 'Baby wanted. Send soon as possible. Love her already'. They would be 'counting the minutes until she arrives'. They would also be counting the dollars.

The Rowes' acceptance of baby Marion was acknowledged with a bill for £50 'for expenses' from St Clare's. The bill – equivalent, in relation to average Irish wages, to €4,800 in today's money – was not itemised, and it is difficult to imagine what it might have related to since the only expenses incurred by the nuns at this point in their dealings with the Rowes were for postage on three airmail letters and a photograph of baby Marion. And Marion discovered in later life that all expenses arising from her birth and stay at Castlepollard had been paid by her natural father, so the money wasn't to cover that either. But even if her father hadn't paid, the local authority would have done so.

The 1952 Adoption Act had made it a criminal offence to charge money for arranging an adoption. Receipted expenditure on such things as lawyers' fees, transport costs and so on could legitimately be passed on to the adopters – and in the Rowes' case, were, in full, at a later date. But the Rowes still weren't asking any questions, and on receipt of the bill immediately sent a Sterling draft for £50, payable directly to St Clare's and encashable at the Munster and Leinster Bank in Stamullen. St Clare's acknowledged receipt of the money by return post. Marion – or Maureen as she now is – says she discovered in later life that the first cheque was followed by several others which her adoptive parents described as donations.

That was all it took. Baby Marion was assigned to Mr and Mrs Rowe. The future course of all their lives had been determined by a brief exchange of letters and the payment of £50 (€4,800). All that remained to be done now was the completion of formal paperwork, such as passport and visa applications, and baby Marion would be ready to go.

Marion's passport application was submitted to the Department of External Affairs by the nuns in Stamullen, and consisted by and large of the documents prescribed by Archbishop McQuaid – essential proofs of the Rowes' Catholicism such as their marriage and baptismal certificates, references from priests, a Catholic Charities home report, and sworn undertakings from the Rowes to bring baby Marion up, and to educate her, in the faith. Without this last document the Department of External Affairs would refuse a passport, even though no such condition applied to adoptions within Ireland. There was also a statement signed by Marion's mother in the presence of a Notary Public in which she 'relinquished all claims to the child for ever' and consented to her removal from the State for adoption abroad by anyone 'deemed suitable' by St Clare's. To the consular officials in the Department of External Affairs, this was a routine application. Everything appeared to be in order, and on the 15 July 1960 baby Marion got her passport, issued in the name of the Minister for External Affairs, Frank Aiken.

By comparison with the Irish passport requirements, the demands of the American embassy for an immigrant visa were distinctly secular.

The Rowes had to guarantee that the 'alien' they were sponsoring for entry to the States – i.e. Marion – would not become a 'public charge'. The 'alien' had to answer such questions as: 'Are you a drug dealer?' 'Do you have leprosy?' 'Are you going to the United States to engage in an immoral sexual act?' 'Are you a psychopath or otherwise mentally insane?' and 'Are you a member of the Communist Party?' On Marion's behalf St Clare's answered 'no' to each question, and on 28 July 1960 her immigrant visa was issued.

Under international air-traffic law, minors under eight years of age had to be accompanied on all flights, so baby Marion needed an escort. There were several options. She could be entrusted to any one of a number of young Irish women who had made themselves known to the nuns as willing volunteers. For the girls it meant a free flight to New York and a few days in America, all at the adopters' expense. Or a children's nurse could be hired for the job, at extra expense. There was even an American company called Shannon Travel Services which specialised in bringing Irish 'orphans' to the States, collecting them by taxi from the orphanage, driving them to Shannon, and engaging escorts for the flight. But in the end the Rowes decided to send a female escort of their own choice from New York. The escort arrived at Stamullen on Monday 8 August 1960 and took custody of baby Marion, all dressed in her best clothes. Next day, baby and escort were aboard the Pan American Airlines afternoon flight from London to New York's Idlewild airport. The total bill from the airline company was a staggering $455, equivalent to €16,000 today. The Rowes were at the airport to meet their little 'alien'.

Just that morning the Rowes had received their first detailed description of their new daughter from St Clare's. Her height, weight, colouring, eating habits and diet were described in minute detail. She had been passed by the doctor as 'perfectly healthy and normal both physically and mentally,' but 'does not walk yet, in fact is not quite standing'. Though Marion was already 14 months old, St Clare's advised the Rowes that her lack of mobility was 'nothing to worry about as children in an institution are slower at all these things than a child in its own home'. There were, after all, 60 children at a time in the nursery, so they weren't getting much personal attention. Marion had no 'particular little habits,' the nuns reported, 'but she can do with a lot of love and affection.'

The Rowes were overjoyed with their new daughter – whose name they changed to Maureen. They wrote fervent thank you letters to the nuns at St Clare's. But they were also worried that Maureen was still not walking and asked the nuns if there were such things as 'walkie pens' in Ireland. Yes, replied St Clare's, 'we have walkie pens over here, but they are expensive, so are more or less beyond us, but we do have one. They are grand for teaching babies to walk'. Next time they wrote, the Rowes enclosed $20 – with the purchasing power of almost €700 in today's money – enough to buy any number of 'walkie pens'.

Although subsequent letters rarely mentioned money, Maureen was to learn from her father Jim in the years ahead that he and Dorothy sent fairly regular donations to the nuns in Ireland. He mentioned sums of $50 and more – not vast amounts to the Rowes, but a fortune to the nuns and equivalent to €1,725 today. Maureen believed her adoptive parents had been made aware of the nuns' expectations in this regard before she arrived in the United States. Certainly someone had told the Rowes that the nuns' account was at the Munster and Leinster Bank, a detail that was never mentioned once in any of the letters from St Clare's. 'Well basically,' Maureen said, 'from talking to my father, they had given donations up to a certain amount a year. I think it was an unspoken understanding. They would always give money. He sent it to the nuns, mailed cheques to them as a gift. He said it wasn't that much but it was over many years. You know he had a good job as an engineer, they had a nice home. Money wasn't a problem.'

As late as September 1966, by which time Maureen was over six years old, St Clare's Adoption Society was writing to the Rowes asking for money, from them or any of their friends, to help 'build a new wing for all our little darlings'. The sisters told them 'we pray for our benefactors every day'. This was the sort of request Mr Rowe would have responded to with generosity. 'He's that kind of person,' Maureen said, 'very generous financially'. Her adoptive parents, she said, imagined that Ireland was an impoverished third-world country and that by sending money they were helping keep babies alive who might otherwise not survive. What was more, she said, 'they were both over 40 years of age. If they hadn't got a child from outside America, adoption would have been closed to them, so they were very, very grateful.'

And there were further expenses in America too, including Maureen's legal adoption and naturalisation. After a compulsory probationary adoption period, the application for full adoption was drawn up in the summer of 1961, a service for which the Rowes' lawyers sent a $150 bill (€5,175 in today's money). Another bill followed – equivalent to €480 today – from an Irish lawyer who had obtained the consent of Maureen's natural mother to the adoption. Finally, on 13 December 1961, Judge Maximillian Moss, presiding over the Surrogate's Court in the Civic Centre of King's County, Brooklyn, approved the adoption and officially sanctioned the change of name.

The only outstanding legal matter was to have Maureen made an American citizen through an application for naturalisation. The Rowes had to appear before a naturalisation examiner (cost $10, equivalent today to €350), and then a judge to answer another series of questions. 'Had they recently divorced or committed adultery?' 'Committed crimes?' 'Become prostitutes, drug addicts, communists or pacifists?' One can only wonder at Maureen's fate had the answer to any of these questions been yes. As it was, their petition was granted. Maureen Rowe, blonde, blue-eyed, three feet seven and a half inches tall, weighing 40 pounds and very nearly five years old, was 'admitted as a citizen of the United States of America'.

The Rowes' adoption experience differed in no significant way from that of most American couples adopting from Ireland in those years. The key factor, common to all, was that children were being adopted sight unseen while the motives of the adopters were barely interrogated. It was strictly adoption by mail-order, the system that had been sharply criticised in 1958 – just two years before Maureen was dispatched to the US – by two of America's leading child-protection bodies: International Social Service and the Child Welfare League of America. But their calls for a change in the law to prevent what they called 'proxy' adoptions had fallen on deaf ears. Maureen Rowe may have escaped the worst consequences of such a system as described by the ISS and CWLA, but, as we shall see, her life as an adopted child was far from the idyll imagined by the nuns back in Ireland.

11. Pat: Against My Will

'Someone always made a run for it, but they were caught and dragged back... I suppose it was like a prison.'

Patricia Thuillier, 1996

When the story of Ireland's baby-export business first emerged in 1996, Patricia Thuillier was in her 50s. With her family grown, she lived with her husband in a well-presented terraced house in one of Dublin's post-war suburban estates, and worked as a nurse with children with intellectual disability. To anyone who didn't know her, Pat would have appeared unexceptional, outwardly busy and confident. But for 34 years Pat's life revolved around a pitiful and destructive lie.[1]

In 1962 Pat had become a single mother. In 1964 her baby boy had been sent to America for adoption. Shortly afterwards Pat married and had four more children. But she never told her husband or any of their children about the first baby. It remained a secret, buried deep inside her. Only when the story of the American adoptions began to unfold, almost three and a half decades after she had had her first child, did Pat tell her husband. 'We were watching a programme on television about those babies when my husband said how awful it was for the poor women. I don't know where it came from, I just said it: "I'm one of those women. I had a baby." It was very emotional. He asked why I hadn't told him all the years we were married, but I just couldn't. I was so ashamed and so afraid of what people would think of me, what sort of a person was I at all? I dreaded rejection.'

Pat's fears of contempt and rebuff had governed her life for 34 years, and her anxieties were well-grounded in experience – not with her husband but with the nuns. In fact, Pat's husband was totally supportive. He told her that any son of hers was his son too. He couldn't agree to her request not to tell their (adult) children, and when he did tell them they all rallied round as well. But they weren't just considerate and understanding. They were angry. Angry at the way their mother had been treated all those years ago; angry at the awful hurt and damage she had suffered as a result of 34 years of suppression and denial. Together, as a family, they set out to find their long-lost son and brother.

It was an exciting quest, full of great expectations and foolish fantasies. The girls joked among themselves: maybe he was Hollywood heartthrob Brad Pitt or billionaire computer genius Bill Gates. For her part, Pat imagined a happy and joyful reunion with the son she had last seen at 18 months of age, when she kissed him goodbye at the side door of the Castlepollard mother and baby home.

Pat was just one of around 300 unmarried young women whose babies were sent to America for adoption by the Sacred Heart nuns from Castlepollard, County Westmeath. From their convent in the old Manor House – once the country home of Lord Pollard – the nuns ran a substantial 120 acre farm as well as a maternity hospital and home for around 120 single mothers and their babies. These mother-and-child facilities were located in a separate, more functional building dating from the 1930s known as St

Peter's, with the nursery on the ground floor, girls' dormitories on the first floor and delivery rooms on top. St Peter's was maintained at public expense, but it also provided single rooms for those who could afford to pay the fees. In all, the nuns at Castlepollard placed around 2,500 'illegitimate' children for adoption, most of them within Ireland.

In Pat Thuillier's case it seems the Dublin priest, Father Michael Cleary, who himself fathered two children, was deeply involved in arranging the adoption of her son. Michael Cleary's role in the whole affair remains somewhat shadowy, but Pat was convinced he played an important part at every turn. Pat got to know Father Cleary when she was training as a children's nurse with the Sisters of Charity at the Temple Hill children's home in Blackrock, County Dublin. It was not a career she had chosen for herself, but then Pat Eyres, as she was then, had few choices in her life.

'I was actually born in a home myself, Sean Ross Abbey in Tipperary, which was also run by the Sacred Heart Sisters. My mother wasn't married. When she got pregnant a second time I was sent to a foster mother. I had a very difficult childhood. My real mother kept my younger sister after rejecting me, and she seemed to have everything. There was always a preference for someone else over me and I wondered why I was the one who was always rejected. I wasn't a happy child.'

In 1958 at the age of 16, Pat went off to Temple Hill to train as a nurse under the direction of the Sisters of Charity who ran the children's home there. 'I wasn't given any choice, but as it happened I liked it. I was just glad to be away. We went to Mass every morning at 6.50 am. I wasn't late once in two years. We worked 12 hour shifts for £2 a week (€200), which was a lot of money to me in those days. I loved the children in Temple Hill. I got very attached to them. Many of them were sent to America to be adopted, but it never occurred to me to ask why or what became of them. I just accepted it as something that happened.'

Temple Hill was attached to St Patrick's Guild, also run by the Sisters of Charity, who over a period of 20 years sent almost 600 children to America for adoption. Unlike Sean Ross Abbey where Pat was born, or Castlepollard where she had her own baby, Temple Hill had no maternity hospital attached to it. It took in 'illegitimate' babies from other hospitals without their mothers.

It was during her training at Temple Hill that Pat first met Father Michael Cleary, who was involved in making arrangements for many unmarried mothers. In 1960 – after seeing scores of children sent to America for adoption – Pat finished her training and was sent to work as a children's nanny with a wealthy family in Dalkey. From there she moved to another post on Carysfort Avenue.

'I had a boyfriend, and I became pregnant. We had arranged to meet this particular night, but it never happened, we never got to see each other. They just came to the house where I was working and took me away. It was a social worker and some other people. Even though I was over 18 years old I just assumed they could do this because I had been in foster care before.' This, Pat thought, was the first critical intervention by Michael Cleary. 'I think it must have been him who told the social worker. He knew I was pregnant. I'd told him I was, even though I wasn't looking for his help. The child's father, Austin, was still talking about getting married. I can't see any other way the social worker would have known but for Mick Cleary telling her.'

It was April 1962 and the beginning of 34 years of anguish for Pat. 'The first night I spent in the Magdalene Home on Sean McDermott Street. That was terrible. Girls were screaming and fighting. I had no idea what was going to happen to me. The next morning the social worker reappeared and took me off to Castlepollard. That journey was the last I saw of the outside world for two years.' On arrival at Castlepollard, Pat, like all the young women, was given a new identity, of sorts. She was no longer allowed to use her own name but would be known as Augusta. Her own clothes were taken from her and replaced by a sort of over-all. 'You couldn't be identified or talk about your home to anyone, but there was one girl from my home town who used to give me copies of the local newspaper to read.' This was against the rules, and getting caught would have resulted in segregation, Pat said.

While there was a strict work regime at Castlepollard, pregnant girls didn't have to do any of the hard labour. 'We just sat around and knitted all the time, knit, knit, knit, that's all we did for days and weeks on end,' said Pat. The hard graft would come later. 'The nuns weren't very warm or friendly towards us,' Pat recalled. 'They weren't liked. There were fights and sometimes the nuns were hit and had things thrown at them. They vetted all our mail, they read letters, coming in and going out. I knew that if I wrote to my boyfriend the letter would never reach him, and I knew if he wrote to me I wouldn't get his letter either. There was an awful lot of fire and brimstone stuff from the priest, Father Regan. He wasn't nice either. We were preached at all the time.'

And there were severe restrictions on movement. 'You couldn't get out of the outside gate, you just weren't allowed. But some girls tried to resist. Lots of them tried to run away, especially on Sundays when we got out for a walk in the grounds without our babies. Someone always made a run for it, but they were caught and dragged back or the Guards would be called and they'd go out and round them up and bring them back again. I don't know of any-one who got away, but the Guards were always being called. I suppose it was like a prison.' But Pat said she was always too afraid to question anything. She kept her head down and kept out of trouble. 'We were told we were privileged being in there, that we'd been taken in by the nuns out of the kindness of their hearts. If we weren't in there we'd end up as prostitutes. That's what we were told the alternative was for us. We were bad girls, we'd had sex. We were shamed. That worried me. I was always timid and afraid and I suppose I believed it.'

Pat's baby, a boy, was born on 29 August 1962. She called him Trevor Augustine Eyres. Because she was breastfeeding, Pat was allowed to stay with Trevor for longer than many new mothers. 'I used to fantasise then about his father coming and taking us both away,' she said, 'but of course he never did.' Soon they were separated, Pat going upstairs into a dormitory with six or seven other girls, Trevor to the nursery. 'At first we were allowed to see our babies three times a day, but then it was reduced to two and finally to just once a day. That was how they tried to wean us off our babies so we wouldn't be so upset at them being taken away for adoption. But of course it didn't work. How could you fail to be devastated by something like that?' Michael Cleary would visit from time to time, bringing a few sweets and toiletries, but when he went to look at her baby he would never go with Pat, only with a nun. 'I think that was because they were discussing the adoption between themselves,' she said. But they didn't discuss it with her.

'Six weeks after your baby was born they reckoned you were fit for work. Most of the girls were put out in the farm, working in the fields or the gardens or with the pigs and cattle. Or they were put to cleaning. Girls worked in the dormitories, the laundry, the kitchens, the dining room, the bakery, the nurseries. I was lucky. I was put into administration. It was my job to give the new girls their "house-names", take their clothes, give them their house clothes, which I used to make as well, and give them their bedding.' Her work was supervised by Sister Isabel, the only nun, she said, who ever showed her any kindness at

Castlepollard. 'She would bring me the odd sweet or biscuit for Trevor and she would let me go to see him more than I was supposed to.'

Pat spent her 21st birthday in Castlepollard. 'It was just like any other day. I was polishing the floors in reception when Sister Isabel came over and gave me a quarter pound box of Cadbury's Milk Tray, maybe six or eight chocolates, and a hanky. That was my 21st birthday. It was straight back to work polishing the floor. There was no one else offering any sort of support or friendship.'

For much of the time the girls' entertainment consisted of imagining what might have been. 'I remember Joe Dolan was playing in a marquee in Castlepollard and we all sat round fantasising, could we get out and see him? Of course we never did. But that was how we spent a lot of our time. We'd go up to the top of the house to see could we hear the music from the town.'

Some of the girls developed relationships with each other which the nuns never discovered. 'There were six to eight girls to a dorm,' said Pat, 'and at night some girls used to get into bed with each other. There was a lot of pairing off. I was invited into bed with girls from time to time, but for some reason it didn't appeal to me and I didn't do it. I knew nothing about lesbianism of course, and it's only looking back now that I understand what was going on. I'm sure it was just for closeness, a bit of human contact, a cuddle. It was so cold and impersonal there, no one ever touched you, no one held your hand or offered any sort of comfort. But when you'd hear a nun coming at night, they'd all jump out of bed and get back into their own beds.'

Pat had always known that she would have to spend a long time at Castlepollard, for although the home was maintained at public expense, the girls still had to pay for their own and their babies' upkeep by working. Their labours, of course, also maintained the Sisters of the Sacred Heart who resided at Castlepollard. Girls were not free to leave until alternative arrangements had been made for their children, whether through adoption or a place becoming available in a home for older children. It had also been clear to Pat that her child would eventually be offered for adoption, but as the weeks turned to months, she put the thought out of her head. On Saturdays she would sit and watch visitors coming, imagining that her child's father might appear one day and take her and the child away. He didn't come, but a lot of American couples did. 'They'd come and look at the babies,' Pat said. 'I remember this one nun who used to show them around. She was very loud: "Oh no, you can't have that one," she would say in her haughty voice, "that one's gone already but come and look at this one."'

Pat said there was a rigorous selection process for the children sent to America. 'They had to be physically perfect, and none of the black babies that were there were ever selected. The nuns inquired into the background of the mother and the father of the child. Background seemed to be very important in making the selection.'

When Trevor was almost 18 months old, on 19 February 1964, Pat was ordered to attend a meeting in the 'big house' – the convent. 'I was told to sit at one end of this long table and at the other end was a man I imagine was a solicitor. In between us were two nuns. I was given a piece of paper and told to sign. I wasn't told what it was I was signing. Nothing was explained to me. And you daren't ask, you just did what you were told and got on with it.' In fact, Pat recalled, this was the third 'signing' she had attended, the others being when Trevor was six months old and a year old. She said that on those occasions she wasn't even allowed to read the papers that were thrust in front of her. The final document she signed read as follows:

I, Patricia Eyres, at present residing at the Sacred Heart Convent, Castlepollard, in the County of Westmeath, Republic of Ireland, make Oath and say as follows:

(1) I hereby relinquish full claim forever to my child Trevor Augustine Eyres, born on the 29th day of August, 1962, and I hereby surrender the said Trevor Augustine Eyres to Catherine McCarthy, known in religion as Rev Mother Rosamonde McCarthy, Sacred Heart Convent, Castlepollard, and I undertake never to make any claim to the said child.

(2) I authorise the said Catherine McCarthy to send my child Trevor Ausgustine Eyres out of the Republic of Ireland for the purpose of legal adoption.

Sworn by the said PATRICIA EYRES at Castlepollard in the County of Westmeath, this 19th day of February 1964 before a Notary Public for the county of Westmeath, and I certify that the Deponent is personally known to me.

Pat, however, said she certainly did not know the Notary Public, the man at the far end of the big table who confirmed her signature, and who certified that he knew her personally. And, as we shall see, at least one of the signatures he said he witnessed was not hers at all.

At no point in any of these proceedings was Pat told what her rights were – or even that she had rights – or advised as to what rights she was signing away, although the Adoption Act required that her right to withdraw her child from adoption at any time before the legal process was completed had to be explained fully to her. But her sense of being shabbily treated was tinged with resignation. 'What alternative did I have? Absolutely none! I could never have got my child out of there – never – they wouldn't have let me leave that home with him. I'd nowhere to go. I had nothing, no money, no job, no home of my own. No one ever discussed adoption with me. I was just told that's what was going to happen. I was too scared to question it. I just accepted it. What else could I do?'

After each of the three signings, Pat said, Father Michael Cleary would mysteriously appear. 'I'd come out of the room where I had just signed whatever was put in front of me and there would be Mick Cleary. He would just appear from nowhere. I know he had an interest in me and my baby. And I know he was very involved in America at the time too, back and forth all the time.' Pat was firmly convinced that Cleary was involved in arranging Trevor's adoption in America.

A couple of days after her last signing, Pat recalled, the child was taken up to Dublin for passport photographs. Official records show that the passport itself was issued by the Department of External Affairs on 8 April 1964, and on the 24 April Trevor was 'discharged' for adoption in America.

'He was 20 months old. That's how long we had been together,' Pat said. 'I was just called over by one of the nuns and told he was going the next day. Up till then I had imagined it wouldn't really happen. But it was happening. I only had a few more hours. I was given a bundle of clothes and told to get him up early next morning, to give him a bath and get him dressed for the journey. I did everything I'd been told. I washed him and dressed him. I remember so clearly, bringing him down to the side door, hugging him, cuddling him and kissing him, and he was just swiped out of my arms by a nun. All I could think to do was run as fast as I could up to the top of the house to look out this small window to try and get one last look at my child. I saw him getting into the car with a nun. The maintenance man, Mr Murray, was driving. That was the last I saw of him.'

At such a traumatic moment there wasn't a single word of comfort for Pat. No one seemed to care that she was in bits. And as someone who felt rejected all her life by her own mother and knew the pain that rejection caused she felt doubly guilty that she was now rejecting her own child, even though that was not something she would have wished. 'I was left numb, just numb. No one offered any counselling or anything like that. I was told I had an hour to pull myself together and get down to the dining room. A nun just stood over me in silence. Then it was back to work, as if nothing had happened. That was it. No cuddles, no sign of any feelings, nothing. You were just left raw.' This was how it was, not just for Pat Eyres, but for the thousands of young women consigned to the religious-run mother and baby homes: heartless, vengeful and cruel – and unimaginably damaging psychologically.

A few weeks later Father Michael Cleary reappeared, this time with news of a job for Pat. He had found her a post in South Dublin looking after a six-month-old baby girl recently adopted by a well-known TV personality. 'I came out of Castlepollard completely raw. I hadn't had my hair done in two years. I was wearing the same clothes I'd worn going in two years earlier. I was so conspicuous. I remember walking down O'Connell Street thinking everyone was looking at me. It was awful. I was trying to pick up the pieces, trying to meet up with old friends who didn't know where I'd been for the past two years.'

Within a few months Pat had met the man who was to become her husband, but she never told him about the baby. She feared that if he knew he too would reject her. After their marriage, carrying such a dark secret took its toll on her health. She suffered from depression and was in and out of hospital. Medical professionals knew of her secret and encouraged her to at least tell her husband, but she couldn't do it. 'I didn't want him to think of me the way I'd been made to think of myself, as bad and shameful, just a step away from being a prostitute.'

When her children were born she never seemed happy with them, but exhibited a great deal of anger towards them. 'You'd have had to live with it to know how bad it was,' said one of her daughters. 'We always used to ask ourselves, why is she like this? Why is she always angry with us? And when we were old enough to have our own lives, she wouldn't let go. She'd go ballistic at the thought of us leaving home. Now we know she was going through mental torture all those years.'

In 1983, on 28 August – the day before Trevor's 21st birthday – Pat's mother committed suicide. The combination of her estranged mother's death and her lost son's 21st birthday sent her health into another tailspin. Almost 13 more years were to pass before she finally managed to break the cycle.

Pat began her search for Trevor in the summer of 1996, after finally telling her husband about her secret in the wake of the American adoption story breaking. Like many natural mothers she was gently encouraged by remarks made by Dick Spring, Tánaiste and Minister for Foreign Affairs. Speaking in Waterford in March that year, Mr Spring had referred to children who had been 'exported to the United States' as having been 'removed from their young and frightened mothers at the most vulnerable possible time in the lives of those mothers.' The 'cost in human suffering,' Spring said, 'may never be known.' In referring to the declarations signed by young women like Pat he said he 'could only imagine the pain that must have been involved.'

While still very far from an apology for the role the State played in exiling thousands of its infant citizens, here for the first time in 34 years was what appeared to be official recognition of the unspoken and unacknowledged trauma that women like Pat had suffered in secret and in silence.

And when Mr Spring declared his fervent wish that they could 'quickly arrive at a point where it will be possible to make information available to people who want help in being reconciled and reunited,' Pat had every reason to hope that she would be given every assistance in finding Trevor.

On 7 May Pat wrote to Dick Spring seeking his help. Critically, what she needed to know was Trevor's adopted name and last known address. With that information she could at least start her search. Five weeks later, on 10 June, Mr Spring replied. There was a file on Trevor, his letter confirmed. It was number 345/96/1681. But either the file, or Mr Spring, got the surname wrong: he spelled it 'Ayres' instead of 'Eyres'. A small detail, perhaps, but a mistake that should not have been made in such a personally sensitive matter. What the file showed, the Tánaiste said, was that Trevor's adoption had been arranged through the Catholic Home Bureau for Dependent Children in New York (a branch of Catholic Charities), and that his adoptive mother was a native of New York State while his adoptive father was Irish-born. The adoption itself, Mr Spring said, had taken place on 3 March 1965. (Another incorrect detail: it had taken place on 4 February.) This was all no doubt very interesting, but what was Trevor's name now and where in New York had he gone?

Well, said Mr Spring, 'the National Archive Act 1986 restricts access to information on files in the National Archives relating to individuals in order to protect information supplied in confidence or which might cause distress to living persons. I am advised,' he went on, 'that disclosure of information of a personal or private kind without the consent of those to whom it relates could constitute an invasion of their constitutional right to privacy.' Consequently, his letter concluded, 'I may not let you have the specific details.' It was a dreadful blow. The promise of help to those seeking reunification with their kin was a puff

of smoke. And Pat wasn't the only one to get this response:
all those seeking assistance from the Department of Foreign Affairs were given the same message.

Pat spoke to an official in the consular section of the
Department. 'I begged him, please don't leave it too late
for mothers like me. We're not getting any younger. Please
give me some information. You're sitting there in a privileged position with my file in front of you. Tell me
something that will help me. Tell mothers like me something that will help them. But he just kept saying he
couldn't. It was confidential.'

Pat didn't give up. She turned to the Catholic Home
Bureau in New York, writing a three page letter to Sister
Una McCormack, detailing her 'dreadful existence' as a
'poor young frightened mother' in Castlepollard in the early
1960s, who was 'never allowed to leave the building,' and
all of whose 'mail was vetted by the nuns.' She complained
to Sister Una that 'this issue is bottom of Mr Dick Spring's
agenda' and said the 'lack of urgency is contributing to the
anguish of birth mothers and adoptees waiting to obtain
the vital information they require.' Ireland in the 1960s, she
said, 'was very unfair to unmarried mothers, and indeed is
not much better now.' What was needed was 'someone to
have enough courage to address this issue, not only for me
but for hundreds of women like me who had to give up
their babies against their will in 1960s Ireland.' Pat also let
Sister Una know that she and her family were 'involving the
media in our search.' Her daughters had written letters to
the press and they were meeting with an American television programme called "20/20" who were interested in her
story and in her search.

On 28 August she got her reply from the 'legal department' of the Catholic Home Bureau. 'New York State law,'
Sister Margaret Carey wrote, 'protects agency case record
confidentiality and prohibits the release of information by

an agency without a court order. Social Service Law Section 372. We wish you well and hope you and your family are enjoying good health.' Sister Carey enclosed a copy of the surrender document Pat had purportedly signed on 19 February 1964, and which formed the legal basis of Trevor's adoption in the United States a year later. On the same day, Sister Sarto Harney, social worker with the only remaining branch of the Sacred Heart Adoption Society at Bessboro in Cork, wrote to Pat confirming the name Eyres was on their records, but advising her to contact the North Eastern Health Board in Drogheda where 'many of the Castlepollard USA files' were held.

Like so many before her and many more since, Pat ended up going from pillar to post. She had identified and contacted the three leading agencies who held detailed information on her son's adoption – the Department of Foreign Affairs, the Catholic Home Bureau in New York, and the Sacred Heart Adoption Society – but to no avail.

In desperation, she wrote again to Dick Spring in September 1996, complaining that information about herself and her son was being withheld from her. The Department responded by again quoting the National Archive Act and pointing out, with unintended irony, that 'the only item of any importance' they were withholding was her son's adopted name and his address. Like the legal department of the Catholic Home Bureau, the Department of Foreign Affairs enclosed a copy of the notarised surrender document Pat was supposed to have signed on 19 February 1964. The point of sending this, presumably, was to remind her that she had not only agreed to her son's removal from the country for adoption, but had relinquished him 'forever'.

But with the two surrender documents fortuitously in her possession, Pat now had startling evidence: the signatures on the two pieces of paper, both bearing the same date, and both witnessed by the same Notary Public, were totally and undeniably different. On one document the signature 'Patricia Eyres' is written in a neat, even hand, the small clear letters sloping backwards. On the other the signature is different in every respect, with larger and more uneven letters, differently formed and falling somewhere between upright and forward-sloping. The difference was blatant and undisguised. One of the documents was used to legitimise the removal of Pat's child from the country, the other to legitimise his adoption in the States. The fact that one was clearly not signed by her may have nullified the entire adoption procedure – had anyone cared to look.

But in the short term Pat was more interested in finding her son than in making a fuss about forged signatures. By various routes – many of them pursued by the American television programme, "20/20" – Pat had finally come up with a name and an address, and contact was made with a 34-year-old male in the States. Excitement in Pat's house was at an all time high. She and her daughters were talking to the Irish papers about the imminent happy outcome of their quest. But it turned out to be a false trail. The final breakthrough came only by subterfuge when a woman who was helping Pat in her search gained unexpected and unassisted access to records that had previously been denied her. What she found was Trevor's adopted name: John Patrick Campbell. Further searches in New York State by "20/20" turned up old school friends and, eventually, the woman who had adopted Pat's child in 1965. When contacted by the people from the television programme, Mrs Campbell revealed the awful news – John was dead.

The programme-makers passed on the tragic news to Sister Una McCormack at the Catholic Home Bureau and asked her to tell Pat. And so it was, one night at the end of October 1996, Pat got a call from Sister Una. She knew almost at once that the news was bad. Sister Una herself broke down in the telling of it. John had died 13 years earlier and the circumstances of his death were themselves tragic. His adoptive parents had given him a car for his 21st birthday. He had been arrested soon after for speeding and detained overnight by the police. The next morning he was found dead in his cell. Pat found that after her son's death three local policemen, including the police chief, were removed from their posts. Suicide was suspected, which would have been remarkable given that her own mother had committed suicide just days beforehand – on the very day John Patrick Campbell celebrated his 21st birthday.

'He had so much to live for,' said Pat, gently fingering three small photographs of her son, sent to her by Mrs Campbell. John was a tall, good-looking young man with fiery red hair and a winning smile. 'I know he got a fantastic home in America,' Pat said. 'His parents loved him dearly.' She had spoken to Mrs Campbell by telephone.

John was in college and he had been accepted by the American Space Agency, NASA. He had a girlfriend, a student nurse, and they were planning on getting engaged. He had a sister in the States who was also adopted from Ireland and she had found her natural mother. 'That fascinated him,' Pat said, 'and he had told his adoptive mother he was going to look for me once he had finished college. He never got the chance. I had hoped for a happy reunion. I never thought I would outlive my child.'

The one small consolation Pat had was that John's adoptive parents had told him from the earliest time that he was adopted, 'and they told him I gave him up because I loved him so much, that I wanted him to have a better life than I could have given him in Ireland. So maybe he didn't think too badly of me.'

Castlepollard ceased to function as a mother and baby home in 1969. It is now a home for people with mental disability. While she was looking for her son, Pat went back on a visit. Although she hadn't been there for 32 years she found her way instinctively to the room at the top of the house from which she had caught the last glimpse of Trevor. 'It's just as it was then,' she said. 'The radiator under the window still bears the marks of where hundreds of girls like me climbed up to see their babies for the very last time. If nothing else, I hope my story will help some of them find the courage to do something about this wall of silence and all this dreadful secrecy.'

Pat Thuillier died suddenly at home in Dublin in October 2010.

* * * * *

In March 1998 I received a moving letter from P.J. Murray whose father, Mickey Murray, was the maintenance man at Castlepollard, the man identified by Pat Thuillier as the driver of the car in which Trevor departed the home in 1964. P.J. had read *Banished Babies* and wanted to let me know that Mickey was 'a good man, honest and hard working'. But, P.J. said, he never spoke at home of what happened at the 'orphanage'. P.J. mentioned the small cemetery attached to Castlepollard where an unknown number of infants lay buried in unmarked graves. 'There was no attempt at equality,' P.J. wrote. The single monument in the cemetery 'asked only for prayers for the Sisters of the Sacred Heart.' And P.J. ended by saying there was 'a strong case for the State to answer to the girls who suffered in these convents. They and their children were wrongfully separated, and someone must be accountable.' A decade and a half later, that accountability is still sorely lacking.

12. Mary, Michael and Kevin: Legitimate Error?

'I arrived in Dublin on the train from Cork, got a taxi to Abbey Street to the office of St Patrick's Guild, and I handed over my child to a nun. I don't remember signing any documents and I don't remember seeing anyone else in the room other than a nun taking the child out of my arms. I just walked out of there onto the street. It was dreadful, parting with your child is so traumatic. If I was in my right mind and had support of some kind it wouldn't have happened that way. But I was alone. That was life at the time and I just had to face it.'

Mary, 1996

It was in August 1961 when Mary Cunningham, a young nurse at Tullamore hospital, realised she was pregnant.[1] She wasn't married. 'I couldn't have told my mother,' said Mary, 'no way could I have told her. My mother was very religious, very Catholic.' Mary was the only girl of four children and her mother had been very protective of her all her life. 'So if she found out that I was pregnant it would have destroyed her. I made up my mind that I would never tell her.'

A doctor friend at the hospital where she worked told Mary about the Sacred Heart Convent at Bessboro in Cork. It had been the first maternity home in Ireland for single pregnant women and girls. Mary decided 'there and then' that she would have her baby secretly with the nuns in Cork. 'The question of keeping the baby afterwards didn't even arise,' she said. 'I had no choice in the matter. My mind was made up for me – wherever or however – it was made up for me.'

At the Cork convent Mary was put to work in the nursery, looking after other women's children. 'I was fairly privileged because I was a nurse and they had me minding the babies,' she recalled, 'but the other girls were out working the fields, milking the cows, bringing in the potatoes, working in the kitchens, cleaning and scrubbing. It wasn't an easy life. We didn't have comfortable facilities, all very basic. But we did have some kind of fun among ourselves to lighten our burden.'

Sister Mary was one of the nuns at the Sacred Heart Convent in those days, working in one of the three nurseries. 'Many people speak of how hard done by the girls were, working in fields, in the laundry, and so on,' she said, ' but no pregnant girl ever worked in the fields.'[2]

They farmed to feed themselves, growing all of their own fruit and vegetables, making jam and pickles, operating a bakery, keeping hens, pigs, sheep and cattle, and producing milk, butter, eggs and meat. 'No girl,' Sister Mary said, 'was put out in the fields against her wishes. Most did not object as they came from farming backgrounds and loved being out in the fresh air. The girls had great fun during the thrashing and hay-making.' Girls who didn't want to work outside 'helped' with indoor tasks like stoking the boiler and sluicing the dirty nappies.

'In the evening,' Sister Mary recalled, 'we listened to the radio, danced to the music, played records and games of cards and draughts. Sometimes we had concerts. The girls used to impersonate the nuns. They had great fun dressing up.' Mr Crowley from Cork fire brigade used to bring boxes of sweets for the girls and their children – of whom there were around 100 at any one time. Santa came at Christmas while at Easter the Cork Junior Chamber of Commerce brought Easter eggs.

Sister Sarto, the senior social worker at Bessboro, described life at the home in these terms: 'No girl was compelled to go out and work. She was asked would she mind. But of course society in Ireland was harsh, but we didn't complain. That's the way it was. Everyone lived that way. The girls that came here, of course, had been rejected by society as well. And yes, it was a harsh regime.'[3]

In the eyes of the nuns at that time, they were dealing with 'fallen women', sinners who had to see the error of their ways and repent. They were engaged in saving souls as well as delivering and disposing of babies. There was nothing joyous about giving birth in a convent. And the harshness Sister Sarto acknowledged seemed to extend into the labour wards. Certainly Mary Cunningham's experience of giving birth was traumatic. It was on the night of 26 March 1962. She was in a locked room, alone, when she went into labour. 'I'll never forget when the morning came, after being in pain all night, I was so thrilled to hear the rattle of keys,' Mary said. 'The door opened and a nun brushed in, pegging her veil across her face. She just glanced at me lying there and said, "Oh there's not a sign of you having your baby yet," and off she went to 6 o'clock Mass leaving me alone again. Kenneth, my baby, was born at 8.00 am. That was very, very traumatic.'

But what followed was even more devastating for Mary. 'It was just three weeks after Kenneth's birth. I was happily minding him and the other babies in the nursery when one of the nuns just walked up to me and said, "There's two bottles of milk and here's a bundle of clothes. Put them on your baby straight away. We've got adoptive parents in America who match up with your background and he's going to America for adoption." I was so shocked and numbed. It was all done so suddenly and without any feeling or sympathy.'

Mary had been told by the nuns that because she was still involved in a serious relationship with Kenneth's father, Michael, it would be unsafe to place Kenneth with an Irish couple here as there was a possibility she and Michael would try to get him back. Adoption in America would rule out this 'danger'. 'I have no doubt whatever that it was a deliberate policy to put the Atlantic Ocean between me and the child,' said Mary. 'The nuns said as much. And they said I would have to relinquish all rights to see him again.' Mary's recollection contrasts with the explanation given by Sister Mary of the Sacred Heart Convent of how it came about that some children rather than others were sent to the United States. 'It was the girls themselves decided,' she said. 'They chose to let their children go to America. Nobody made them. It was their own free choice.'[4] The Sacred Heart Convent in Cork sent just 100 babies to America, a relatively small number compared with the other Sacred Heart homes in Roscrea and Castlepollard, which sent 750 between them.

At the time when she first learned Kenneth was going to America, Mary assumed because of the suddenness of it all that he was going more or less immediately, a belief that was strengthened by the fact that she was put on a train that very day and sent up to Dublin to hand her baby over to St Patrick's Guild who, she was told, had arranged the adoption.

'Well, I got on the Dublin train, but I was absolutely in bits. I'll never forget it. I had my little baby in my arms wrapped in a shawl. I had two bottles of milk. I sat down opposite two old ladies, and I was crying. These two ladies helped me change the child because I just couldn't cope. It seemed such a long journey, and I cried all the way to Dublin. When I got there I got a taxi to Abbey Street where I handed my child over to a nun. That was the last time I saw him for 33 years.'

Mary, of course, was just one of hundreds of girls and young women who passed through St Patrick's Guild every year. Sister Frances Elizabeth, one-time Superior, wrote of them: 'These unfortunate girls are of good class with, usually, excellent backgrounds. In most cases it is imperative that they return to their employment within a fortnight, or less, after the birth. Many of them are working in such places as government offices, solicitors' offices and commercial offices, schools or hospitals.'[5] Sister Elizabeth also emphasised the need for secrecy: 'In such circumstances the greatest secrecy is not merely desirable but essential. Should there be a shadow of suspicion or scandal the girl's whole future might be in jeopardy.'

Mary Cunningham, of course, felt the need for secrecy, especially from her 'very religious, very Catholic' mother, and, ironically perhaps, she was to find the most willing accomplices in the nuns of St Patrick's Guild who prided themselves in cultivating attitudes of concealment. It was religion that demanded such concealment and it was the religious who provided it, like some self-fulfilling prophecy. No one, it seems, had any idea about the possible long-term psychological problems that could arise from feeling compelled to keep secret something as traumatic as the birth and relinquishment of a child.

Michael, who worked in a bank, also felt he could not openly admit to having fathered an 'illegitimate' child. To do so could have jeopardised his job. 'My family would have been a big concern, of course,' said Michael, 'but also my peers, people in the bank. I couldn't have told them. The consequences could have been serious.' Under the circumstances, Michael said, he tried to take a positive view of having his son adopted in America. 'The way I felt at the time was, well, going to America was good for the child.

It was a developed society and he was going to get a good home. It was very easy to convince oneself that he was going to get a home better than the one we could give him. But I regret not having had the moral courage to face down society and do the decent thing and get married and hold on to our baby, but I just wasn't able to do it.'

The need for secrecy also meant that frightened women like Mary Cunningham weren't in any position to insist that their rights be upheld in the course of having their children adopted. It is, of course, probable that Mary Cunningham signed whatever documents were necessary to make Kenneth's adoption in America possible, but she has no recollection of doing so because of the state she was in – a factor that might have called into question the legality of the entire procedure. 'I blanked out everything,' she said, 'except handing my child over to a nun. That image is firmly in my mind, but I remember nothing at all of who else was there or whether I signed anything, or what I signed if I signed.'

The Department of External Affairs insisted that a mother like Mary give her consent before it would issue a passport enabling her child to travel abroad for adoption. But all that the officials in the Department saw was the piece of signed paper. They could not even begin to imagine the circumstances in which women like Mary signed these 'legal' documents. The chances are that when she handed over Kenneth, Mary Cunningham signed a document, much like the one signed by Pat Thuillier, that would have included phrases to the effect that she 'relinquished full claim forever' to her child, that she 'surrendered the said child to Sister… of St Patrick's Guild' to enable her to make the child 'available for adoption to any person she considers fit and proper inside or outside the State.'[6]

The precise form in which a mother's consent was obtained varied from institution to institution and also changed over time, and although the legal status of such documents has never been tested it must be seriously in doubt. A document like this would certainly not be adequate in legalising an adoption *within* Ireland because the mother could not delegate her consent to others. But in Mary Cunningham's case it wasn't just the nature of her 'consent' that was in question. Something else happened that was clearly and seriously improper. But she was only to find out about it more than thirty years later. In effect, Kenneth was sent *illegally* to the United States.

In October 1962, when Kenneth was almost seven months old, Mary and Michael got married. Michael takes up the story: 'When we got married we assumed that Kenneth was already in America. That's what we'd been told. "He's going straight to the US within days," so we assumed we had no access. It was only afterwards, when we found him again thirty-odd years later that we realised he was still in Dublin long after we married. St Patrick's Guild knew Mary and I were still together. Now with the baby still being in Dublin, I'd have expected contact to have been made with us. It came as a great shock to learn he was in Dublin for 20 months before he was sent to the United States and we were married for more than twelve of those months.'

By marrying, Mary and Michael had 'legitimised' Kenneth's birth, and under the 1952 Adoption Act it was a criminal offence to send a 'legitimate' child out of the country for adoption abroad. The nuns probably knew nothing of their marriage, but it is not clear if they tried to find out. (Ironically, a Supreme Court decision in the late 1970s – that the distinction between 'legitimate' and 'illegitimate' children in the Adoption Act was unconstitutional – had the effect of retrospectively legalising Kenneth's removal from the country in 1963). At the time of Mary and Michael's marriage, Kenneth was in the care of the Sisters of Charity at Temple Hill 'orphanage', home to most of the children sent for adoption by St Patrick's Guild. Kenneth – or Kevin as he now is – often wonders how he was treated during those 20 months of institutional life: was he picked up and talked to? Was he cuddled and shown real affection? Or was he just left lying in a cot?

The process that was to culminate in Kenneth's dispatch to the States began in November 1962, the month following Michael and Mary's marriage. On the 5th of November, Sister Xaveria, the nun in charge of St Patrick's Guild, wrote to a Mr and Mrs Bates of New York who had applied to her for a baby to adopt. She sent them a copy of Archbishop McQuaid's requirements for the adoption of children outside the country and told them when these were met to the satisfaction of His Grace 'we will select a nice little baby for you.' The required documents were duly procured by Mr and Mrs Bates, sent to Sister Xaveria and approved by Archbishop McQuaid. All that was left to be done was for the nuns to select a baby boy, and the one selected was Kenneth Cunningham.

'If we had known that our child was still in Dublin when we married,' said Michael, 'an obvious choice would have been to go and take our baby back. We were in a predicament of course, because we had told no one about the baby before we married and Mary still couldn't tell her mother. So we couldn't suddenly produce this baby out of the blue and say it was ours. But we could have overcome that by adopting our own baby, telling everyone we had adopted a baby. But we didn't get that choice. We didn't know it was there for us.'

All together it was a shoddy business, but one founded on the notion that neither Mary nor her baby had any rights worth considering. None of this became apparent until 1995 when Mary and Michael finally found their (by now) 33-year-old son, Kevin Bates. Kevin was able to tell them that he had arrived in America in November 1963 –

at precisely the time of President Kennedy's assassination, and some 13 months after Mary and Michael had married, and 20 months after Mary had handed him over to the nuns at St Patrick's Guild. If this came as a shock for Mary and Michael, Kevin, too, was astonished to learn that not only had his natural parents married but they had gone on to have six more children. He had six full brothers and sisters in Ireland. It was all the more poignant since Kevin had grown up in America as the only child of a couple who, although devout Catholics, had divorced when he was in his teens.

'Well, all my life I've lived knowing there's a woman out there somewhere in Ireland who gave me up,' Kevin said.[7] 'A father never entered into the picture. I almost thought I was born by immaculate conception. Then I learn of Michael's existence and I think, gosh, what am I going to do now? I've waited all these years to know who Mary was, how am I going to cope now with knowing Michael? Having given birth to me, and then relinquishing me, there they were in Ireland, married. It's amazing that I wasn't in that family.'

And while Kevin wondered who his mother was back in Ireland, Mary never stopped thinking about the child she had given away. 'You know, this was our life all along – where is he? How is he? We would see American soldiers fighting wars around the world and we'd sit glued to the television wondering – is he in the Army? Is he one of those soldiers? Has he been killed? It never left us. And of course it was a secret between us. No one knew until very late on. And a lot of it we never talked about even between ourselves. It was too painful. You just lived with it inside.' It took a serious toll on Mary's health over the years, but after finding Kevin she said she had begun to recover.

It was January 1995 when Kevin flew into Dublin. 'The flight over was surreal,' he said, 'knowing I was leaving a part of me behind in America, but also finally getting back to Ireland, to a place where I thought I was destined to be, a place where I felt like I belonged.' Meeting all his brothers and sisters – 'people that looked like me' – was an emotional experience. 'All through your life if you are adopted you look for people that look like you because you want to find some type of identification. So this reunion was just an amazing revelation. It was such a good feeling to finally feel like I belong somewhere, and they wanted me. And I wanted to be there with them. It felt like I'd never left them before. It was remarkable. And we were all so alike, our temperaments were so similar. We all laughed and smiled the same way.'

But such a resolution to their sundered lives was not always in prospect. Finding each other had not been easy and St Patrick's Guild seems to have been a part of the problem rather than part of the solution. Mary first started to look for Kevin in 1980. 'Well of course I was looking for Kenneth because I didn't know what his name had become since he went for adoption,' Mary said. 'I could never really accept that he was in America. I secretly hoped he was in Ireland all along, Cork, Donegal, I didn't mind where because Ireland is small enough to find someone. But America's not only far away, it's so big as well. How could you ever find someone there? I suppose that was the thinking behind sending him to America, that we'd never find him again. But I really secretly believed he was in Ireland.'

When she started inquiring, the first thing Mary was told was that she would have to tell her mother about the baby and the adoption. But her mother was quite elderly and Mary could not tell her after all these years. She was also told that she would have to have counselling. 'It was just like shutting doors in my face. It was a big setback and I didn't do anything more for over a decade.'

In the meantime, 3,000 miles across the Atlantic, Kevin had commenced his search. 'I wanted to trace, to find out if my natural mother was okay, and let her know I'm okay. It was an innate feeling, something inside. I couldn't really describe all the reasons why, other than to move on in my life. I was 30 years old when I decided to search in earnest.' In April 1991 Kevin went on vacation to Ireland. 'One day,' he recalled, 'I got a chance to visit Sister Gabriel, the senior social worker at St Patrick's Guild in Dublin. It was a short meeting, maybe 20 minutes. My goal was to find out did anyone know where Mary Cunningham was. Sister Gabriel brought a file to the meeting, but she didn't let me see it. She's a woman of very few words, communicating when I asked questions but she never came out openly and volunteered information. She did give me some snippets of non-identifying information: my natural mother was a nurse, my natural father was in banking, that was all. She said she didn't know where Mary was, and, whether she knew it or not, she certainly didn't say my mother and father had married. I think there was a lot of information there I wasn't being given.' Kevin asked a lot of questions but got very few answers. 'In the end I gave her my address in America and said to get in touch if Mary ever came looking for me.'

Mary did come looking. It was early in 1994, as she recalled, just three years after Kevin visited Sister Gabriel. 'I phoned several times but I was always told Sister Gabriel wasn't available, she was at a meeting, or she was away. Eventually I got an interview with her. It was quite startling. She told me my son had been to see her in 1991. And I asked, "well, what's his name?" "Oh," she said, "I can't give you that." So I said, "didn't he leave his address with you?" And she said "he did, but I can't give you that." And I said, "couldn't you just give me an idea of whereabouts he is in the States?" And she said, "Oh no I can't do that."'

It was a huge blow to Mary. 'I came home really down-hearted. What could I do? Sister Gabriel said she would write to my son, so I rang her every few weeks after that to see was there any news. Eventually she said she had written to him and the letter had come back – he had moved house. I still kept ringing. It was heartbreaking. There was no news. "We'll keep praying, just keep praying," she'd say, "something will happen if we pray." But nothing happened.' Mary felt devastated, frustrated and angry all at once. 'I wasn't getting anywhere and here was my son looking for me and here was I looking for him. We both wanted to meet. There were no secrets any more. And still nothing was being done, and I couldn't understand this.' After each call to Sister Gabriel she was left feeling drained and dejected.

'I just wonder why I wasn't contacted after Kevin's visit to St Patrick's Guild back in 1991.' Mary said. 'Three years had passed before I found out he'd been there. I mean Ireland is a small place and it would have been easy enough to find me if anyone had bothered to look and say: "your son wants to meet you and here's his address". I can't understand why that wasn't done. They might say they were protecting me, but I believe Kevin had a right to know regardless of me. After all, I had given birth to him. He wanted to know his roots. He was in pain and he was left in limbo.'

Michael decided to join in and see if he could move things along. Three of his sisters were nuns, so he was both experienced in dealing with them and sympathetic to their vocation. 'Mary was getting so frustrated we decided I'd go with her to see Sister Gabriel,' he said. 'We knew she had our son's name and address, and the purpose of my going was to at least get that and then we could do our own searching. So up we went and she was very nice to me, very helpful, except she wouldn't give me what I'd come for. I asked her several times – just give me his name and last known address. All she would say was, "Oh, you'll be pleased to know it's a good Irish name". Now whether Bates is a good Irish name or not I don't know, but that was hardly the point as she wouldn't even tell me what the good Irish name was. I found it very difficult to accept that here she was sitting in front of us with his file in her hands and his name and address right there and she wouldn't give it to us.'

To Michael it seemed that Sister Gabriel was working under some rule or other. 'She wasn't emotional about it or anything, just clinical. There were rules she had to abide by – that was how it appeared – and nothing but nothing was going to make her break those rules, whatever they were. In our case, of course, it was well known and documented that both sides wanted to find each other, and we were all mature adults, so why she didn't show some flexibility I just don't know. Anyway, we came away empty-handed.'

It was on Michael's mind that if he had Kenneth's new name, and a fairly recent address, he could have gone to the United States himself. 'I was retired, I had plenty of time. But she wouldn't tell us where to begin. She did say she would do everything she could herself. But nothing happened. Nothing at all.'

Finally giving up all hope of progress through St Patrick's Guild, Mary made contact with a woman in Dublin called Enda who helped people trace lost relatives. Enda carefully took down all her details. Back in the States, Kevin too had taken a new initiative, bypassing St Patrick's Guild. 'I got information from my computer, names and addresses of people who helped adopted people trace their roots. So I sent a letter off to a woman in Dublin, Enda, and she telegrammed me straight back. I was out of town on business for a few weeks, and when I got back and saw this thing in my mailbox, I thought it was a telephone bill, so I just left it lying there until the end of the month. When I finally opened it, it said "I've good news, call me."'

It was an astonishing coincidence that Kevin and Mary had been in contact with was the same woman, Enda. 'Well, I talked to Enda early in the morning,' Kevin recalled, 'and she said she had found my birth mother, Mary, and she said "you'd better be sitting down for this bit – your birth mother married your birth father and they had a family. You've got four brothers, two sisters, a dozen aunts and uncles, and 38 first cousins and they can't wait to meet you." I was shocked, as happy as a person can be, just overjoyed, very emotional. The tears were flowing.'

The same day Enda contacted Michael and Mary and told them she had found Kenneth, now Kevin. Late that night Mary rang her son in America. 'Kevin answered. I felt so excited. "Hello, is that Kevin?" "Yes, who is this?" "This is your mother." I can't tell you what was said. It was so emotional, the relief on both sides, you could feel it 3,000 miles away.'

Kevin recalls their first call like this: 'She rang. I picked up the phone and she introduced herself. "Hello this is Mary, this is your mom, how have you been?" Although I'd already shed so many tears earlier that morning after talking to Enda, I was choking up inside. What do you say to your mother after 33 years? I never really imagined that I would ever find her. And on top of that to find I had a father and a family as well. It was all too incredible.'

Mary believes her positive experience in reuniting with Kevin holds out hope to other mothers who gave a child up for adoption and who are now worried about the prospect of confronting that child as an adult. 'I'm sure all mothers who gave a child up for adoption are aching – part of their heart is gone like mine was. And 3,000 miles of ocean between mothers and children who were sent to America is an added complication. But don't give up. I faced up to Kevin expecting to be rejected, expecting to be given out to, expecting him to say "you dumped me". And

I was prepared for him to say "now I've found you, you can go to hell". But he didn't. He was thrilled. And all those children need that, and the mothers will find relief too. For each one just knowing the other is alive, hopefully well, and not bearing grudges, that's a great relief.' And now, fifteen years after their reunion, Mary says it has all gone 'swimmingly': they talk regularly by phone and she and Michael have been to visit Kevin in Virginia and he, too, comes to Ireland to see them.

When Kevin thinks back to the circumstances in which he was placed for adoption, any grudges he harbours are most certainly not against Mary. 'Thirty years ago it was a different world. I don't think Mary had any choice. I don't think Mary felt she had the power to keep me, she felt forced to give me up. It was a control thing and I don't think that was fair. I know it has been a very painful experience for Mary not to have seen me grow up and to have lived with the guilt of giving me up and being powerless to do anything about it. That, I think, is the worst part of it, and we can't go back and change that. For me, there was a spot in my heart that was empty for years. You've lost your roots, you've lost your heritage, all the possibilities of another life that has been denied. You lose your identity, the foundation of who you are, the person you are supposed to be.'

These feelings, Kevin made clear, did not arise because of any unhappy experiences in his adoptive family. 'I've had a great life in America, my parents loved me dearly, but there is a deep sense of loss, very deep inside me. As much as my life has been happy and wonderful, there's a sorrow at not knowing where you came from. And then there's the pain in trying to reconcile these two aspects of your life. It can exhaust you sometimes. I think that like many other adopted people I've been on a journey. We all have different roads. My journey was to find my natural parents, and my goal was to fill the void inside my heart. I know I'm one of the lucky ones.' Mary agrees: 'We are the lucky ones. How many mothers are out there wondering where their child is?'

And it was no thanks to St Patrick's Guild that Mary, Michael and Kevin turned out to be among 'the lucky ones'. Yet in a statement issued in response to questions, Sister Gabriel pointed out that St Patrick's operates a professional tracing service which aims to help reunite adopted children with their natural mothers. She quoted figures. St Patrick's Guild had placed over 4,000 children with adoptive parents, 572 of them children who were sent to America between 1947 and 1967. Since it began offering a tracing service in 1981, Sister Gabriel said 1,513 of the adoption files had been opened, 113 of them relating to American adoptions. But just 12 of these had resulted in reunions – half the rate of domestic reunions.[8]

'It is the policy of St Patrick's Guild to help adoptees and birth mothers in any way we can, within our very limited resources,' Sister Gabriel said. But 'until funding is put in place it is inevitable that there will be long delays in satisfying people's requests.'

'There seems to be a lot of holding back or putting off, and what's that going to do for all these mothers and adopted children?' asked Mary. 'It's the adopted children really who are attempting to get to their roots and they are being prevented from doing it. But we've moved into a different age. Surely now is the time to let everything come out into the open and not be coming back in 30 years time and saying yes, it should have come out.'

13. Maureen - Seek and Ye Shall Find (But Don't Hold Your Breath)

'When you know that the church has all the information, they have your file sitting right there in front of them, and they won't tell you anything, that's very frustrating, and very hard. It's a control thing. They separated you from your mother in the first place. So they are going to try and keep you apart now. They might think it's for the best, but they have no right to make those decisions on behalf of adults'.

Maureen, 1996

Maureen Rowe found out she was adopted when she was about seven years old.[1] 'I was playing in my parents' room one day and I remember opening the bottom drawer in their dresser looking for something and there was this silver box. Of course being a child I opened it and it was full of paper. What caught my eye – I'll never forget it – was a newspaper clipping, pictures of babies, with a headline like "these babies need homes." The children looked really desperate. And there were other papers, letters, documents, more pictures, photographs of a baby girl. There was an Irish passport – although of course I didn't know that's what it was at the time – and an airline ticket. I saw my name on some of the papers and I knew this had all something to do with me, but I didn't know what.'

Maureen took the box downstairs and asked her mum and dad, Dorothy and Jim. That was the first time they acknowledged she was adopted. They told her a shocking story about a car crash in Ireland in which her real mother and father had been killed. 'They told me I had been thrown clear and landed on some grass and I had no one to love me so they had brought me to America and had become my mum and dad.' My first reaction was confusion then grief, like my real mum and dad were both dead and I'd never known that before. It was terrible, just terrible.' But the Rowes must have decided their invented story could cause problems in later years, for shortly afterwards they told Maureen a different story: that her natural mother wasn't dead but just hadn't been able to look after her. 'I thought, great. I was so glad she was alive. I suppose it was then a seed was sown, you know, that I'll find her one day. But of course as a kid that's just fantasy.'

Maureen's early childhood was full of conflicting images and impressions. 'When you're adopted it's like you're there but you're not fitting in. I was blonde and blue-eyed and all my family were dark. I didn't look like anybody. And I was very outward going, quite extrovert and carefree really, but my parents were the exact opposite, quiet and reserved and very strict and proper. Well, her more than him really. There was a basic clash of personalities, certainly between me and my adoptive mother. We were so totally different.'

The whole thing about being Irish was also a source of confusion. 'Well, from what they told me about Ireland I had this vision of a desperately poor third world country where children were left to starve. But from the Irish in New York, and especially from St Patrick's Day, I had this image of people who just got drunk. It was awful because no one explained anything to me. I suppose my parents didn't know. They didn't know about Irish history and culture, they had no Irish background at all. So I was left with this picture, from St Patrick's Day really, of the Irish as people who dyed their hair green and drank green beer and ate green cakes. It was weird. I was kind of repulsed by it and yet I knew this was where I was from.'

But if her Irish identity remained a source of anguish for Maureen, Catholicism served her no better. 'Church was the big deal. I knew a lot more about the whole Catholic tradition than I knew about Ireland, that was for sure. My parents were very Catholic, very, very Catholic. It was church, church, church. And of course I went to a Catholic school. You could say I was steeped in Catholicism.' But Maureen never found the doctrine easy to accept. 'In school, I was always raising questions, like about the wealth of the church and how that fitted with Jesus overturning the money changers. And about priests drinking. And just why this and why that. I never accepted anything without asking why, and of course they didn't like that. I was made sit in the corner and told I was a sinner and to stop asking questions. I'd get banged about a bit as well. I remember before confession once, saying I didn't have any sins to confess and being told to make a few up. Of course when I said that would be telling a lie and a lie was a sin, I was in big trouble. You couldn't question anything. It was all very controlled, very strict. Every area of your life they tried to control. I just couldn't take it.'

When Maureen was ten years old her school called her parents in and told them they didn't consider Maureen a suitable pupil. She was taken out of the school and put into the public school system. 'When I left Catholic school and went public, they were very, very angry about that. In fact they were furious, especially my mother. She was very upset that I wasn't going to get a Catholic education. I remember they even tried to bribe me to stay in Catholic school by telling me I'd get a car when I was old enough if I went to a Catholic University. I was just a child. You don't think that far ahead when you are a child, so promises like that really didn't have any impact. But looking back I can see now how important the whole Catholic education thing was to them.'

Only in later life, when Maureen looked more closely at the box of papers she had found as a child in her parents' bottom drawer did she see the copy of the affidavit Jim and Dorothy Rowe had signed all those years ago. They had sworn a solemn oath that if the nuns in Ireland gave them a child they would educate her in Catholic schools, all the way through to university. 'When I saw that affidavit and read it, I understood why they had reacted as they did when I left the Catholic school system. I had made them break their word. My mother especially was obsessed about it. It really had a huge impact on her and on the way she treated me. I can now see it was around then she really got to be very harsh towards me. She had wanted to make me turn out like her, and it wasn't happening.'

It was around this time that Mrs Rowe added a new dimension to the story about Maureen's adoption. 'She started telling me I had been an unwanted baby, that my real mother didn't love me, that she had abandoned me, and that I should show more gratitude to her for taking me in. It was all this stuff about how awful and terrible my natural mother had been and how wonderful she was to have given me a home. I suppose it was to make me feel guilty as much as grateful, you know, because I wasn't turning out to be such a good Catholic after all.' Harsh words were followed by harsh treatment, but Maureen doesn't like to dwell on that side of the story.

For the next 25 years of her life, Maureen lived with this image of herself as an unwanted, unloved, abandoned baby. 'All my life I carried that, because of the way it was presented to me. She never missed an opportunity to tell me I owed her a great debt of gratitude. And living with the thought that your natural mother just abandoned you – that was baggage you carry all your life.'

And there were other negative factors too. Despite the fact that both Jim and Dorothy Rowe had met Archbishop McQuaid's health requirements, by supplying a doctor's certificate stating they were both 'in very good health', Mrs Rowe, in fact, had suffered from rheumatoid arthritis since she was 20 years old, 20 years before she adopted Maureen. She was in a wheelchair for much of Maureen's adolescence, which added to the difficulties that already existed between mother and daughter. It was clear that no independent check had been carried out on the state of Mrs Rowe's health. Someone in her condition would have had difficulty adopting a child in Ireland.

At the same time, curiosity about her natural mother continued to grow in Maureen. 'Just who was this woman, and did she really abandon me? You fantasise about her being a wonderful and famous person, beautiful, rich, all that sort of stuff, and you imagine a terrible mistake was made, or a wicked person took you away, anything so you weren't just dumped.'

In childhood little can be done to satisfy the urge to know, but at 18, newly independent, with a job and a flat of her own, Maureen decided to have a go. It was the beginning of a painful search that was to take another 18 years to complete. She described it as '18 years of frustration, like banging my head off a brick wall, knowing someone had this information and they just weren't going to give it to me.' As a first step she wrote to the nuns at Castlepollard, saying she had lost her original birth certificate and could she please have a replacement. This was a document she had never seen before. Within weeks she had in her hands the official record of her birth, her mother's name included.

That's when I had to make my mind up – did I want to find her or not? Was I going to get into something here that might end in tears for everyone? I mean, I'd been told she didn't want me, so why should it be any different now, and why should I go looking for someone who abandoned me in the first place? But then I'd say to myself, well that's someone else's opinion, that she didn't want me. She hasn't told me that herself. I haven't heard it from her. "I don't want you, please don't bother me, you're being a pain". If I heard that from her then I could let this thing rest. I have to know was I wanted, what was the situation, was it difficult, did she ever think about me, did she just walk away and say "okay, bye now, that's it, and don't ever come looking for me"?

Maureen's first efforts to find her mother were dispiriting. 'When I knew her name I got in touch with Father Regan at Castlepollard. It was amazing, because he knew me, he called me by my birth name, Marion. He got me to write her a letter and said he'd forward it. Then I'd get back to him and he'd say he had no reply and maybe I should just accept that she wasn't interested. That kind of made me think well maybe she doesn't want to know, maybe I should just let things lie. And so I backed off for two or three years and did nothing.'

In the meantime Maureen had married. Her husband was in the hotel business and they were comfortably well-off. To anyone who didn't know her well, Maureen seemed to have everything and certainly no reason for discontentment. But she was still carrying this burden of uncertainty about her own origins. It just nagged at her all the time. Then she got pregnant. 'Suddenly I started thinking again about her in a concentrated way, you know, that she was pregnant with me once, what was it like for her? What happened that made it all work out this way? And where is she now? What is she doing? Has she any other grandchildren?

Have I any brothers or sisters? All these things go on in your head. So one day I just picked up the phone and rang Father Regan again at Castlepollard and a secretary answered. She said, "Oh are you one of those children from the United States?" When she said that I had the weirdest feeling, I wasn't alone, there were others like me, other people who must have been doing what I was doing, trying to find out who they were, what had happened in their lives. It was funny knowing other people out there were feeling the same way as me.'

Maureen was put through to Father Regan, and even though a few years had passed since they last spoke, he still remembered who she was and called her Marion. 'I knew he was just putting me off, distracting me, giving me little bits of information. He'd tell me a little bit about her, like the colour of her hair, her height, her background, but never enough to help me find her, and that would be it. And I found out afterwards that not everything I was told had been true. I was told my mother's father was a clock-maker and had a shop. In fact he worked for the post-office. I had been told my mother was a nurse when she was really a teacher. So for years I was looking for the wrong person.'

Maureen wrote several letters to her mother, care of Father Regan. 'Of course as I was to find out later my mother never received any of my letters. I don't think they wanted me to find her, they didn't want it to come to a conclusion. It was a control thing. They had separated us and they were going to keep us apart. They probably thought it was for the best, you know, put all that behind you and get on with your life. But what right did they have to make such decisions?'

Father Regan, of course, was a traditionalist. He had come into the adoption business when the prevailing theory favoured closed adoptions, a system in which, once separated, mother and child were never to see one another again. Father Cecil Barrett spelled it out in his definitive guide to adoption practice. "The child will never know his own parent... he will never know his mother,' Barrett wrote, and 'she knows that she will never see her child again, that she will never know him.'[2] Helping reunite adopted people with their natural mothers was not part of the Church's agenda.

In her frustration Maureen considered coming to Ireland to confront Father Regan face to face. 'One time I said to him, "am I going to have to come over there to get this information out of you? There's no problem with me getting on a plane and coming over." I was thinking, put the heat on a bit, he doesn't want to look me in the eye and tell me his lies. So he told me then she wasn't in Ireland any more, that she had actually lived in America and then the Bahamas, and she had married. But he wouldn't tell me her husband's name and of course he wouldn't give me her address. After a while it finally dawned on me that he just couldn't care less. I wasn't so much resentful as frustrated. I felt I was being treated like a child and that was difficult. I wasn't a kid, I was 36, not three or four.'

Then in 1992 Maureen made contact with a social worker at a Dublin adoption advice agency. The social worker wrote to Father Regan on Maureen's behalf, but he didn't reply. The advice agency next wrote to Sister Sarto Harney, senior social worker with the Sacred Heart Adoption Society in Cork. The Sacred Heart nuns had run Castlepollard where Maureen had been born. When Castlepollard ceased to function as an 'orphanage' the records had gone to Sister Sarto. When Sister Sarto wrote back to the social worker in Dublin she gave some useful information: Maureen's mother had originally been from North Dublin.

In February 1994 the adoption advice agency wrote again to Maureen to say they had contacted Father Regan by phone and he had given them some startling news. It was something that gave Maureen great hope: her mother had actually contacted Father Regan at Castlepollard back in 1963 looking for information about her child's whereabouts. Amazingly, through all their correspondence and telephone conversations over a period of a dozen years or more, the priest had never once divulged this information to Maureen. Father Regan also told the social workers that 'due to confidentiality' he was not prepared to pass on the last address he had on file for Maureen's mother, an address in the Bahamas. This infuriated Maureen as she felt that if she had the address she could start to trace her mother. What was more, the address had now been on the priest's files for more than 30 years. Maureen feared the trail could have gone cold. 'If I'd had that address when I contacted Father Regan the very first time, look how much closer I would have been to her – fifteen years instead of thirty.'

By the summer of 1995 the social workers were reporting 'deadlock' as far as Castlepollard was concerned. Father Regan was 'out sick' and no one was handling his work. Father Regan died a few months later without casting any further light on the whereabouts of Maureen's mother.

In the meantime Maureen had written to the Angel Guardian Home in Brooklyn, the people who had helped organise her adoption back in 1960. They replied with a lot of standard information based on a review of her file: her date of birth and weight at birth; the fact that she cut her first tooth at five months, had arrived in the United States in August 1960 and was adopted in December 1961. The file said there was no 'serious mental or physical illness in the family', and that her mother was 'a pleasant, friendly girl of average weight and height with blue eyes and brown wavy hair.'

For the first time since she had started to look for her mother, Maureen found a reference to her father. According to the Angel Guardian Home: 'There isn't any information on the putative father. He did not acknowledge paternity or contribute to your support.'

'My response to that was, what a creep,' Maureen said. 'And then you would wonder, was it rape? You know, you hardly every think about the father. I suppose it's the way our society is in these situations. You don't really expect the father to stick around. You look for your mother because you would have expected to have been with her even if she wasn't married. So when you learn something about your father, and it's negative, I suppose it just reinforces something that was there already. I mean you wouldn't have expected anything different.'

But if there was nothing in the response from the Angel Guardian Home that would help her find her mother, the Dublin social workers at least had one final suggestion as to where Maureen might turn for help: a woman called Anne who specialised in tracing and reuniting, and who didn't charge for her help. Anne knew how the system worked, where the public records were and how to access them and cross-reference them.

'So I got in touch with Anne. She asked me to send all my papers and she would do her best. It was amazing, within six months she had found my mother. I'd been looking for 18 years.' Anne had worked independently of the Church. She had traced Maureen's mother's family in north Dublin and through them, without divulging anything about the reasons for her search, had discovered a current address for Maureen's mother. She was living with her husband in the United States.

When Maureen found out how close she now was to making the contact she had craved for so long she became nervous. 'You know I was still thinking all this stuff I'd been told as a child, that my mother didn't want anything to do with me. But Anne helped me think positively about a reunion. She was able to explain what it had been like for single mothers in Ireland in the 1950s, the pressures on them, the lack of support. I began to understand a little bit better that there was a lot more to this than rejection. I began to feel compassion towards my mother. This would be important for her as well as for me. She would be able to know that I was well, that I had a family, that she was a grandmother to six smashing kids. And that I had no resentment towards her. Making contact now would bring a sort of closure to what was a painful experience for both of us.'

Maureen didn't rush the contact. 'I prepared myself. I got all these books and articles about adoption from the birth mother's point of view. I read and read, especially about the worst scenarios. I suppose I prepared myself for the worst and hoped for the best. I didn't know what I was going to find. Did she want to be contacted? Did she care? Anne made the first approach, discreetly, to see if Maureen's mother wanted to be contacted by her daughter. The answer was yes, she did. 'So Anne gave me her phone number and I called. It was difficult on the phone, you know, emotional, but still sort of anonymous. She was in Florida, I was in Virginia. We agreed to meet, so I flew down to her. Meeting your own mother face to face after 36 years – that's some experience. There was no resentment on my part at what she had done and no anger from her that I had suddenly burst into her life. She was wonderful.'

In the course of the first meeting with her mother and in subsequent conversations, Maureen was to make some startling discoveries. 'My mother told me that a few years after my birth she had written to Castlepollard and left her address and said if ever Marion comes looking for me this is where I am. And she wrote to the nuns: "any news of Marion?" And she looked in the States, but every avenue was just shut in her face. They'd just tell her, "look, forget about it."

Maureen's mother confirmed this. 'I visited Castlepollard on occasion and met with Father Regan,' she said. 'He knew where I was in the Bahamas and the States, but I never got any letters from him at any time. And I used to correspond with the Mother Superior at the orphanage and would get replies from her six months later. But she never indicated she knew anything about Marion.'

Maureen is convinced it was a deliberate policy not to help reunite them. 'They knew she was looking for me and they knew I was looking for her but still they wouldn't give either of us the information. They just weren't going to do it. There was still that control, being treated like a child when you're not a child: we'll make your decisions for you, and we decide you're not going to find her.'

Maureen also learned of the circumstances which led to her being born in Castlepollard. Her mother had been seeing a man quite a few years older than herself, Jan, who was a 36-year-old Dutchman working in Dublin. When her mother got pregnant, far from denying paternity Jan had found a flat for them both to live in. But in the meantime Maureen's mother had turned to a priest she knew for advice and he forbade her from 'living in sin' with her child's father. As Jan was a Protestant who had been married once before and divorced, marriage in Ireland to a Catholic girl was out of the question.

Partly to get her away from Jan and the 'occasion of sin', and partly to avoid scandalising her family, the priest arranged for Maureen's mother to have her baby in Castlepollard. Maureen was told by her mother that Jan had contributed financially while she was at Castlepollard, information that flatly contradicted the dispiriting news Maureen had been given by the Angel Guardian Home about her father denying paternity and contributing nothing towards her support.

Maureen also learned that Jan had come to see them both after the birth but had been turned away by the nuns. Nor had he simply abandoned his daughter. In fact he had proposed taking baby Marion back to Holland, but Maureen's mother didn't want to give her up: she was determined to keep her and look after her herself.

The unconventional relationship between Maureen's mother and father had little chance of success in the Ireland of 1960. They would have to go their separate ways. Maureen's mother stayed on with her baby at Castlepollard for a few months. She had no complaints at all about her treatment. As a private, paying client – unlike most girls who were there at public expense – Maureen's mother was not required to do any manual work, and was treated with common decency if not respect. Money, as always, talked to the nuns. But the Sisters at Castlepollard put pressure on her to agree to give her baby up for adoption. She resisted. They then informed her that her baby was sickly and would require greater care and attention than she could hope to provide as an unmarried mother. This was untrue. The child had had a stomach disorder in early infancy, but at the time of going to America she had been given a completely clean bill of health.

Finally, sometime before the baby's first birthday, the nuns got their way. Maureen's mother admitted defeat and agreed to let her baby be offered for adoption. 'But only on condition,' she said, 'that they send me news of how she was doing from time to time, and the occasional photograph.' None of these were ever sent to her despite the fact that Jim and Dorothy Rowe wrote regular letters to the nuns, full of news about the baby's progress along with lots of photographs.

Learning so much about her origins was a life-changing experience for Maureen. 'To find out the truth, to discover that you were wanted, that you were loved and that your mother only parted with you under awful circumstances, that was a life-changing experience for me. It was such a boost to my self-esteem. And to see that I look like her, this is a wonderful experience because when you are adopted you don't look like anyone. Suddenly you know you came from somewhere, that you belonged somewhere, that you have a real past, you didn't just appear from nowhere. That's all so important for adopted people, that if you're not adopted you just can't understand it. But no one should have the right to keep it from you.'

There was a final piece of the jigsaw missing: Jan, Maureen's birth father. She discussed with her mother whether or not she should look for him, and her mother encouraged her to do so. But where would she begin? Telephone directories are a useful starting point, but even though his surname would have been uncommon in America it was probably quite ordinary in Holland. By chance Maureen just happened to have computer access to all listed telephone numbers in Canada and she just keyed in her father's name one day to see what turned up. There were a couple of entries for the same surname, but none had 'J' as a first initial. She tried one anyway and after a convoluted conversation about family trees with the man on the other end of the line, she discovered that she was talking to Jan's brother. It was a staggering coincidence, a chance in a million. She told him why she wanted to contact Jan, and he promised to come back to her soon with information. A couple of days later he called with a telephone number. Jan was in Cape Town, South Africa.

'I called him straight away and he answered the phone. I just came out and said it: "You had a baby in Ireland." Well, he said straight back, "yes I did have a baby, is it you? Are you Marion?" He said the same name, he remembered the name. He was so excited, he seemed so happy. "I've thought about you all these years," he said. "Where have you been? What have you been doing?" He just couldn't believe that I had done the search and I had found him. He was so accepting and so excited.'

Next time Maureen called Jan it was on his birthday. 'He told me then he had tried to get in to see me but the nuns just slammed the door in his face. He said he was so sorry now that he had accepted their right to do that, he hadn't fought them, just turned round and went away again. He explained that being divorced there was no way things could have worked out in Ireland. He had no rights. He wasn't allowed to see me. He wasn't asked about my future. Now, he's old and he never had that opportunity.' Jan finally visited Maureen in America in late 1996, spending five weeks with her and her family. 'He was so open about it all,' Maureen said, 'but also so angry about the way we had all been treated by the Church.'

Maureen may be one of the lucky ones. Not only has she found her mother and her father, but she has come through her experiences remarkably intact and the reunions have proved amicable. But she has strong feelings about the obstacles that were put in the way of her tracing her mother. 'I don't think any priest or any nun has the right to keep records secret that could help reunite people. If mothers – or fathers for that matter – don't want the contact, let them say so themselves: "sorry, I just can't cope with you in my life right now", not have someone else say it for them. And it's even worse when the people telling you, "no, we can't put you together" are the same people who pulled you apart in the first place.'

14. Deny Till They Die

'It must be borne in mind that no official records exist of Irish children who were sent abroad for adoption in the past… No information is kept on Irish children who were adopted under the laws of foreign countries.'

Austin Currie, Minister of State for Children's Policy
Dáil Éireann, 5 March 1996

'… there are up to 1,500 detailed adoption files which… contain the names and dates of birth of the children concerned, the names of their birth mothers, the names and details of their adoptive parents…'

Dick Spring, Minister for Foreign Affairs,
Waterford, 7 March 1996

By the early 1960s the American adoption business had gone into decline, although it would be the early 1970s before it stopped altogether. The figures that chart its descent are quite dramatic. Between 1949, when records began, and 1961 – a period of 12 years – approximately 150 children were sent to the United States on average each year. But over the next 12 years up to 1973, the average was just 30 a year.

In the early 1960s, ironically as its adoption workload declined, the Department of External Affairs tried to extricate itself from responsibility for the American baby traffic by having the whole business shifted onto the shoulders of the Adoption Board. But Peter Berry, Secretary General in the Department of Justice, which then had responsibility for the Board, opposed the idea, and although his reasons were never made clear it could simply have been that, like many others, he had little faith in the Board's ability to do a proper job. Having failed to pass responsibility in that direction, one passport official came up with a startling plan for disposing of all 'illegitimate' children from the State.

Early in 1962, the official calculated that approximately 550 'illegitimate' children a year were 'surplus' to domestic demand. US adoptions, he said, would take about 150 of these annually, but that meant the number of children dependent on institutional care would be growing at a rate of 400 a year. The official proposed a coordinated campaign involving the Department, Archbishop McQuaid and Catholic Charities to clear the orphanages of these 'unwanted children' by advertising their availability in the States and making 'a positive effort... to have them all adopted.'[1]

But when the official discussed the matter with McQuaid's adoption advisor, Cecil Barrett, by then a Monsignor, he discovered that the figures he had been working on were very out of date. 'Adoptions within the country are proceeding so satisfactorily,' the passport officer then noted, 'that neither St Patrick's Guild nor the nuns at Navan Road have any children available for adoption abroad.'[2]

Times were changing. Major social and cultural shifts were underway in Irish society as a whole, and it was these, rather than any decision on the part of the nuns to actually stop the traffic, that were responsible for the decline in child exports in the 1960s. With the advance of urbanisation in Ireland, adoption was becoming more popular – even fashionable. In 1967, for example, 97 out of every 100 children born in Ireland to unmarried mothers were adopted *within* the State. The average yearly figure for the 1950s had been 56 Irish adoptions per hundred 'illegitimate' births. But the other side of this equation also needs to be noted: when the small number of continuing US adoptions is factored in, we are left with the fact that fewer than two out of every 100 unmarried mothers kept their children, indicating the extent to which these young women still felt compelled – and in many cases *were* compelled – to give up their babies. As Irish adoptions increased further, the American traffic declined at a pace. Again, the figures are quite dramatic. Between 1949 and 1961, an average of 12 out of every 100 'illegitimate' children born each year were sent to America. From 1962 until 1973 the yearly average was just 2 per hundred.

And by the 1970s another significant factor had come into play: the payment of state benefits to single mothers. As the number of children born each year to unmarried women soared – virtually doubling between 1964 (1,292) and 1974 (2,515), Irish society was at last forced to come to terms with its own reality. The single mother's allowance had the effect of enabling more women to keep their children rather than giving them up for adoption. It was no coincidence that the number of adoptions within Ireland itself peaked in 1975 when 1,287 'illegitimate' children were adopted. Although church pressure continued to be applied to many unmarried young mothers to give their babies up for adoption through the 1980s and into the '90s, the number of babies available for adoption continued to decline. An additional factor was the legalisation of abortion in Britain in 1967, which enabled a growing number of Irish women to terminate unwanted pregnancies by travelling to the UK. And as fewer and fewer Irish children became available for adoption, and as Ireland became a wealthier society, more and more childless Irish couples turned to other, less developed or poorer countries in search of children to adopt, turning the situation that had prevailed in the 1950s and 60s on its head. From exporting babies, Ireland has become a net importer of children. Inter-country adoption, the new name for baby exports, is supposed to be tightly regulated under the umbrella of the Hague Convention on the Protection of Children. But as Ireland's own sorry history in this area shows, rules are made to be broken and unscrupulous operators will always find ways to procure babies from unfortunate mothers on the one hand, and locate people with deep pockets to acquire them on the other. Issues such as these have arisen in just about every country where Irish people have adopted children in recent years, countries like Russia, China, and Vietnam where critical matters – such as informed and freely given maternal consent, and the extent of corruption among public officials – continue to provoke concerns. So much so, in fact, that at the time of writing in 2011, the Adoption Authority's website carried a stark and frequently repeated warning that if they find evidence of cash payments for babies adopted abroad they will refuse to recognise the adoption in Irish law. Yet from some would-be inter-country adopters, there have been loud and persistent demands for a relaxation in Ireland's now thoroughgoing process of assessment for those who want to become adoptive parents. Again, Ireland's own experience shows, tragically, that it is when the tests of suitability are lax or poorly enforced that child welfare is most at risk. Unfortunately there are plenty who would still deny the lessons of history.

Meanwhile, as Ireland's own child export programme faded out, and as many of those who were involved moved on or died, memories dimmed. Dust settled on the files. It had become a non-subject. A whole new generation of Irish citizens grew up in a radically changing society, oblivious to this episode in their nation's history, an episode which most of them – with more progressive attitudes to women's rights, contraception, sexual relationships, single motherhood, and child welfare – would find shameful. But it was not a story that would stay buried forever. Too many people had been hurt, too many powerful human emotions denied. Yet when the long-suppressed saga finally did begin to emerge, in a confused and incomplete way in the spring of 1996 – quarter of a century after the baby traffic ceased – the nuns who had organised it kept quiet while the State, which had facilitated it, kicked for touch.

The tale of Ireland's infant diaspora began to emerge only in the wake of other disturbing revelations about the treatment of children in days gone by. Given the endless flow in the intervening years of clerical abuse stories and stories of the systematic brutalisation of children in religious-run institutions, coupled with all the tribunals of inquiry and harrowing official reports, it can be difficult to remember just how new and utterly sensational it all was in the mid 1990s. There was a deeply controversial television documentary, *Dear Daughter*, on the appalling abuse of children by nuns in a Dublin orphanage at Goldenbridge. That programme itself had come after the first tentative revelations of clerical child sex abuse which in turn followed the scandals of Bishop Eamon Casey and Father Michael Cleary who had secretly fathered children. But the subject of the Church and sex was a minefield for those in power. After all, a Government had fallen in November 1994 over the botched handling of an extradition warrant for the paedophile priest Brendan Smyth.

Against the backdrop of these faith-shattering episodes, former Aer Lingus employee, Anne Phelan, phoned a morning radio chat show and told of her encounters in the early 1950s with American military personnel who openly talked of buying children from Irish orphanages.[3] This was just the beginning. Pat Kilmurray phoned to say he used to take American couples around the orphanages in his taxi so they could inspect the babies on offer.[4] Rosemary Walsh, who had worked in the visa department of the American embassy, recalled the special days that were set aside each month to deal with around 20 children at a time who were going to the States to be adopted, all brought in by nuns. And she remembered, too, the 'fabulous wealth' of the American adopters, as seen in their affidavits.[5]

It was becoming apparent that this was something more than a few chance cases here and there. It had the appearance of something organised, something large scale.

Yet no one seemed to have an overview. No one could say – or, more accurately, was prepared to say – when it began or when it ended. No one seemed to know how many children were involved, or the circumstances in which they were taken from the country. Who had been behind it? Was money a primary consideration? Where did all the children come from and where did they end up? Had it been legal?

The emerging, if still utterly confused story took a more sinister turn when Maggie Butler, who had been sent to America by St Patrick's Guild in 1951, revealed that after years of searching for her natural mother, she had discovered that her mother's name had been falsified on birth records, making it impossible for Maggie to find her.[6] And what was more, the nuns, who she believed knew her mother's true identity, had misled her and would give her no help. We know now, of course, that falsifying birth records and lying about it in later years were common practice among the baby exporters, but when Maggie Butler first spoke about her experience she wasn't always believed.

Then came the first firm proof that substantial numbers of children were involved in the American adoptions: Nora Gibbons, then senior social worker with the child welfare organisation Barnardos, revealed that they were already dealing with around 200 Irish-born people sent to the US for adoption who were trying to unravel the secret of their origins. Many of them, Gibbons said, were finding it impossible to discover anything because of falsified birth records.[7] The State's own Adoption Board put out a statement admitting that it was aware of this problem, which, it said, was faced not only by those sent to America but by unknown numbers of children adopted within Ireland as well. And some adoption societies had colluded in it.[8]

All this emerged in a matter of days, and although the pieces of the jigsaw were slowly falling into place, to complete the picture and make sense of it all some sort of authoritative statement was needed from those in possession of the facts. The opportunity for the State to tell what it knew came when the matter was raised in the Dáil on 5 March 1996. But what came out was not illumination but simply more confusion. Alan Shatter, then a backbench TD on the Government side and an expert in family law, had asked the obvious questions: How many children were sent abroad? What agencies or individuals were involved? What records had been kept? Was the natural mother's consent obtained in all cases?[9] Shatter went on to demand a formal inquiry into the whole affair, 'for the sake of many hundreds, if not thousands of children who were effectively exiled from the State in which they were born'.

But when Austin Currie, Junior Minister responsible for the care of children, rose to reply, it was clear he was already on the defensive. He was here, he said, to deal with 'allegations'. Contradicting the public mood of astonishment over the emerging revelations, Currie said the former practice of exporting children to America had been 'well known', although the exact number involved was not.[10] 'It must be borne in mind,' Currie said, 'that no official records exist of Irish children who were sent abroad for adoption in the past as no such records were required to be kept by public authorities.' This was an astonishing statement, a seeming assertion that the State had no responsibility for what had happened, no duty of care towards thousands of its own infant citizens.

Austin Currie's statement contained no words of regret, no sentiments that would bring comfort to those, like Pat Thuillier or Mary Geraghty, who had suffered so much. Currie said he was considering a contact register to help people adopted within Ireland, but be doubted if it was possible to extend it to those adopted in the United States.

The Junior Minister went on to deny Shatter's demand for an inquiry and in the process issued a rebuke to those who asked critical questions. 'Given the dearth of information regarding arrangements that were made some 30 or 40 years ago,' Currie said, 'I do not see how it would be practicable at this stage to conduct an investigation into a practice which was widely known at the time and which does not appear to have been considered unacceptable.' The implication seemed to be that if it was acceptable then, it could not be queried now. It was a cold, if not chilling performance.

Austin Currie, however, had misled the Dáil on two counts, no doubt unintentionally. Many people did find the practice of exporting 'illegitimate' children unacceptable, including people in authority at the time. And there *were* records – individual records for every single infant who was given an 'adoption passport', as well as voluminous official files relating to Church and State involvement in the whole affair.

Listening to the growing clamour on the nation's airwaves, Caitriona Crowe at the National Archives had been reminded of a file she had spotted the previous Christmas.[11] It had come from the Irish embassy in Washington and contained around 20 names of Irish children sent to America for adoption in the early 1950s. She retrieved the file – on the day of the Dáil debate – and on closer reading she spotted a reference to another file that had come from the Department of Foreign Affairs at Iveagh House. Next day she located that file. It was massive, containing separate records on no fewer than 1,500 children who had been exported before 1964. And there was more to come: the Department of Foreign (formerly External) Affairs subsequently located a further 500 or so personal files covering the later years. In addition to the personal records, there were several enormous policy files containing memos, minutes, reports, correspondence – the sort of paperwork on which civil servants seem to thrive.

On the discovery of the individual records in the National Archive, Caitriona Crowe proposed privately to the Department of Foreign Affairs that essential information be made available, on a confidential basis, to Barnardos, so they could assist and counsel natural mothers who were looking for their now grown children as well as children who were looking for their mothers. The Department of Foreign Affairs, however, said no. Instead of putting the information into the hands of those who could have used it, the Department decided to take legal advice on issues of confidentiality and the right to privacy of those involved. Such a course of action, obviously, could tie the whole thing in knots for the foreseeable future. The matter was put in the hands of Austin Currie to resolve. It was an inauspicious beginning.

In the meantime, Dick Spring, Tánaiste and Minster for Foreign Affairs, decided to go public on the existence of the records. As chance would have it, Spring had a fitting engagement: the very day after the files were found he was due to speak in Waterford on the theme of 'Creating a better world for our children'. It was here he unveiled the discovery of the first batch of children's files, announcing, '… there are up to 1,500 detailed adoption files, which… contain the names and dates of birth of the children concerned, the names of their birth mothers, the names and details of their adoptive parents…' It was a potential treasure trove of information.

Spring also revealed details of some of the policy documents, including ones indicating the close involvement of Archbishop McQuaid back in the early 1950s. For the first time it became clear that this whole business had been organised and operated by the religious, under John Charles McQuaid's intense sectarian gaze. Then, on the same day as the State opened its own policy files, the Archdiocese of Dublin decided to open a small file of documents and correspondence relating to the American adoptions from McQuaid's archive. It was the first time any of McQuaid's voluminous papers had come into the public domain.

Dick Spring seemed to have read the public mood more accurately than Austin Currie. His Waterford speech was the first acknowledgement by anyone in authority that a lot of hurt and damage had been done. Spring was critical of the practices of 40 years ago when so many babies were 'removed from their young and frightened mothers at the most vulnerable possible time in the life of these mothers,' and sent off, 'hopefully to a better life, but at what cost in human suffering we may never know.'

'We have no way of knowing who suffered most in these situations,' Spring went on, 'and we hope that the children involved, at least, went on to have happy and fulfilled lives with their new adoptive parents. But we know from at least some of the stories that that wasn't always true, and that some of these children have spent many years trying to find out why they were abandoned, as they saw it.' And outlining the practice of compelling young mothers to sign away all rights forever to their children, Spring said, 'one can only imagine the pain that must have been involved.'[12]

Spring's revelations of a large-scale, highly organised baby traffic, spanning almost three decades, and his acknowledgement of the pain and suffering that resulted from it, set a new tone. A few days later, on 9 March, Austin Currie told RTÉ news, 'All I can say is that our hypocritical past is catching up with us, and a lot of things are now being revealed that were very carefully hidden in the past. The extent of human misery is now being exposed.' It was a complete reversal of Currie's defensive and insensitive Dáil speech of just four days earlier.

The newspapers reflected the growing sense of anger in the community at large. 'Banished children of Erin' ran one headline.[13] 'Ghosts of our hidden history return,' said another.[14] 'Stark days of revelation' was the heading over an *Irish Times* editorial. The writer was in sombre mood: 'When the social history of our times is written, the early months of 1996 will figure as a period of stark revelation, a final drawing away of the veils from a darker, hidden Ireland. These days and weeks have marked a convergence of suppressed grief, of buried secrets and of enduring pain.'[15]

Another journalist waxed more lyrical, writing that 'every dog-eared file is a small conspiracy of officially-sanctioned dishonesty... a pocket sized slip of shoddy contemporary history.'[16]

Spring had another opportunity to flesh out the story when he had to reply to questions in the Dáil on 14 March 1996. On this occasion Spring named the Irish adoption societies that had been involved and revealed the role played by a powerful American religious body, Catholic Charities. But he also conveyed two incorrect impressions about the role played by the Irish State.[17] First of all he described the nuns who sent children abroad as their 'legal guardians', implying that the courts had conferred some legal status on the nuns and that everything had therefore been done perfectly properly. But the nuns rarely, if ever, went to the trouble or the expense of having themselves appointed legal guardians to the children in their care. The legal basis on which a great many children were dispatched overseas was, and remains, far from clear. Mr Spring also told the Dáil that his Department had required each branch of Catholic Charities, who handled most of the Irish adoptions at the American end, to be 'approved as a child placing agency under the law'. What he did not say was that this elementary safeguard was only introduced in 1956 by which time over 1,000 children had already been sent to the States and placed for adoption.

The effect of Spring's remarks was to reassure the House and the public that even if what happened in the past was regrettable it was all done in accordance with law and proper procedures. As this book has been at pains to show, this was far from accurate. No one knows how many Irish infants were dispatched to unsuitable adopters, or how many couples who had been refused an American child to adopt still managed to get one from Ireland. But the files from Dick Spring's own Department certainly suggest that the numbers in these categories were significant. Finally, no mention at all was made in the Dáil about the murkier dealings in babies, the black market that operated widely in Ireland in the 1950s and 60s, a black market that is also clearly acknowledged in the official files. The full story hadn't even begun to emerge.

Yet, as far as the State was concerned, the only unresolved matter was what to do with all the personal files and the information they contained. Again, in this regard Dick Spring's remarks may have misled some. He told the Dáil that he hoped 'a way will be found to make the information available to the people concerned'. To the hundreds of adopted people who were trying to trace their roots in Ireland, and to the smaller but not insignificant number of natural mothers looking for their children in America, this sounded like the answer to their prayers. But, as we shall see, it turned out to be nothing of the sort. And in the meantime, the first port of call for adopted people coming in search of their mothers was the adoption society that arranged their adoption in the first place. For many, if not most, this proved a deeply frustrating experience.

The nuns who ran these societies would tell anyone seeking to trace their natural mother that a definite 'guarantee of confidentiality' was given to these unmarried girls and women when they turned to the nuns with their crisis pregnancies. These undertakings, they argued, had to be kept – in the same way as a binding contract must be adhered to. But there was never any legislative requirement to give such guarantees, and no documentary evidence of their existence – either across the board or in individual cases – has ever been produced. What is more, it is stretching things to describe the relationship between nuns and the unmarried mothers they dealt with as a 'contract'. Even if something loosely resembling a contract or agreement was reached, the process was carried out from very unequal positions, to the extent that the nuns were effectively in a position to demand anything they wanted, and the shamed and humiliated mothers had little option but to accept the nuns' terms, however unreasonable, and however inadequately understood those terms might have been. Secrecy – which would seriously damage the health of many of these women – was itself a function of conservative Catholicism.

While the nuns' assertion that a binding guarantee of confidentiality was given to every unmarried mother in their care remains unsupported by documentation of any kind, what written records there are from the period tell a very different story: when an unmarried woman was offered confidentiality it was never absolute. Father Cecil Barrett was the Catholic Church's foremost expert on adoption policy in Ireland throughout the period in question, and in his eyes the need for secrecy was part of the programme of moral rehabilitation and nothing else.

Barrett held that 'professional secrets' of the sort that existed between the nuns and unmarried mothers were 'the most binding of all,' but still far from binding in all circumstances. They could be broken, Barrett argued, if for example 'an unmarried mother was about to cause grave spiritual harm to her child' – a coded way of referring to the danger of her handing the child over to a Protestant. The 'professional secret' could also be broken to 'save' the mother from moral harm, if for example she proposed continuing an unmarried relationship with the child's father.

In Barrett's book – and there was no other – an unmarried mother's secret could be divulged to protect the interests of the church and faith. Regardless of the social and personal consequences for the woman, and regardless of any promises of confidentiality that may have been made to her, there was no binding contract.[18] And there is no reason to believe the nuns held views contrary to Cecil Barrett's.

Interestingly, Barrett had nothing whatever to say about the status of the mother's privacy should her child, in later years, come seeking information about her. Such an event was unthinkable to Barrett and the nuns. No mother was ever offered guarantees in this respect. All the undertakings went in the other direction: that she would never try to see or make contact with her child.

When viewed this way, it seems safe to say that the secrecy ordered by nuns to shroud an unmarried mother's 'sin' was not imposed primarily for her benefit at all. Secrecy was part of the nuns' control agenda, not a service offered out of kindness to the unfortunate women caught up in the Church's regime of suppression and deceit. At a wider level, too, it could be seen as a device that enabled Irish society at large to sustain the myth of pre-marital chastity, so important in denying women control over their own sexuality. Pretending that women did not become pregnant outside marriage was one way of denying that women could enjoy sexual relationships with men who were not their husbands.

But while the adoption societies continued to frustrate adopted people searching for their identity, what of the State's undertakings in 1996 to do everything it could to help?

Gene Autry – one of the babies whose birth at St Rita's nursing home and subsequent illegal handover to an American military couple had been the subject of a major Garda investigation in 1954 – had extensive dealings with the Department of Foreign Affairs in this period. Gene, whose story was told in Chapter 5, had only discovered in 1997 – when he was already 44 years old – that he had been adopted from Ireland. But when he turned to the Department of Foreign Affairs for help in tracing his natural mother, he was politely told that as his file was now in the National Archive, and as the National Archive Act of 1986 forbade the release of personal information that might cause distress to another living person, there was nothing they could do for him. The official writing this, of course, had no knowledge of whether Gene's natural mother was alive or not, but it was the standard response to everyone in Gene's position. Certainly the Department made no effort to discover his mother's current status, nor, if she were alive, would it try to contact her and ask if her name and address could be passed to her son. The very least the Department could have done was see that the official, public birth record was corrected and that Gene's natural mother's name replaced that of Mr and Mrs Autry on his birth certificate – as the law required. That way they could have enabled him to find his mother's name without breaching the terms of the National Archive Act, if that was what really concerned them. But instead, Gene was given what was considered 'non-identifying' information from his file – much of which was simply incorrect and quite misleading. There is no reason to believe this was done with the intention of confusing him, but it does indicate that those in possession of information vital to Gene's search for his origins were, to put it at its mildest, insensitive to the effect that their misleading advice might have. And of course Gene was just one among hundreds of people sent to America for adoption who were now knocking on the Department's door, and there is no reason to suppose any of the others fared any better.

Gene was told at the outset that the file from the Garda investigation into his birth at St Rita's was 'restricted' and could not be made available to him, yet this author obtained it on request from the National Archive. Gene was also told the 'good news' that Minister Austin Currie was setting up a contact register to help adopted people and their natural parents contact each other, should they so wish. He wasn't told Currie had ruled out extending this to the American adoptions. The final piece of information that was provided to Gene Autry also proved unhelpful: the pre-1963 birth records from St Rita's, he was told, were in the custody of the Eastern Health Board. But when he contacted the Eastern Health Board, they denied having them. But Gene never gave up trying, and finally he persuaded an official in the Department to tell him the first letter of his mother's name, which was not in itself identifying information. The letter was T. With remarkable patience, Gene bided his time, returning some time later to see if anyone could tell him how many letters there were in his mother's name. Another bit of luck: an official told him this time that there were seven letters. No doubt their intentions were humane, but the fact that they had to turn a very painful human dilemma into something akin to a crossword puzzle, so as not to be seen to be actually *helping*, just served to highlight how inadequate and outdated the law in this vital area is.

Gene Autry was one of the lucky ones. Using the information he had gleaned from Department officials he was able to narrow his search down sufficiently to produce a positive result. In the end, he traced his natural mother and in the process discovered she had gone on to marry his father and between them they had produced seven more children – full brothers and sisters for Gene who now enjoys a close relationship with his extended family in Ireland – but with little thanks to officialdom.

Citing the National Archive Act as a reason for withholding information from Gene Autry – and hundreds of others who were searching at the same time – was somewhat disingenuous. If the individual adoption files had been removed from the Archive and reinstated in a government department, this restriction would have been removed overnight. And if that couldn't be done, there was another option: the information in the personal files in the State Archives is duplicated in the files of the adoption societies who sent the children to America, and those files are not subject to the National Archive Act. The 1952 Adoption Act empowers a State agency, the Adoption Board/Authority, to enter the premises of registered adoption societies and copy their records. So, if it wished, the State could have obtained the information people were seeking unrestricted by the National Archive Act. The fact that no one was willing to take any of these options suggests that the State itself had no serious intention of finding ways to make the information available. In fact, it had another stock argument in its armoury for denying information to adopted people.

For two years after the American adoption story first broke, adopted people seeking information on their origins, or mothers on the whereabouts of their adopted children, were told that while the State really wanted to help, nothing could be done for them because the whole issue of who was entitled to know what was currently before the courts. The official position was summed up by then Junior Minister for Children, Frank Fahey, who in reply to a parliamentary question on the subject in March 1998, declared that the 'the establishment of a comprehensive legal framework for post-adoption contact between birth mothers and adopted persons and access to birth records is a priority. However,' he went on, 'it would not be prudent to proceed with the necessary enabling legislation at present as there are a number of legal and constitutional issues awaiting clarification following the hearing of a Supreme Court case,' in which judgment was still awaited.[19]

The case concerned two women who had been informally adopted prior to the introduction of legal adoption. They had gone to court asking that the institution who dealt with them as babies be compelled to release the identity of their natural mothers – information the institution was refusing to hand over. The Circuit Court sent the matter to the Supreme Court for a ruling. In April 1998, the Supreme Court issued its findings.[20] This was a judgment about arrangements made before the introduction of legal adoption in 1953, not about people who had actually been adopted. Legally adopted people's circumstances might have been found to be different since they were governed by a specific piece of legislation, the Adoption Act. Nevertheless, the judgment has been held by all government agencies to be directly relevant to adopted people as well. It was a complicated ruling, and one that brought no immediate benefit to those seeking information. The court found that while every child had a constitutional right, under Article 40.3, to know their natural parents' identity, unmarried mothers who had given their children up also had a right to privacy. It was, the ruling said, a matter of balancing these conflicting rights, something the courts would have to do in individual cases that would come before them.

One Supreme Court judge, Ronan Keane, was highly critical of the Oireachtas for not clarifying these issues by way of legislation. 'The Oireachtas,' he wrote in a dissenting judgment, 'have failed to avail of the many opportunities which have been presented to them of dealing with these issues. That does not, in my view, justify the courts in undertaking such a task for which they lack, not merely the expert guidance available to the legislative arm, but also, and more crucially, the democratic mandate.' With the Supreme Court ruling now issued, and with Justice Keane's admonishments to spur them on, the Government might have been expected to move swiftly to do what they had long promised – legislate to provide for adoption information once the Court had its say. Instead, they did the opposite, using the judgment to argue that their hands were now tied.

Yet a huge anomaly seems to hang over the Supreme Court judgment, for while the Court upheld a *right* to privacy, the law of the land explicitly *prohibits* privacy in matters of birth. By law, every birth that occurs in Ireland must be registered in the Register of Births, Deaths and Marriages, and each entry must include the name and address of the child's mother, whether or not her child was subsequently adopted. Any member of the public – and that includes all adopted people – may view the register on demand. And for all mothers, regardless of whether their child was adopted or not, giving false information to achieve privacy – such as a bogus name or address – is a serious criminal offence. In the matter of giving birth, the law on registering the basic facts makes no distinction between women whose children were given up for adoption and women who kept their children. They are all treated equally. It was the Supreme Court that said those who gave their children up must be treated differently by being afforded a constitutional 'right to privacy'.

But even though all birth certificates are public documents, the problem for an adopted person trying to access the public record of their own birth is that they are not permitted to know their natural mother's name, and probably don't even know where they themselves were born – the two key ways of accessing information in the register. This is a consequence of Ireland's closed adoption regime. And if an adopted person asks the Adoption Board (now Authority) for a copy of their birth certificate, the Board is not legally obliged to provide it – even though it is a public record. In fact, for many years the Adoption Board simply refused all requests for birth certificates without exception, asserting that the law precluded them from doing otherwise. But the courts have held that by imposing a blanket ban on the release of birth certificates, the Board was misapplying the law, and they instructed the Board to assess each application on its merits and act in the best interests of the adopted person. As a result of this judgment, the Adoption Authority says it now issues more birth certificates to applicants than it refuses, including in cases where the natural mother has objected. Although the numbers involved are small, this seems to make nonsense of the Supreme Court ruling, and provides further proof that the whole system is in disarray. (Where a birth certificate was issued to an adopted person without the natural mother's consent, that person was required to swear an affidavit that they would respect their natural mother's privacy and agree not to try to contact her other than through the Board or the original adoption society.)

The 1998 judgment also sits unhappily alongside the European Convention on Human Rights as well as the UN Convention on the Rights of the Child, which the Irish State has ratified and which enshrines the right of all children to know their parents and to establish their full identity. Under the circumstances, it seems astonishing that the 1998 Supreme Court ruling has been allowed to go unchallenged by a State which purports to take its international obligations seriously.

The powers that be, of course, will point to what they regard as significant advances since the American adoption story first broke putting the whole issue of adoption information firmly on the agenda. First, there is now a National Adoption Contact Preference Register – as promised by Austin Curry in 1996. But it took *nine years* to get it up and running, and in the course of drafting enabling legislation, successive Fianna Fáil governments went so far as to propose that an adopted person who tried to contact a natural parent where the parent had registered a desire not to be contacted, and likewise a parent who tried to contact reluctant children, would be liable to prosecution for harassment under the Non Fatal Offences Against the Person Act. This is a criminal offence, potentially punishable by imprisonment. This astonishing proposal was contained in legislation first submitted in 2001 by then Minister of State for Children Mary Hanafin and subsequently championed by her successor in that role, the late Brian Lenihan. The proposal was not proceeded with, largely it seems because of the storm of protest it engendered rather than because its authors realised they had made a dreadful *faux pas*.

It was March 2005 before a National Adoption Contact Preference Register was launched (by Brian Lenihan) amid a fanfare of publicity. Every home in the country was sent a leaflet about the new service. Adopted people, natural parents, grandparents and siblings were all invited to register, and where there was a match, contact would be facilitated. The leaflet was to be re-circulated at regular intervals to encourage more and more people to register, but it never was. The rate of matching people who do register has been incredibly slow, and the numbers tiny. Some 50,000 people have been adopted in Ireland. Each of them had two natural parents and four grandparents and most of them probably have natural siblings. Yet, at the time of writing, only 450 matches have been achieved through the official register, involving 900 people – less than a third of 1% of the 300,000 or so people who could have joined the scheme.[21]

The Adoption Authority maintains the Contact Register, but when it matches two people who are looking for each other – two consenting adults – it does not put them in touch directly but refers their details to the adoption agency that arranged the adoption in the first place, and there they join a queue, waiting for advice and counselling before they are put in touch with each other. For some adopted people and natural mothers, having to go back to the very organisation that separated them – perhaps in a legally and ethically questionable way – is a deeply frustrating and alienating experience. Yet the Adoption Authority seems content to leave matters as they are.

Another frequently cited reform for making good past wrongs has been the creation of nationally applicable standards in the area of information and tracing for adopted people and their natural parents. For many years past one of the most frequently heard complaints from those searching for a parent or child was that the adoption societies who were charged with helping people in this area operated widely different standards. Put bluntly, some offered a modicum of assistance while others were downright obstructive. This problem was highlighted most dramatically in 1996 in the wake of the American adoption story, when frustrated and angry adoptees and natural mothers told of how they were consistently lied to by the adoption societies – and by specific nuns running the societies. Lives already troubled were being made intolerable and urgent action was needed to bring order to the chaos. But it was to be 2007, eleven years later, before the Adoption Board, along with the adoption societies, initiated the Standardised Framework for the

Provision of a National Information and Tracing Service. This framework sets national standards and provides guidance for those offering information and tracing services around the country, but at the time of writing four years later again, the Standardised Framework, which only reached the piloting stage, was again under review. What is more, it remains entirely voluntary. If its attempt to standardise procedures were to be really effective, the guidelines would have to be enshrined in legislation.

The one certain way to clean up this appalling muddle in the area of adoption rights would have been for the Oireachtas to legislate – as Justice Ronan Keane pointed out back in 1998.

In almost every western democracy but Ireland adopted people have significant rights to information on their birth records. In Scotland, all adopted people have been entitled to their original birth certificates as of right on reaching the age of 17, a right that was extended to adopted people in England and Wales by the 1976 Adoption Act. In Northern Ireland the 1987 Adoption Order extends the same rights to adult adopted people there. In Germany similar rights apply from the age of 16. Belgium and Portugal also allow access to such information as of right. Since 1956, adopted children in Holland could access their full adoption records from the age of 14. In 1979 this was lowered to 12. In Germany the age has always been 16. An adoption information commission in Canada found in 1985 that the facts surrounding an individual's adoption belong to that person, no matter where they are stored, and also that revealing those facts had not been shown to cause harm.

In 1985 New Zealand introduced an Adult Information Act permitting adopted persons, on reaching the age of 20, to apply for information on the identity of their natural mother. Natural mothers may likewise apply for information on the adoptive identity of their 20-year-old offspring. Both sides have a right of veto, but in practice it is rarely used. In the first five years of the Act, 8,500 reunions were facilitated, and of these only six resulted in serious complaints.[22]

Ireland's most recent legislation in this area is the 2010 Adoption Act, steered through by Fianna Fáil's Minister of State for Children, Barry Andrews. The new Act was heralded by the chairman of the Adoption Authority, Geoffrey Shannon, as a 'world-class piece of legislation' that would mark a 'new era' for Ireland. But, spectacularly, the Act failed completely to address the issue of adoption information and the right of people adopted in the past to know their origins. To the astonishment of many it also failed to legislate for open domestic adoptions in the future, although an earlier Act in 1991 allowed for openness in inter-country adoptions, thereby creating a two-tier system, with children adopted from abroad enjoying greater rights to know their origins than children adopted within Ireland. (While open domestic adoptions do now take place in Ireland, they have no legal basis and depend entirely on the goodwill of all concerned.) Commenting on the 2010 Adoption Act, the Adoption Rights Alliance remarked: 'Barry Andrews managed to enact an Adoption Bill without including a single provision for adopted people's rights.' Mr Andrews countered: 'The accusation that the Government is at pains to preserve the ethos of secrecy redolent of a darker period in Irish history is wide of the mark.' He, too, cited the 1998 Supreme Court judgment as the critical determinant of State behaviour in this area and ended by saying: 'it is my intention to introduce legislation that will balance in a proportionate manner the rights of all parties involved in adoption information matters – the child, the birth parents and the adopted parents.'[23] That promise, as we have seen, has been made repeatedly without fulfillment, and Mr Andrews never got the opportunity to prove he would deliver where others had failed. His party, Fianna

Fáil, which had ruled without interruption since 1997, was voted out of office in the election of February 2011.

In March, Ireland got a new Government – a Fine Gael-Labour coalition. Alan Shatter, an expert on family law and long-time critic of the chaotic nature of Ireland's adoption legislation, was appointed Minister for Justice. On the appearance of the first edition of *Banished Babies* in 1997, Mr Shatter, then a backbench TD, wrote a letter of congratulations. 'On a personal level,' he told me, 'I have found the lethargy shown by the State in addressing the issue of access to original birth records and the provision of information to facilitate those sent abroad to trace their origins extremely frustrating.' In the new administration too, Frances Fitzgerald – another forceful critic of past adoption practices – was given the first ever full cabinet post as Minister for Children. 'It is universally accepted,' she had told the Dáil in 1997, 'that denial of access to information about one's origins is denial of a basic human right... These cases coming to public attention reveal considerable human unhappiness and heartbreak, and the minister must now introduce measures to deal with this. We must have action at official level.'[24]

With two ardent champions of adopted people's 'right to know' now occupying the very positions from which change must come, radical reform seemed possible. The ball was finally at their feet. But, yet again, the ball has been kicked into touch. Questioned on *Today with Pat Kenny* on RTÉ radio shortly after coming to power, Ms Fitzgerald indicated she might legislate for *future* adoption rights, but would do nothing for people adopted in the past. 'I think you can bring in tracing legislation,' she said, 'not going backwards but from current best practice going forward that the child would have access to birth certs, to detailed information.' And she acknowledged how badly this would go down among the people whose cause she had seemed to support 15 years earlier: 'There will be people who will be very disappointed hearing that,' she told RTÉ.[25]

One of them was Grainne Mason who immediately wrote to the papers: 'I know the hurt, upset and sheer devastation this decision will bring to the thousands of adopted adults who are searching… Our mothers carried us for nine months, gave birth to us, cared for us for days, weeks, months and, in some circumstances, years before we were given up for adoption and to be told that we will not have a right to know her identity is simply not right. We are not asking for her bank details, credit card account, alarm code or passwords, just her name and where she (and indeed, we) come from. Is this too much to ask for?'[26]

Speaking in the Dáil on 21 July 2011, Ms Fitzgerald seemed to indicate that her thinking on all of this was dictated by the complexities of 1998 Supreme Court judgment which found that unmarried mothers whose children were given up had a constitutional right to privacy. 'Legislation to provide for information and tracing,' she said, 'is in preparation within my department and is a priority.' But then came the inevitable rider: 'This is a sensitive and complex area, and it will be necessary for the legislation to balance the constitutional rights of mothers whose children were adopted with those of adopted people seeking to trace their birth families.' The claim that the matter is 'complex' is one that was rejected nearly fifteen years previously by an acknowledged leading professional in this area. 'I want to nail the suggestion that this is a hugely complex issue,' the expert said. 'It is an issue that has been properly and adequately addressed in a variety of other countries with the degree of insight and sensitivity…' He went on, 'I urge the Minister to proceed hastily with bringing the necessary legislation before the House.'[27] The speaker on that occasion was family lawyer, now Justice Minister, Alan Shatter.

* * * * *

Many adopted people and natural mothers who continue to feel frustrated by the entire system had hoped that the 1998 judgment, which they see as seriously flawed, might have been challenged rather than taken as gospel.

It may seem astonishing that fifteen years after the American adoption story first broke, putting the whole adoption information issue onto the political agenda as never before, there has been so little advance. Legal obstacles and concern for the 'sensitivities' of all involved may indeed play a role, but in continually prevaricating over access to information that might help reunite adult adopted people and their natural mothers, the State and the adoption societies are also protecting themselves. It is now clear that not everything in the past was done in a legal and above-board manner. The conditions in which many young mothers 'consented' to the adoption of their children could well mean the consent itself had no legal validity. Others never signed consent documents at all, but had their signatures forged. Yet consent – and informed consent at that – has always been a fundamental requirement in Irish adoption law since the first Adoption Act came into force in January 1953. On the other side, there are adopted people returning with unhappy stories to tell, of adoptions that did not work, stories that might raise awkward questions about how individual adoptions were arranged and how unsuitable people managed to acquire children, particularly when the State had the final say before adoption passports were issued. Other adopted people have learned from their adoptive parents that considerable sums of money were sent to the nuns back in Ireland, a practice that has never been acknowledged or accounted for by the recipients who fear being accused of 'selling' the babies in their care. And, again, the State has never shown any interest in investigating this aspect of the baby business.

Under all these circumstances, the prospect of aggrieved but frequently submissive natural mothers getting together with unabashed and confident adult adoptees to 'compare notes' cannot be a welcome one for agencies – whether of Church or State – whose past practices could not withstand close scrutiny. By keeping mothers and offspring apart, a multitude of past sins, errors and shoddy practices by all those involved can be kept from view.

In case anything written here be thought of as insensitive to the feelings of natural mothers who are still desperately trying to keep their secrets, it should be said that contemporary research suggests a greater openness on the part of natural mothers than is frequently assumed. In one major investigation, three out of every four natural mothers contacted reacted with moderate to strong enthusiasm. Only one in six refused a reunion, but in the end, all were coaxed round. Other studies suggest that only one natural mother in 10 will refuse to meet her offspring, and for most of these mothers the reasons are fear of rejection and feelings of guilt rather than an absolute desire for secrecy.[28] Anecdotally, too, there is considerable evidence to suggest that natural mothers who at first resisted contact have experienced great relief once they have changed their minds. Gentle persuasion, and an opportunity to discuss issues with their peers – rather than the dissuasion some Irish adoption societies are believed to have engaged in – can be the essential ingredient.

For many, if not most adopted people, the purpose of their search is not to establish a permanent relationship with their natural mother, but more modestly to find out the circumstances of their birth and adoption and, if possible, something of their family health history. They feel they need such information so as to move on in their lives. There is no doubt that many searches and reunions do not have happy outcomes, but these can rarely be predicted. Nor, adopted people feel, can the danger of unhappy outcomes in general be used by those in control of information as a justification for withholding it in all cases. As one person put it: 'We are seeking the *truth*, and if the truth is bad news, well so be it, it's still better than a sugar coated lie.'

The culture of secrecy, which is proving so hard to overcome, also protected men of course. It is conveniently forgotten that for every shamed natural mother there was an anonymous natural father, most of them desperate to cover their tracks. How many of these men occupied positions of power in relation to the women they made pregnant? How many were employers? How many men of the cloth? How many politicians? How many were guilty of incest? How many of sexual assault and rape? How many were other women's husbands? In the production of tens of thousands of 'illegitimate' children in Ireland during these years, how many sexual taboos were broken? And in the determination to keep the doors locked on the adoption files, how many male – and prominent male – reputations were still being protected?

In Ireland, where the Church-induced culture of secrecy probably went deeper and lasted longer than elsewhere, the tendency for natural mothers – especially those from the earlier years – to remain hidden may well be stronger than research suggests it is elsewhere. Some of the mothers are already dead – as adopted people returning from America have discovered – their pain never acknowledged, their secrets never shared. And as the first edition of this book stated at its conclusion: *unless something is done in the very near future to actively encourage and assist the process of reunion, many more of the now elderly natural mothers won't live long enough for their adopted children to find them.* In the intervening years this, sadly, has come to pass in a great many cases, making the final words of the first edition even more compelling: *that it seems to be the unstated intention of those who continue to think up excuses for keeping information under lock and key to deny till they die.*

Tables

Figures for Ireland's foreign adoptions are far from definitive. The tables below are derived from a database constructed by the Department of Foreign Affairs in 1997. Because of overlaps and different methods of recording cases down the years, total numbers differ when calculated under different headings. It is important to note that the Department only kept records from the end of 1950 onwards. Approximately 170 entry visas were issued by the American embassy in Dublin between July 1949 and the end of 1950, but there is no record of how many children were taken or sent to America, or anywhere else, before July 1949. There is no record whatever of 'illegitimate' Irish children who were adopted in Great Britain and Northern Ireland, or taken from those jurisdictions to other countries for adoption. The overwhelming majority (98%) of the recorded foreign adoptions were to America, but children were also sent to 16 other countries.

Table 1: Annual Totals

Year	Number of 'illegitimate' births	Number of Adoption Passports	Foreign adoptions as % of births
1951	1588	122	7.7
1952	1619	193	11.9
1953	1340	128	9.6
1954	1310	182	13.9
1955	1234	184	14.9
1956	1173	111	9.5
1957	1032	122	11.8
1958	976	146	15
1959	959	141	14.7
1960	968	145	15
1961	975	125	12.8
1962	1111	107	9.6
1963	1157	65	5.6
1964	1292	51	3.9
1965	1403	43	3.1
1966	1436	21	1.5
1967	1540	20	1.3
1968	1558	10	0.6
1969	1642	8	0.5
1970	1709	4	0.2
1971	1842	1	0.05
1972	2005	2	0.1
1973	2309	2	0.1
1974	2515	0	0
TOTAL		**1933**	

Note: The annual passport totals have been gathered from a number of Department of Foreign Affairs documents. Annual figures for 'illegitimate' births come from the Central Statistics Office. When the 170 US entry visas for July 1949 to the end of 1950 are added the total comes to 2,103.

Table 2: Destinations by Country

Australia	2
Austria	1
Canada	2
Egypt	1
France	1
Germany	4
Great Britain	18
India	2
Ireland	6
Italy	3
Lebanon	2
Libya	1
Peru	1
Philippines	1
Saudi Arabia	1
South Africa	3
Turkey	1
United States	1911
Venezuela	1
TOTAL	**1962**

Note: These figures do not include the 170 or so US visas issued between July 1949 and the end of 1950. When these are added the total comes to 2,132. There are some unexplained anomalies with these figures. For example, it is not clear why there should be an entry under 'Ireland' unless these were foreign nationals resident here at the time of obtaining a passport for a child they intended adopting in another country. It is also unclear why Great Britain should be included as no passport was necessary to travel there, although it is possible the recipients of the children intended adopting them elsewhere, for example, US military personnel stationed in the UK after World War II who would take children back to America.

Table 3: American Destination by State

State		State	
Alaska	1	Missouri	96
Arizona	8	New Jersey	233
California	116	New Mexico	3
Colorado	11	New York	517
Connecticut	28	North Carolina	1
Florida	5	North Dakota	4
Hawaii	1	Ohio	100
Idaho	1	Oklahoma	2
Illinois	273	Oregon	4
Indiana	6	Pennsylvania	73
Iowa	6	Puerto Rico	1
Kansas	36	Rhode Island	4
Kentucky	1	South Dakota	3
Louisiana	30	Tennessee	1
Maine	1	Texas	140
Maryland	16	Virginia	10
Massachusetts	46	Washington State	7
Michigan	46	Washington DC	9
Minnesota	7	Wisconsin	21
Mississippi	27	Unidentified	5
		TOTAL	**1900**

Note: These figures do not include the 170 US visas issued between July 1949 and the end of 1950. Their inclusion brings the total to 2,070.

Table 4: Children's Origins by Institution

St Patrick's Guild	515
Sean Ross Abbey	438
Castlepollard	278
St Patrick's Home	254
St Clare's Stamullen	130
Sacred Heart Convent Cork	98
Catholic Women's Aid Adoption Society, Cork	37
St Joseph's Convent, Croom	29
All Protestant Adoption Societies	24
St Bridget's Orphanage	14
Miscellaneous	101
TOTAL	1918

Note: When the 1949-50 American visas are added, the total comes to 2,088. The extent to which the Department's figures understate the actual numbers can be seen from the fact that St Patrick's Guild's own records show that they sent 572 children to America for adoption, an addition of 11%. The Guild's records cover the period from 1947 when they sent their first child to the US.

Note on Sources

Documents referred to as the 'McQuaid Papers' are in the Dublin Diocesan Archive, Archbishop's House, Drumcondra, Dublin 9. References to archive material from the Department of Foreign Affairs have been abbreviated for convenience. Documents cited are contained in eight large 'policy files' located in the National Archive in Dublin. The file titles are as follows:

345/96/I:	Enquiries regarding Irish law relating to the adoption of children, 1942-54
345/96/II:	Enquiries regarding Irish law relating to the adoption of children, 1953-57
345/96/III:	Enquiries regarding Irish law relating to the adoption of children, 1958-60
345/96/1/1:	Report to Government regarding adoption of Irish children abroad, 1956-67
345/96/1/ 2:	National Conference of Catholic Charities: annual meeting 1957
345/96/545:	Irish children alleged to be illegally registered as American citizens, 1952-57

350/280:	Statistics relating to the issue of passports to children who are travelling abroad for the purpose of legal adoption, 1955
350/297:	Correspondence with the Department of Health regarding the issue of passports to children in County Homes, 1956-57

Note on Monetary Conversions

When converting monetary values from the 1950s and early '60s to today's equivalents, I have first converted to Euro where appropriate (conversion rate: €1 = Ir£0.787564) and then multiplied by a factor of 76. This method of calculation is based on official figures for average earnings which have risen from around £7 a week in the early years (€8.90) to €675 a week in mid-2011. The dollar-punt exchange rate was constant at $2.8 to £1 throughout the period in question.

Endnotes

Part 1: Prologue
1. *New York Times*, 29 July 1949
2. *San Francisco Call Bulletin*, 15 November 1949
3. *San Francisco Chronicle*, 15 November 1949
4. *San Francisco Examiner*, 15 November 1949
5. *Ibid*

1. A Happy Hunting Ground
1. DoEA 345/96/I, internal memo, Kenny to Commins, 13 October 1952
2. DoEA 345/96/I, note to Minister, 5 November 1951
3. DoEA 345/96/I, Horan, internal memo 9 November 1950. Horan reports communication from a Mr. Lefreniere of the US embassy to the effect that 140 US entry visas were issued to Irish babies for adoption between July 1949 and September 1950, an average of 10 per month, giving a total of 170 to the end of 1950.
4. McQuaid Papers, 'American Adoptions,' undated type-script.
5. *The Irish Times*, 8 October 1951
6. DoEA 350/28
7. DoEA 345/96/I

8. All figures from the Central Statistics Office.

9 . Barrett, C., *Adoption: the parents, the child, the home*, Dublin 1952, pp.17-18

10. *Ibid*, pp.23-24

11. Dervan, M., *The Problem of the Unmarried Mother*, Mercier Press, Cork, 1961, p. 12

12. While they banned foreign adoptions, however, the British authorities still sanctioned the shipment of thousands of children from orphanages and homes throughout Britain (including Northern Ireland) to Commonwealth countries where they were placed in institutions – many run by Irish Christian Brothers. The aim was to release them into society when they were old enough to marry and reproduce, thereby boosting the Anglo-Saxon presence in these countries. Many of the children were exported against their wishes and without the knowledge of their parents. See Margaret Humphreys, *Empty Cradles*, Corgi, London 1995. For the story of the sexual and physical abuse of many of these children by Christian Brothers, see the documentary, *Betrayal*, by Mike Milotte and Mary Raftery (RTÉ *Prime Time*, November 2001). See also the 2011 feature film, *Oranges and Sunshine*, directed by Jim Loach.

13. *New York Times,* 24 November 1950

2. McQuaid's Rules, OK?

1. DoEA 345/96/I, Schafer, *St Louis Globe*, to Passport Office, 9 May 1950

2. DoEA 345/96/I, Hughes to DoEA, 17 November 1949

3. DoEA 345/96/1, DoEA to Hughes, 21 November 1949

4. DoEA 345/96/I, various papers

5. DoEA 345/96/I, Dept Health to DoEA, 12 December 1949

6. Schafer, *op. cit.*

7. DoEA, 345/96/I, Dept Health to DoEA, 12 December 1949

8. McQuaid Papers, copy of Brown's letter to St V de P, 8 March 1950

9. McQuaid Papers, handwritten note on Barrett's letter to Mangan, 22 March 1950

10. DoEA 345/96/I, W.J. Gilligan, Hon Sec St v de P to Rev Brown, 24 March 1950

11. DoEA 345/96/I Assistant Secretary to Secretary, 5 September 1950

12. Barrett, *Adoption*, 1952, pp. 42-43

13. McQuaid Papers, Sr Elizabeth to Fr Mangan, 4 June 1951

14. Statement to the author from Sr Gabriel Murphy, Senior Professional Social Worker, St Patrick's Guild, June 1996

15. Sr Frances Elizabeth to Mr & Mrs M.J., correspondence in the author's possession.

16. McQuaid Papers, Sr Frances Elizabeth to Fr Mangan, 25 March 1950

17. McQuaid Papers, Fr Mangan to Sr Frances Elizabeth, 25 March 1950

18. McQuaid Papers, Sr Monica to Fr Mangan, 23 & 24 March 1950, Mangan to Monica, 25 March 1950

19. *New York Times*, 18 March 1950

20. McQuaid Papers, handwritten memo, undated

21. DoEA 345/96/I, Horan to Garda Superintendent, 27 February 1952

22. McQuaid Papers, Barrett to Mangan, 30 March 1950

23. Minutes of the Meeting of Standing Committee of Directors of Catholic Charities, Washington, 19 May 1950, Catholic University, Washington

24. DoEA 345/96/I, Hugh McCann, Irish embassy in Washington to DoEA, 23 May 1950

25. *Ibid*

26. DoEA 345/96/I, McCann to DoEA, 23 June 1950

27. DoEA 345/96/I, Lennon to Gallagher, 4 September 1950

28. Gallagher to Secretary, 12 July 1950

29. DoEA 345/96/I, Horan to Gallagher, internal memo, June 1950

30. DoEA 345/96/I, Gallagher to Secretary, internal memo, 12 July 1950

31. *Ibid*

32. *Ibid*

33. McQuaid Papers, Barrett to Mangan, 29 May 1951

34. McQuaid Papers, Sr Frances Elizabeth to Fr Mangan

35. J.H. Whyte, *Church and State in Modern Ireland 1923-1979*, Gill & Macmillan, Dublin 1980 pp. 192-3

36. McQuaid Papers, 'American Adoption of Irish Children', undated.

37. McQuaid Papers. This is the earliest version of this document. Later versions appear in various files, but the amendments are slight.

38. 'American Adoptions of Irish Children' *op. cit.*

39. DoEA 345/96/I, Berry, Justice, to MacDonald, DoEA, 2 November 1950

40. DoEA 345/96/I, Horan memo, 29 December 1950

41. DoEA 345/96/I, Sean Ronan, DoEA, to Donal Scully, Irish Consulate, New York, 5 June 1951

42. DoEA 345/96/II, 'Documentation to be submitted with Passport Application for Catholic Illegitimate Child', undated. The 'not shirking natural parentage' condition was added to the Department's regulations at an unknown date, some time after the initial rules were set down.

43. DoEA 345/96/I, Horan memo, 29 December 1950

44. Dáil Debates, Vol. 125, Col 781

45. *The Irish Times*, 12 April 1951

3. Me Tommy, You Jane

1. .*Saturday Chronicle*, 11 November 1951

2. *The Irish Times*, 30 October 1951

3. Florrie Kavanagh gave this account of the entire episode to the *Sunday Express*, 11 November 1951

4. *Daily Mail Weekend*, 10 October 1998

5. *Sunday Chronicle*, 11 November 1951

6. Dáil Debates, 21 November 1951, Vol 127, Col 6

7. DoEA 345/96/I (340/12/114) 'Deputy Kyne's Question re Thomas Kavanagh/ Jane Russell' addressed to the Minister.

8. DoEA 345/96/I, Memo to Secretary of Department from MR, 12 November 1951

9. *Manchester Guardian*, 16 November 1951

10. *Sunday News*, 20 April 1952

11. *Manchester Guardian*, 1 January 1952

12. *Sunday News*, 20 April 1952

13. Interview with John Peoples, Jane Russell's agent, June 1996

14. Letter from Bruce Mohler, National Catholic Welfare Conference, to Msgr Cecil Barrett, Catholic Social Welfare Bureau, 31 March 1958, archives of the Migration and Refugee Services, US Catholic Conference.

15. DoEA 345/96/I, O'Beirne to Dept Secretary, 19 December 1951

16. Handwritten and initialled note on O'Beirne's memo, dated 29 December 1951

17. DoEA 345/96/I, Letter from T.J. Horan, 14 January 1952

18. *The Irish Times*, 8 October 1951

19. DoEA 345/96/I, Telex, Horan to Woods, 31 December 1951

20. DoEA 345/96/I, Horan to Molloy, 16 January 1952

21. DoEA 345/96/I, Horan to Molloy, 21 November 1950

22. DoEA 345/96/I, 29 December 1950

23. DoEA 345/96/I, Horan to Molloy, 16 January 1952

24. DoEA 345/96/I, Horan to Chief Superintendent, 4 January 1952

25. *Ibid*

26. *Ibid*

27. DoEA 345/96/II, Brogan to Commins, DoEA

28. DoEA 345/96/I, Ms R Kenny, memo 2 November 1951

29. Quoted by Elizabeth Marriott, 'A National Tragedy', in *Hampshire Life, Daily Hampshire Gazette* Magazine, 8-14 May 1998.

30. Interview with Mary Theresa Monaghan, Dublin 1998. All subsequent quotations are from letters and documents provided by Ms Monaghan to the author.

31. *Daily Mail*, Weekend, 10 October 1998

32. *Ibid*

33. *Chicago Tribune*, 6 July 1955

34. DoEA 345/96/I, Horan to Molloy, 24 January 1952

4. A Hard Act To Follow

1. DoEA 345/96/I, Horan to Molloy, 24 January 1952

2. J.H. Whyte, *Church and State in Modern Ireland, 1923-1979*, p. 276

3. DoEA 345/96/I, Wm, Fay, DoEA, to Irish embassy, Washington, 25 April 1952

4. This distinction between 'legitimate' and 'illegitimate' was found to be unconstitutional by the Irish Supreme Court in the late 1970s. But the effect of the Supreme Court decision was not to give 'illegitimate' children the same rights as 'legitimate' ones – ie the right not to be exported – but rather to legalise the export of 'legitimate' children as well. But by this time the American traffic had already come to a halt.

5. McQuaid Papers, Letter from Department of Justice to Fr Chris Mangan, 4 November 1952

6. *Ibid*

7. *The Primal Wound: Understanding the Adopted Child*, Nancy Newton Verrier, (Lafayette, California, 1993) provides a thoroughgoing account of the psychological damage that can be wrought by separation, and in particular the feeling – and enduring dread – of abandonment.

5. A Major Inquisition

1. DoEA 345/96/545
2. DoEA 345/96/I, Horan to Molloy, 21 November 1950
3. DoEA 345/96/I, reference dated 26 August 1950
4. Interview with Anne Phelan, November 1996, Dublin
5. DoEA 345/96/545, Kennan, DoEA, to Berry, Justice, 25 June 1954
6. Flaherty quoted in *Ibid*
7. DoEA 345/96/545, D.I. John Flaherty's report, 9 July 1954
8. *Ibid*
9. *Ibid*
10. Lynda Harden, now Hargrave, provided all the details about her personal story by way of email correspondence.
11. The names of all the American Air Force couples as well as the babies' natural mothers, have been blanked out from the official Garda investigation file. However, thanks to an oversight, the name 'Autry' remains visible in one document. One day, out of the blue, I received a query from an American man called Gene Autry who was desperately seeking information about his origins, having just discovered, in 1997, that he had been born in Ireland and adopted. He had had no idea he was an anonymous baby in a Garda investigation file. By comparing what information he had gathered with the details I had obtained from the files, I was able to identify Gene of as one of the 'St Rita's 8' and provided him with all the information about his origins and unorthodox acquisition by the Autrys from the Garda file. Gene subsequently discovered much more from his adoptive mother and shared that information with me.
12. Copy of Marie Keating's letter to Mary Autry supplied by Gene Autry.
13. DoEA 345/96/545, Kennan, DoEA, to Dutko, US embassy, 27 November 1954

14. DoEA 345/96/545, Kennan to Fay, internal memo, 19 October 1954

15. *Ibid*

16. *Ibid*

17. DoEA 345/96/545, Private Secretary to Minister, 22 October 1954

18. DoEA 345/96/545, Minister's minute, 25 October 1954

19. DoEA 345/96/545, Kennan to Morrissey, internal memo, 13 January 1955

20. DoEA 345/96/545, telex 83, Kennan to Kirwan, telex 136, Kennan to Woods, telex 212, Woods to Kennan, January 1955

21. DoEA 345/96/545, Fr Keane's original reference quoted in Kennan to Morrissey, internal memo, 13 January 1955

22. *Ibid*

23. DoEA 345/96/545, Morrissey to Rynne, internal memo, 20 January 1955.

24. Handwritten note on above memo.

25. *New Haven and Connecticut Register*, 2 February 1955

26. DoEA 345/280, Garda Siochana, Metropolitan Division, Alleged Trade in Irish Children for American Couples, 15 February 1955

27. DoEA 345/280, Kennan, DoEA, to Berry, Justice, 11 March 1955

28. DoEA 345/280, Berry to Kennan, 2 April 1955

29. DoEA 345/280, Morrissey to Woods, internal memo, 13 April 1955

30. DoEA 345/96/545, Morrissey internal memo, 28 April 1955

31. DoEA 345/96/545. An undated handwritten note on the margin of Morrissey's internal memo to Rynne of 20 January 1955 states 'instruction subsequently cancelled by Minister after further discussion with Mr Morrissey'.

32. DoEA 345/96/545, Cosgrave's note on Morrissey's internal memo to Minister, 20 May 1955

33. DoEA 345/96/545, Morrissey, DoEA, to Adams, US embassy, 31 May 1955

34. DoEA 345/96/545, Kenny to Kennan, internal memo, 21 February 1955; Kennan to Morrissey, internal memo, 24 February 1955

35. DoEA 345/96/545, J. Shields, Irish embassy, Washington to Secretary, DoEA, 12 June 1957; Morrissey to Secretary, internal memo, 19 June 1957

6. From Cock-Up...

1. DoEA 345/96/II, Angel Guardian Home to Sr Monica, St Patrick's; Mother Rosamund, Castlepollard and Sr Barbara, Sean Ross Abbey, 12 May 1954

2. DoEA 345/96/II, Reddy to Barrett, 11 February 1955

3. DoEA 345/96/II, O'Grady to Barrett, 7 July 1955

4. DoEA 345/96/II, Barrett quotes the Kansas letter in a letter of his own to Ms Kenny at the DoEA, 20 August 1955

5. DoEA 345/96/II, Quealy's circular and related correspondence.

6. DoEA 345/96/II, Barrett to Morrissey, 14 July 1955

7. DoEA 345/96/II, 'Discussion with Monsignor O'Grady at the Department on the 16th January 1956'

8. DoEA 345/96/II, Morrissey to O'Grady, 8 December 1955

9. *Ibid*

10. DoEA 345/96/II, Morrissey, DoEA to Sean Ronan, Irish Consul in Chicago, 22 September 1956

11. DoEA 345/96/II, 'Discussion with Monsignor O'Grady', *op. cit.*

12. DoEA 345/96/II, Ronan, Chicago, to Woods, DoEA, 29 August 1956

13. DoEA 345/96/II, Morrissey to Ronan, 22 September 1956

14. DoEA 345/96/II, Welfare Dept., Madison, Wisconsin to Sean Ronan, Chicago Consul, 22 September 1956.

15. DoEA 345/96/1/2, National Conference of Catholic Charities, Annual Meeting 1957, report from Sean Ronan, Chicago Consul, to DoEA, Dublin

16. DoEA 345/96/II, covering note to Minister, 3 February 1956

7. ... To Cover-Up

1. DoEA 345/96/1/1, 'Report to Government re Adoption of Irish Children...', various drafts

2. DoEA 345/96/III. This file contains further drafts of the Report

3. Dáil Debates, 10 April 1956, Col 8

4. *Ibid*

5. Dáil Debates, 19 June 1956, Col 473

6. DoEA 345/96/II, Garda report quoted in J.J. McCarthy, Dept of Justice, to Woods, DoEA 22 March 1956

7. Dáil Debates, *op. cit.*

8. Dáil Debates, 18 July 1956, Col 1227. It transpired in the subsequent debate that Mrs O'Carroll had misunderstood the terms of the Adoption Act as it affected foreign adoptions. She had mistakenly believed that the Act banned the export of children over one year of age rather than under one year. And she had taken up the cases of Anthony Barron and Mary Clancy largely because both were over one year of age when removed from Croom hospital, something which she thought was a criminal act. Had she not made this simple error – a consequence of the impenetrable language of the Adoption Act – the Dáil debate would not have taken place at all.

9. Dáil Debates, 18 July 1956, Cols 1227-8

10. *Ibid*, Col 1229

11. *Ibid*, Cols 1369-70

12. *Ibid*, Cols 1371-72

13. *Ibid*, Cols 1373-74

14. *Ibid*

15. *Longford News*, 24 September 1955

16. DoEA 350/297, Morrissey, DoEA to Health, 26 June 1956

17. *Ibid*, Dowling, Health to DoEA, 31 July 1956

18. *Ibid*, Hargadon, Health, to Dublin Board of Assistance, 26 January 1957

19. *Ibid*, Health to DoEA, 14 February 1957

20. *Ibid*, Morrissey to Secretary, internal memo, 6 March 1957

21. *Ibid*, Morrissey, DoEA to Health, 8 March 1957

22. DoEA 345/96/1/1, internal memo, O'Riordan to Gallagher, 9 October 1961

23. DoEA 345/96/1/1, O'Riordan internal memo, 30 January 1962

24. McQuaid Papers, Cecil Barrett to Bruce Mohler, Director, National Catholic Welfare Conference, Washington, 17 February 1958

25. *New York Times*, 1 August 1958

26. Kevin Murtaugh wrote to me after the first edition of *Banished Babies* was published in 1997. After several letters had passed between us, he opened up and told me his full and very disturbing story.

27. Kieran McGrath, *The Irish Times*, 11 November 1998

28. *Kentucky Post*, 7 December 2007

29. *The Primal Wound: Understanding the Adopted Child*, Nancy Newton Verrier, Lafayette, California, 1993

30. Quoted in *Journey of the Adopted Self*, Betty Jean Lifton, Basic Books, New York 1994, p.102

31. *Ibid*, p. 103

32. *Ibid*, p. 107

8. A Very Grave Offence

1. Interview with Karl Mullen, Dublin, 1997
2. The names of Wedderburn and Woulfe are fictitious; real names have been changed for legal reasons.
3. This account of the Garda investigation was given to me by a departmental official who had sight of the file. The file itself was never released for public inspection.
4. *Irish Press*, 20 January 1965
5. Interview with priest, May 1996
6. DoEA 345/96/II, Fr Brogan, Chicago to Ms R Kenny, DoEA, 8 May 1957. The other two were Fr Cecil Barrett of the Catholic Social Welfare Bureau, and Ms Rita Kenny, an official in the Passport Office.
7. RTÉ, Today Tonight, 9 April 1991
8. Interview with former member of the Adoption Board involved in the investigation.
9. Interview with the social worker, March 1996
10. Interview with Sr Sarto, Cork, June 1996

9. A Troublesome Priest

1. Interview with Msgr Bryan Walsh, Dublin, June 1996
2. DoEA 345/96/I, Fay to Irish Consulate in New York, 8 August 1952
3. DoEA 345/96/II, Fr Bernard Brogan, Chicago, to Rita Kenny, DoEA, 8 May 1957
4. McQuaid Papers, Barrett to Mangan, 30 March 1950

10. Jim and Dorothy: No Price Too High

1. The name 'Rowe' is fictitious, but all other names are real. This account of the Rowes' adoption of an Irish baby is based on the correspondence between them, the Angel Guardian Home in Brooklyn and St Clare's Adoption Society in Co Meath. Mrs Rowe (deceased) kept every letter she received from the Angel Guardians and from the nuns in Ireland. She also meticulously copied by hand every letter

she sent them, and retained copies of all official documents, affidavits, receipts, airline tickets, etc.

11. Pat: Against My Will
1. Interview with Pat Thuillier, December 1996

12. Mary, Michael and Kevin: Legitimate Error?
1. Interview with Mary and Michael Geraghty, June 1996
2. Untitled, undated two page typescript given to the author by Sr Mary.
3. Interview with Sr Sarto, June 1996
4. Interview with Sr Mary, June 1996
5. DoEA 345/96/I Sr Frances Elizabeth to Ms Ennis, Private Secretary to Minister, 26 June 1952
6. Sample surrender/consent form provided by Sr Sarto, Sacred Heart Convent, Cork.
7. Interview with Kevin Bates, Leesburg, Virginia, USA, May 1996
8. Statement from St Patrick's Guild, in response to queries, 19 June 1996

13. Maureen: Seek And Ye Shall Find (But Don't Hold Your Breath)
1. Interview with Maureen, Virginia Beach, USA, May 1996, and subsequent conversations. Additional details from her mother.
2. Barrett, *Adoption*, pp. 48-52

14. Deny Till They Die
1. DoEA 345/96/I/I, internal memo, 13 February 1962
2. DoEA 345/96/I/I, internal memo, 1 March 1962
3. *Gay Byrne Show*, RTÉ Radio 1, 4 March 1996
4. *Gay Byrne Show*, 7 March 1996
5. *Gay Byrne Show*, 4 March 1996
6. *Morning Ireland*, RTÉ Radio 1, 6 March 1996

7. *The Irish Times*, 7 March 1996

8. *The Irish Times*, 6 March 1996

9. Dáil Debates, 5 March 1996, Shatter's speech is at Col 1458-59

10. Currie's speech is at *ibid*, Col 1459-62

11. Caitriona Crowe told how she located the files to *The Irish Times*, 9 March 1996

12. Quotations are from Spring's prepared script, dated 7 March 1996

13. *Sunday Tribune*, 10 March 1996

14. *Sunday Independent*, 10 March 1996

15. *The Irish Times*, 9 March 1996

16. *Irish Independent*, 8 March 1996

17. *Dáil Debates*, 14 March 1996, Cols 432-34

18. Barrett, *Adoption*, pp 28-30

19. Dáil Debates, 4 March 1998, Cols 440-41

20. Supreme Court judgment in the case of *I.O'T. and M.H. v Rotunda Girls Adoption Society* (1998)

21. The Adoption Rights Alliance, who suggested the 300,000 figure, say it is a conservative estimate.

22. Eileen Farrelly Conway, *Search and Reunion in the Adoption Triangle*, Trinity College, Dublin, 1994, p. 11

23. *Irish Examiner*, 23 April 2010

24. Quoted in *Irish Examiner*, 20 July 2011

25. *Ibid*

26. *Irish Examiner*, 9 June 2011

27. *Dáil Debates*, 9 April 1997

28. Conway, *op. cit.*, p. 31

Index

Protestant Adoption
    Societies 52, 66, 236
Protestant fostering
    services 25, 33
Protestants 23, 35, 44, 47,
    52, 61, 64, 66-7, 109,
    131, 196, 213
psychological damage
    associated with
    adoption xiii, 13, 67,
    119-121, 152, 173, 209,
    212
publicity xii, 5, 19, 27-9,
    41, 49, 51, 71, 86, 98,
    100, 109-10, 130, 220
Puerto Rica 235
Purcell, Mary 28

Q
Quigley, Michael, Fr 95

R
race, as a factor in US
    adoptions ix, 14-15,
    51-2, 85, 132, 158
Raftery, Mary 241
Reddy, J.J., Msgr, Catholic
    Charities 91-2
Regan, P.J., Fr 143, 155,
    190-93, 196 *see also* St
    Clare's Adoption
    Society
Reuters 29
Rhode Island 95-6, 235

Riflin, Joel, 'The Ripper'
    120
Romania 9
Roscrea, Co Tipperary 22,
    24, 126, 172 *see also*
    Sacred Heart nuns and
    Sean Ross Abbey
Rotunda Hospital 71
Routledge, George 45
Rowe, Dorothy & Jim 139,
    141-3, 145, 148-150,
    188-9, 197
Rowe, Marion (Maureen)
    139, 144-150, 185-199
RTÉ ix, 210, 224-5
Ruislip 79
Russia 9, 203
Russell, Jane 40-51, 58-9,
    61
Ryan, James 85

S
Sacred Heart Church,
    Donnybrook 77 *see also*
    Donnybrook Catholic
    Church
Sacred Heart Adoption
    Society, Sacred Heart
    nuns 5, 12, 24, 54, 56,
    91, 112, 118, 126, 129,
    143, 152-3, 158-9, 165,
    168, 169-70, 172, 192,
    236 *see also* Bessboro,
    Castlepollard, and Sean
    Ross Abbey